studies in christian existentialism

lectures and essays by JOHN MACQUARRIE

PROFESSOR OF SYSTEMATIC THEOLOGY

UNION THEOLOGICAL SEMINARY, NEW YORK

The Westminster Press
PHILADELPHIA

STUDIES IN CHRISTIAN EXISTENTIALISM

Library of Congress Catalogue Card No. 66-21808

Published by The Westminster Press
Philadelphia, Pennsylvania

TO THE REVEREND RICHARD GARY
PRIEST-IN-CHARGE OF SAINT MARY'S, MANHATTANVILLE
IN THE CITY AND DIOCESE OF NEW YORK

Preface

In October, 1963, I gave the Birks Lectures at McGill University, Montreal, on "Some Heideggerian Themes and their Theological Significance." I wish to thank the Faculty of Divinity at McGill University for the honour which they did me in inviting me to give these lectures and for their hospitality during my stay in Montreal.

The Editor of the McGill University Press talked with me about the possibility of publishing the lectures, and as a result of our discussions it was decided to put together a larger volume containing not only the Birks Lectures (Chapters 4-6 in this volume) but a number of other lectures and writings on related subjects. Among these are the English Lectures given at Andover Newton Theological School in October, 1963 (Chapter 17), a paper prepared in connection with the Consultation on Hermeneutics at Drew University in March, 1964 (Chapter 11), and my inaugural lecture at Union Theological Seminary in October, 1962 (Chapter 1).

The pieces have been arranged in a definite sequence which is divided into five parts. Part I serves as an introduction and defends the kind of approach to theology which is developed in the remainder of the book.

Part II discusses the philosophical presuppositions of this approach, while Part III develops the conception of an existential method in theology. Part IV considers (not polemically, I hope) the claims of some alternative approaches. Finally, Part V applies the theological conceptions that have been developed to specific Christian doctrines.

All of the pieces here presented have been specially revised (and some of them almost entirely rewritten) for this volume, but some of them have already appeared in more or less different forms in various periodicals. I wish to express thanks to the publishers of these periodicals for their kindness in permitting me to make use of this material, especially to Union Theological Seminary, New York, for material in Chapters 1 and 7 from *Union Seminary Quarterly Review*, Vol. XII and XVIII; to the World Alliance of Reformed Churches, Geneva, for material in Chapter 2 from *The Reformed and Presbyterian World*, Vol. XXV; to The S.P.C.K., London, for material in Chapters 3 and 12 from *Theology*, Vols. LVIII and LIX; to T. & T. Clark, Edinburgh, for material in Chapters 8, 13, 14, and 15 from *The Expository Times*, Vols. LXXI, LXXII, LXXIV and LXVIII; to the Epworth Press, London, for material in Chapter 9 from *The London Quarterly & Holborn Review*, Vol. CLXXXVI; to the British Broadcasting Corporation, London, for material in Chapter 10 from *The Listener*, Vol. LXVII; to The General Commission on Chaplains and Armed Forces Personnel, Washington, for part of Chapter 12 from *The Chaplain*, Vol. XVI; and to The National Association of Biblical Instructors, Philadelphia, for material in Chapter 16 from *The Journal of Bible and Religion*, Vol. XXXI.

J.M.

UNION THEOLOGICAL SEMINARY

NEW YORK

April, 1964

Contents

In Defense of Theology PART I

How Is Theology Possible?

1

Soon after I first became a teacher of theology, I was invited to take part in an interesting university teachers' conference. Its aim was to do something toward combatting the unfortunate results of the increasing specialization of studies, whereby a theologian, let us say, is in the dark about science, while an engineer finds philosophy unintelligible. The plan was to get a representative from each major field to explain as clearly as possible to scholars from other fields just what was the nature of his own studies. Knowing that I would have scientists, classicists, lawyers, medical men and, indeed, all sorts and conditions of scholars in my audience, I took great care to prepare a paper which, I fondly hoped, might transmit the theological theme on a wave-length that could be picked up by all present. The hope was speedily shattered in the discussion that followed the paper. A physicist said something like this: "The speaker was quite intelligible until he introduced the word 'God' into his talk. This word does not stand for anything within my range of concepts or experience, and so every sentence in which it was used was to me meaningless, and the whole paper became unintelligible. Will the speaker kindly tell us what the word 'God' signifies?"

These remarks were, of course, somewhat disconcerting to me at the time. But it soon became clear to me that my scientific colleague had rendered me a valuable service. He had taught me a first principle of hermeneutics, namely, that there must be at least some basis of common ground between an interpreter and his audience if the interpretation is to get under way. He had shown me further that in a secular age one may not assume that language about God affords a universally intelligible starting point for an interpretation of the Christian faith. Above all, he had raised for me very acutely the question: "How is theology possible?" For if theology is the interpretation of our Christian faith in God, and if this interpretation is not merely an academic exercise within an esoteric Christian community but has become, in the words of the founders of Union Theological Seminary, "impressed with the claims of the world," so that it must address the world, then where is a beginning to be made?

Whether we are Christians or secularists, we share our humanity. Is this then the common ground from which a theological interpretation can begin today? Christianity is a doctrine of man as well as of God. John Calvin, as is well known, having remarked that true and solid wisdom consists almost entirely of two parts, the knowledge of God and the knowledge of ourselves, went on to say that "as these are connected together by many ties, it is not easy to determine which of the two precedes and gives birth to the other."[1] Calvin himself began with the doctrine of God, and this is probably the logical place to begin, and was also an intelligible beginning in an age when most people took religion very seriously and could discourse in a theological idiom. But in a secular age, we have to consider the alternative.

Someone, of course, may object here that Calvin began with the doctrine of God for quite another reason—namely, that man can be properly understood only in the light of God. Every Christian would agree that this is true, but it is a truth which by no means rules out the possibility of taking man as the starting point for an interpretation of the

[1]*Institutes of the Christian Religion* (London: James Clarke, 1953), I, 37.

Christian faith. If man is, as Christianity asserts, a creature of God and dependent on him, then this should show itself in a study of man. It should be possible to see man as fragmentary and incomplete in himself, so that we are pointed to God; and if we can see man in this way, then we can go on to a fuller understanding of him in his relation to God. The advantage of such a procedure is that it would help us to answer the question put by people like my scientific colleague at the conference. If we can begin from the humanity which we all share, and if we find that this humanity points beyond itself for its completion, then we have, so to speak, indicated the place of the word "God" on the map of meaningful discourse. Union Theological Seminary's President, Henry P. Van Dusen, has written some time ago: "It is an accepted premise of Christian thought that all the major beliefs of its faith are mutually involved and interdependent. It should be possible and legitimate to make one's start from any one of them, and approach all the others through it."[2] Let us then accept his statement, and see how far it is possible to travel along the road that begins from man himself.

Our question then is, "What is man?" or, to put it more concretely, "Who are you?" Obviously this question admits of many answers, according to the context in which it is asked. It could be answered, "I am a British subject," or "I am a Protestant," or "I am a graduate"; and each of these answers might be quite adequate and appropriate within a particular context. To elicit the Christian answer, and to see how it makes sense, we must first understand the kind of question to which it claims to give the appropriate response. A German writer, Hans Zehrer, tells us about "the man from the hut." This man was a refugee from the East, now living in an overcrowded hut in what had once been a military camp. Once he had had a wife and two children as well as numerous friends, once he had had a home and a well stocked farm, once he had had what we call the comforts of life and a secure place in society. Now all these have been stripped from him and he is thrown back on himself. For the first time, the question "Who are you?" has thrust itself

[2]*Spirit, Son and Father* (London: A. & C. Black, 1960), p. 3.

on this man in a radical way. As Zehrer formulates it: "Well, tell me, who am I, then, and what am I living for, and what is the sense of it all?"[3] We are likely to ask the question about ourselves in this radical way only very rarely. It may even be the case, as some philosophers tell us, that we shrink from the question and screen ourselves from it. Yet perhaps everyone faces it at least once in his life. To this question, "Who are you *at bottom?*" the partial and superficial answers that normally suffice for the question "Who are you?" are no longer adequate.

Perhaps our secularist friend will cut in at this point with the brusque observation that this radical question about ourselves just is *unanswerable.* In a sense, he would undoubtedly speak correctly. For if we are to answer so radical a question about ourselves, would it not be necessary for us, so to speak, to detach ourselves from ourselves, and to stand back so as to view all time and all existence, and thus learn where we fit into the scheme of things? Manifestly it is impossible to do this. So if the question "Who are you?" has disturbed us, would we not do well to put it out of our minds as an insoluble enigma?

We might gladly do this, and perhaps for a large part of our time we might succeed in doing it. But surely we are deceiving ourselves if we believe that we can get rid of the question altogether. If it is true in one sense that *we cannot answer the question*, it is paradoxically true in another sense that *we cannot help answering it.* For this is no speculative question, such that we could take it up or lay it aside at pleasure. It is the question of ourselves, and because we have to live and make ourselves, the question is demanding an answer all the time. In every policy that we adopt and in every unrepeatable action that we perform, we are giving an answer and taking upon ourselves an identity. Always and already, we have decided to understand ourselves in one way or another, though such self-understanding may not be explicit in every case.

These reflections introduce us to the basic polarity of our human existence. We are on the one hand *limited*. We find ourselves thrown into an existence, and we cannot by any means step out of this existence

[3]*Man in this World* (London: Hodder & Stoughton, 1952), p. 13.

in order to get a detached objective view of it. Thus we can never know with certitude its why and wherefore. On the other hand, we are *responsible* for this existence. Every day we have to take the risk of deciding to understand our existence in one way or another. It is little wonder if to some this polarity seems to be just an insoluble contradiction, so that human existence is essentially an absurdity and foredoomed to failure. "Man," Jean-Paul Sartre tells us, "is a useless passion. To get drunk by yourself in a bar or to be a leader of the nations is equally pointless."[4] But before yielding to such pessimistic conclusions, let us ask if it is possible to understand our existence in a more hopeful way. If we are willing to entertain such a possibility, then we are ready to consider what Christianity tells us concerning ourselves.

The Christian answer to the question "Who are you?" frankly acknowledges the polarity or tension that lies at the core of all human existence. The finitude and precariousness of man's life is a familiar theme in the Bible—his origin from the dust, the limitation of his power and knowledge, the brevity of his life and the inevitability of his death. At the same time, there is the theme of man's freedom and distinctive place in the world—he has dominion over nature, he aspires after ideals and realizes values, he is under judgment as one who is accountable for what he makes of his life and his world. There is here no flight from the human condition, no comforting concealment of its dilemma. Man has to walk the razor edge between his finitude and his responsibility.

A further element in the Christian understanding of man seems to heighten the difficulty of making sense of human existence, and to carry us just as far as Sartre in the direction of hopelessness. This further element is the doctrine of sin. There is a pathological disorder in human life, a radical alienation deep within our existence, and on account of it we fall down on one side or the other from that narrow precipitous path along which we have to walk. Sometimes, perhaps in protest against optimistic humanism, theologians have exaggerated the doctrine of sin, especially in some of their formulations of the ideas of

[4] *L'Être et le néant* (Paris: Gallimard, 1943), pp. 708, 721.

"original sin" and "total depravity," but all of them agree with the New Testament in maintaining the universality of sin and its gravity.

Some theologians, such as Reinhold Niebuhr, have seen the essence of sin in pride, so that sin is interpreted as man's attempt to be rid of the finite pole of his existence and to exercise an unlimited freedom. Niebuhr, however, has been criticized for his alleged neglect of the sins of indulgence, which would seem to arise rather from an attempt to be rid of the pole of freedom and responsibility, in seeking to descend to the level of a merely animal existence. But in either case, man becomes untrue to the being that is his. He refuses to accept himself as *at once* free and finite. Of course, although he may not accept his destiny, he cannot escape it either, and hence comes the language of "alienation" in regard to sin. Sinful man is estranged from himself by his refusal to take upon himself an identity which on the other hand he cannot completely discard, an identity which includes both the poles of his freedom and his finitude.

This Christian understanding of man, as so far expounded, is just as desperate and radical as Sartre's. But of course, Christian theology does not remain at the point of despair. It must bring us to this point, to make clear its conviction that *there is no human solution to the human problem.* If man is abandoned to his own resources in the world, then Sartre seems to be right; our life is a useless passion and its ineluctable outcome is failure. But must we halt here? Already the analysis of the situation points to another possibility, though only as a possibility. This is the possibility of *grace*—a power from beyond man which can heal his estrangement and enable him to live as the being which he is, the being in whom are conjoined the polarities of finitude and responsibility. This possibility of grace seems to be the only alternative to despair if we are to take as honest a view of the human condition as Sartre does, and not conceal from ourselves how insoluble is the enigma of man in human terms.

But where are we to look for grace? Clearly, we cannot look to the world of things. That world knows nothing of our predicament. Sartre indeed feels nausea for its solid plenitude of senseless being, which throws into poignant relief the isolated lot of man as the fragile existent that is "condemned to be free."[5] We may not share Sartre's disgust, but clearly a lower order of being cannot *of itself* provide grace, even though it might become a vehicle of grace. Are we then to look to other persons? Sartre is inclined to see other persons chiefly as obstacles to the ambitions projected in one's own existence. We would hope that we did not share such an egocentric understanding of life, and would acknowledge that a man can be helped and strengthened by his fellows. But is even this the source of grace we are looking for? Clearly not, for without depreciating the help that one may receive from another, we must not lose sight of the fact that all men are in the human situation together and that sin and its divisiveness are universal.

If grace is to be found anywhere, it must come from beyond the world of things and the society of human beings, though it may indeed come through these. We are directed toward a transcendent source of grace. This is neither a senseless nor a speculative idea, but rather a question of life and death that arises directly out of the structure of our own existence. It is the question of God, for "God" is the word which the religious man uses for the transcendent source of grace. When people like my sophisticated colleague ask what the word "God" signifies, we can only invite them to ask themselves in a radical way "Who am I?" for this question of man already implies the question of God or is even, as Bultmann says identical with it.[6] The quest for grace allows the word "God" to find its place on the map of meaningful discourse; and with it, other theological words find their places—"finitude" may be equivalent to "creatureliness," and "sin" may acquire its full signification as "separation from God."

So far this is a meagre result. We have raised only the *question* of God. Nothing has been said about his reality, and the very word "God" remains as a formal expression with a bare minimum of content. It is of

[5]*L'Être et le néant*, p. 515.

[6]*Jesus Christ and Mythology* (New York: Scribner, 1958), p. 63.

course important that we have found this question to be one that is raised by the very structure of our existence, for this provides the orientation that enables us to see the possibility of theology as a meaningful and important area of discourse. But can we now go further?

In asking the question of God, man must already have some idea of God, for every question has its direction, and it is impossible to seek anything without having some understanding of what is sought, however vague and minimal that understanding may be. The next step toward grappling with our problem is simply a phenomenological exploration of the question of God itself. What is the structure of this question? How should it properly be formulated? What is already implicit in the question? What conditions would have to be fulfilled for it to receive an affirmative answer?

We must remember that our question is the *religious* question of God, and that it has an *existential* structure. That is to say, it is not a theoretical or speculative question, raised by the intellect alone and asked in a general, disinterested way, but a practical question posed by the whole being of man, who has to exist in the world and decide about his existence. Perhaps the question of God can be raised in a purely theoretical way, but this would not be a question of any direct interest to theology, and perhaps it would not even be a manageable question. We could think, for instance, of the question of God as a *cosmological* question, in which "God" would stand for an explanatory hypothesis, put forward to account either for the world as a whole or for certain events in the world. For a long time men did try to account for many happenings in terms of supernatural agencies. With the rise of science, however, we have learned to look for our explanations in terms of factors immanent in the natural process itself. The famous remark of Laplace to Napoleon, "I have no need of that hypothesis," simply expresses our modern attitude to the world as a self-regulating entity. Science, of course, stops short of the ultimate question of why there is a world at all, but this is simply an acknowledgement that for the finite human intellect which is within the world, such a question is unanswerable. The religious question of God, as existentially structured, is different from any theoretical question about an explanatory hypothesis. We are not looking for some invisible intangible entity to the existence of which we might infer. Perhaps we are not looking for an entity at all, or for anything that could be conceived as a possible object among others.

These remarks at once suggest that we must be highly suspicious of the traditional formulation of the question of God—a formulation which runs, "Does God exist?" For this question already contains implicitly the idea of God as a possible existent entity. The question is parallel to such a question as, "Does there exist another planet beyond Pluto?" This is not at all like the religious, existentially structured question of God. This latter would need to be formulated in some such way as, "Can we regard Being as gracious?" It is a question about the character of Being. Either Being may have the character of indifference toward man, in which case he is thrown back on himself and must understand himself in a secular way; or else Being has the character of grace, so that human life can be lived in the strength of a power from beyond man himself, and ceases to be the tragic contradiction, the useless passion, which it would be in the absence of grace.

"God" is the religious word for Being, understood as gracious. The words "God" and "Being" are not synonyms, for Being may have the character of indifference, and in that case it could not be called "God" nor would any religious attitude towards it be appropriate. "Being" can be equated with "God" only if Being has the character of grace and is responsive to man's existential predicament. Now Being cannot itself be regarded as an entity, for it is manifestly absurd to say "Being exists" or "Being is." Being does not itself belong within the category of particular beings—or "entities", as they may be called to avoid confusion—of which one can assert that they either exist or do not exist. In Heidegger's language, Being stands to entities as the wholly other, the *transcendens,* the non-entity which is yet "more beingful" (*seiender*) than any possible entity. But if God is equated with Being as gracious, then the question, "Does God exist?" involves what British analytical philosophers have taught us to call a "category mistake." The question is not whether some entity or other exists, but whether Being has such a character as would fulfil man's quest for grace.

Can we see more clearly what conditions must be fulfilled if Being can be recognized as God? We have seen that the question of God arises from man's estrangement from himself, and from his inability to bring into unity the poles of finitude and freedom which together constitute his being. These two poles must remain in perpetual and frustrating conflict if there is no positive relation between the Being out of which man has emerged as a finite centre of existence, and the values and aspirations toward which, in his freedom, he aims as at the goal of his being. If Being has the character of grace and can be identified with God, the condition to be satisfied is that the Being out of which man arises coincides with the end of his freedom, thus bringing into unity the polarities of his existence and healing his estrangement. Among modern theologians, this idea comes out most clearly in Paul Tillich, who has two typical ways of talking about God, namely, as "ground of being" and as "ultimate concern." But precisely the same structure is discernible in the more traditional accounts of God. For instance, Oliver Quick writes: "God is the alpha and omega of all things, the source from which they proceed, the end toward which they move, the unity in which they cohere."[7] The language here is perhaps cosmological rather than existential, but this description of God has precisely the same structure as the one at which we arrived by an existential and ontological route.

This must suffice for the phenomenological description of the question of God. The question has, so it is hoped, been clarified, and we see better its meaning and requirements. But the matter cannot be left here. If it were, I might be accused of showing that theology is a possible study of the possible, rather than showing that theology is possible as a study of the most concrete reality. But what kind of evidence can we

[7]*Doctrines of the Creed* (London: Nisbet, 1938), p. 18.

now seek, to bring content into the hitherto formal structures of the analysis?

It is clear that even if in what has been said I have been engaged in some kind of philosophical or natural theology, I have cut myself off from the rational or deductive style of natural theology, by which so many theologians of the past sought to ground their subject and to establish the reality of its matter. Apart from the fact that their arguments have been largely discredited by modern criticism, I have tried to show that their speculative approach was a mistaken one and that their leading question about the existence of God involved a logical defect in its formulation. In any case, their speculative approach, if we may call it such, was an artificial one, for all those who tried to prove the existence of God already believed in him, and must have had a more primordial source for their conviction than their own arguments. Where then are we to look?

At the risk of lapsing into theological incomprehensibility, I must now boldly introduce the word "revelation." Yet this is not a word that need frighten us. Clearly, nothing whatever can be known unless in some way it reveals or manifests itself. Of course, something more than this obvious commonplace is implied in the theological idea of revelation. When it is said that the knowledge of God is revealed, the word is used to point to a kind of knowledge distinct from that which we attain through our own effort of thought. The knowledge of God, it is claimed, comes to us as a gift, and to indicate its distinctiveness by the word "revelation" is simply to remain true to the phenomenological analysis of belief in God, for such belief testifies that it arises through God's making himself known to us, rather than through our attaining to the knowledge of him. The Bible never suggests that man has to strain his mind to figure out a shadowy Something behind the phenomena. There is indeed recognition of man's innate quest for God, but it is maintained that God himself meets and satisfies the quest. Man does not search out God, but rather the reverse is true. One of the greatest of the Psalms begins: "O Lord, thou hast searched me and known me!"[8]

[8]Ps. 139: 1.

and goes on to describe the ubiquity and inevitability of the encounter with God.

What kind of language is this? Of what kind is this knowledge of God, where that which is known towers above us, as it were, and it is as if we ourselves were known and brought into subjection? Perhaps we glimpse an answer to these questions if we consider three possible ways in which we may be related to that which presents itself to us in such a way that it becomes known to us. The first case is our everyday relation to things, as objects of which we make use or have knowledge. They are at our disposal, and even by knowing them, we acquire a certain mastery over them; for instance, we can predict natural phenomena and be prepared for them. The second case is our relation to other persons. This "I-thou" relation, as Martin Buber has taught us to call it, is of a different order, for the other person is not my object and is not at my disposal. I know him in a different manner. The relation here is one between subjects. It is a mutual or reciprocal relation, founded on the same kind of being—personal being—on both sides. Now it is possible also to envisage a third kind of relation in which there is presented to us Being itself. In this kind of relation, we do not have the other term of the relation at our disposal, nor do we stand to it in a relation of equality, but rather we are grasped by it, our eyes are opened to it, and we are brought into subjection to it, but in such a way that something of its character is disclosed to us, so that to some extent it becomes known to us.

Correspondingly, we may say that there are three modes of thinking. We think of things in objective terms, and this presumably is the commonest type of thinking. We think of our friends differently, as those with whom all kinds of relations are possible that are impossible with things. And it is possible to think too of Being which, though it towers above us, does not annihilate us but rather communicates itself and gives itself in the experience of grace. To talk of revelation does not mean an abrogation of thinking, but only that all our thinking is not of the same pattern. Tillich talks of the ecstatic reason which still does not cease to be reason.[9] Heidegger speaks perhaps more soberly of the thinking that is submissive (*hörig*) to Being.[10] Whatever expression we may prefer, this is the kind of thinking that makes theology possible. Theology is the task of sifting and explicating and interpreting God's encounter with man, as this is recollected in tranquility.

If someone is still asking, "What does all this prove?" then the answer must be in line with what has already been said—it *proves* precisely nothing, for the kind of philosophical (or natural) theology that has been sketched out here is not demonstrative but descriptive. Perhaps what we take to be the encounter with God is an illusion; perhaps it is all explicable in terms of a naturalistic psychology; perhaps all our talk of sin and grace and existence and Being is only mystification. These are possibilities that cannot entirely be excluded, even when within the community of faith the experience of grace has begun to produce the fruits of wholeness and serenity in place of estrangement and anxiety. The impossibility of demonstration in these matters is simply a consequence of what we have learned from the analysis of man himself—that he is finite, that he is not the godlike but rather the worm's-eye view, that so long as he is *homo viator* he lacks the unclouded clarity of vision, and must go forward in the attitude of faith, and in the risk of faith.

But on the other hand, if nothing has been proved, at least something has been described. The way has been described that leads from man's confrontation with himself to his confrontation with God and, with the aid of concepts drawn from contemporary philosophy and theology, this way has been shown to possess a coherent pattern, an intelligible structure, and its own inner logic. When challenged to produce the credentials of his subject, the theologian cannot in the nature of the case offer a proof, but he can describe this area of experience in which his discourse about God is meaningful, he can ask his questioner whether he recognizes his own existence in the Christian doctrine of

[9] *Systematic Theology* (Chicago: University of Chicago Press, 1951), I, 124.
[10] *Was ist Metaphysik?* (7th ed.; Frankfurt: V. Klostermann, 1955), p. 13.

man as finite, responsible and sinful, whether he finds hidden in himself the question of God. The theologian can also show that faith is not just an arbitrary matter, and he can make clear what is the alternative to faith. Beyond this, perhaps, he cannot go, but is not this sufficient? For it brings us to the point where we see that this discourse about God has to do with the most radical and concrete matters in life, the point where, exercising our freedom in finitude in all the light that we can get, we decide to take either the risk of faith or the risk of unfaith.

The Service of Theology

2

The very title of this essay may occasion some lifting of eyebrows. Is not theology the most authoritarian of subjects? Has it not consistently sought to be the master rather than the servant? Does it not lay down dogmas to which men are expected to conform? And whatever the word "dogma" may have signified originally or however it may be understood among professional theologians, has it not now acquired in ordinary usage the meaning assigned to it in one of our leading English dictionaries: "an arrogant declaration of opinion"?

There was a time, so we are told, when theology was the most venerated of all branches of study, but that time is long since past, and today its stock has fallen very low. Theology is despised by those who stand outside of the Church. They doubt whether it is a genuine branch of serious study at all. They question whether it should still be taught in our universities. They remember that theologians have in the past interfered with the progress of various sciences, and tried to impede them. They cannot see that theology has any service to render. Moreover, theology is also despised by many people within the Church. When the average congregation is looking for a new minister, it rarely attaches much importance to theological qualifications. It looks for a popular preacher, an active pastor, an able organizer, but it mistrusts the so-called "academic" type, for it must be acknowledged that theology often seems as remote and useless to the ordinary church member as it does to the secularist.

These considerations, however, merely show that theology, like everything else, can become perverted. If theology sets itself up as a heterogeneous collection of infallible information about every subject under the sun, then it rightly earns the contempt of the scientist. And if it should happen, as James I. McCord has recently expressed it,[1] that theology gets "divorced from the life of the Church" and "has been betrayed into sterile intellectualism and scholasticism," then it is rightly suspect in the eyes of the ordinary church member. It would seem therefore that before we can properly discuss the service of theology, we must be clear about what theology is and about what it is not.

A book such as H. R. Mackintosh's *Types of Modern Theology* illustrates the bewildering variety of forms which theology may take—and of course there are other forms besides those which Mackintosh considers, some of which have emerged even in the generation or so that has elapsed since his book was written. Underlying each type of theology there is a distinctive conception of what theology is. How are we to decide which is the correct conception—indeed, how are we to know whether there is any one correct conception? Perhaps there are different styles of theology, just as there are different styles of art, and perhaps each one can claim its right and justification. It may help if we consider briefly two extreme points of view.

On the one hand, some apologists have made the claim that theology is an empirical science. They endeavour to narrow the gap between theology and other branches of learning, to minimize the offence which theology gives to the secularist, and to argue that as an empirical science theology is as securely based as any other empirical science, and has as much claim to a place in the spectrum of university

[1]In *The Reformed and Presbyterian World*, XXV/2: 70.

studies. Superficially, the word "theology" looks much the same as the word "geology." One would mean "discourse about God" and the other "discourse about the earth." But whereas the earth is visible, tangible and generally accessible to the senses, God is not so. The similarity of designation between the two branches of inquiry conceals a radical difference. The claim that theology is an empirical science affords a good example of an apparently important assertion which, on examination, needs to be qualified to such an extent that the original claim is eroded away to something relatively insignificant. When we examine the claim about theology, we find that it involves a twofold equivocation. There is firstly an ambiguity in the adjective "empirical." As commonly used nowadays, this adjective is applied to that which can somehow be tested by sense experience; but as the apologist who claims that theology is an empirical science uses the word, the meaning is qualified or stretched to cover experiences which are allegedly nonsensory. Secondly, there is a similar ambiguity in the noun "science." W. C. Dampier is perhaps not far from common usage when he defines "science" as "ordered knowledge of natural phenomena,"[2] but the apologist who claims that theology is a science will usually also lay claim to a knowledge of more than natural phenomena, and he must once more stretch the meaning of the term which he uses. I do not wish to deny that a wider meaning can be given to the expression "empirical science" than that which is commonly given, or even that it may be unfortunate that the range of "empirical" and "science" has been narrowed down in modern times. But I do wish to point out that in view of the current usage of words, it is so highly misleading to speak of theology as an "empirical science" as to be almost positively incorrect; and by the time the misapprehensions have been removed by the suitable qualification of both the adjective and the noun, the original assertion has become quite shadowy and probably unimportant. Nothing is to be gained by minimizing the difference between theology and all

[2] *A History of Science* (3rd ed.; London: Cambridge University Press, 1942), p. xiii.

other "-ologies." Such a procedure can only be irritating to the philosopher and the scientist, and confusing to the theologian himself. We must clearly recognize that theology is somehow *different* from other branches of learning.

At the opposite extreme, there are those who think of theology as a purely esoteric body of knowledge. This knowledge is claimed to be based on a divine revelation, and is held to be completely discontinuous with any other knowledge that we may have. It is self-contained and self-authenticating, it can be neither confirmed nor disproved by human reason, and the extreme advocates of this point of view seem to claim that it can indulge freely in paradox and antinomy, and it can even rejoice in absurdity. But supposing that what we get to know through divine revelation is "wholly other" or "qualitatively different" from what we get to know in other ways, the knowing is not itself qualitatively different from other knowing—if it were, we could not speak of "knowing." Such knowledge could not even *contradict* our natural knowledge unless it were in logical relations with it. Divine revelation is presumably something which is unique in its nature, and calls into play a special mode of knowing. Theology, however, as reflection upon and explication of such revelation, is not identical with the revelation. It is a branch of inquiry which must have regard for logic, and part of its task is to clarify the relations between what it claims to know and what we get to know in other disciplines. The theologian, if he is not going to live in a private world, must be prepared somewhere to emerge from the circle of theological ideas. If he gains nothing by minimizing the difference between his subject and other branches of study, he loses everything by making that difference absolute. It is part of his service—and this at least is implied in the name "theo*logy*"—to make his discourse as intelligible as possible (*pace* Kierkegaard and the "knight of faith").

Theology, we have argued so far, is different from what is commonly called an "empirical science," and yet it is not so different that there can be no relation between theology and other fields of knowledge. We must now try to work out these characteristics of theology in such a way as to arrive at a clearer understanding both of the nature of a genuine theological inquiry, and of the service which it renders.

Let us suppose that an overseas visitor to England is watching a game of cricket for the first time in his life. He sees one man bowling the ball, and another hitting it with his bat, he sees the batsmen running the length of the pitch and running back again, he sees the field changing over, and it all means nothing to him. And when the batsman steps out of his crease and pats a few blades of grass with the back of his bat, the visitor is completely mystified. Nothing in the game has any significance for him, and he wonders why the British are able to work up such enthusiasm for it. In such cases, we would attempt an explanation. We might get a book of rules and instruct the visitor in them. These rules tell us how the game is actually played. When we had got to the end of them, the visitor might say, "Well, I begin to see what they are doing, and that there is some method in their madness, but nevertheless I think it is a remarkably stupid game." If we ourselves, however, were cricketers, we might feel that he was hardly as yet qualified to pass so sweeping a judgment, and we might pass on to a different kind of explanation. We could put a bat in his hand, stand him at the wicket and send down a few balls—in other words, we could induce him to participate in the game. Only then, the cricketer would maintain, could our visitor begin to understand properly what this game really is—what it demands in the way of alertness, what skills it develops, and so forth. Possibly the visitor might become interested and begin to share something of the enthusiasm of the players. But if he still thought it a very stupid game, it is hard to see what more could be done for him and it would seem that we would have to give up trying to explain.

To the outside observer in the twentieth century, the life, work and worship of the Christian Church may seem as odd and unintelligible as the game of cricket to the visitor in our analogy. Once again, of course, it is possible to give some kind of explanation from the outside. The observer can be instructed in the history of religion and in the development of Christianity as an historical phenomenon. He can be instructed in the psychology of religion and shown the ways in which religious attitudes originate. These subjects do, in fact, have their place in any study of religion. But when everything has been said that can be said under these headings, we have still only scraped the surface of the problem of explanation. We have still not arrived at theology, in the proper sense.

Theological explanation is of the second kind mentioned in our analogy—it is explanation which necessarily involves participation. It is from the inside, not from the outside. This is the point at which the theologian is in a radically different position from the natural scientist. The scientist is, so far as possible (and this qualification is demanded because it may be that all knowing involves some degree of participation), detached from his subject-matter and aims at purely objective description. The theologian is dealing with something that can be understood only through becoming involved in it. It is not just an accident of style that in some of the greatest theologians of the Church, such as St. Augustine and St. Anselm, we find that prayer and exposition stand side by side in their writings and that they pass almost imperceptibly from the one to the other. Theology is grounded in faith; it is faith expressing itself, faith making itself articulate.

It need hardly be said that in the New Testament sense of the word, "faith" does not stand for a mere belief. Faith includes belief, but it includes also obedience. It is an attitude of the whole personality. Hence arises one of the peculiar characteristics of theological language which, as some of our logical analysts express it, is at once descriptive and prescriptive. That is to say that it does not deal with intellectual abstractions but always relates to the concrete situations in which men live and act and choose. It may be recalled that in the exchange of correspondence which took place between Adolf von Harnack and Karl Barth in 1923, one of Harnack's accusations was to the effect that Barth was transforming theology from a science into a form of preaching. Perhaps these men represented extreme positions, but Barth was right in so far as he saw that a genuine theology cannot be just an academic study of religion but is rather the explication of a faith by which men live. Preaching, in its turn, as the proclamation of the acts on which the faith of the Church rests, must be theological if it is to be more than an emotional appeal or entertaining rhetoric. The congregation which is looking for a popular non-theological preacher does not want a preacher at all.

Because it is rooted in faith, theology is a necessary part of the Church's service. Like all other Christian service, it is at once a gift and a task. The knowledge which comes with faith is described in the New Testament as a gift of the Spirit: "The revelation of the Spirit is imparted to each, to make the best advantage of it. One learns to speak with wisdom, by the power of the Spirit, another to speak with knowledge, with the same Spirit for his rule."[3] Yet the Christian who has received such a gift of the Spirit has a duty to grow "richer and richer yet, in the fulness of its knowledge and the depth of its perception."[4] The service of theology is to pursue and promote this growth in the knowledge and understanding of Christian faith. The faith of the ordinary church member is often implicit rather than explicit. Situations arise in which he needs guidance. Theology is serving the Church when it makes clear the bearing of the Christian faith in such situations, and theology itself is never in danger of becoming "academic" in the bad sense so long as it keeps in touch with these situations. St. Paul's theological insights find expression in letters written to help the local churches with their problems, and theological advance has taken place since his time wherever the faith has been interpreted and elucidated in relation to the Church's concrete problems, needs and opportunities.

The situations will be of many kinds, and the questions will arise in varying contexts. They may arise in the field of doctrine, as with the advent of a hostile philosophy, such as Marxism; or in the field of church order, as in efforts toward reunion; or in the field of personal

[3]I Cor. 12: 7-8.
[4]Phil. 1: 9.

conduct, as in the face of new moral problems such as those presented by techniques of contraception and artificial insemination; or in the field of social ethics, as in the matter of racial tensions. The boundaries between systematic theology, practical theology and Christian ethics are fluid, but in each case the service of theology is the same—to enable the Church to see each question clearly in the light of the revelation of God in Christ.

Although I have laid considerable stress on the need for theology to be related to the life and experience of the Church, this should not be taken to imply a completely subservient attitude. It may sometimes be the duty of theology to criticize accepted beliefs or practices of the Church. This internal criticism is itself a service, and so that it can be properly exercised, the Church should ensure all reasonable freedom in theological discussion.

Up till now I have spoken of the service which theology renders within the Church. I seem to have left aside the visitor from overseas in our analogy, the man who had no conception of cricket at all. Has theology any service to give to those who are outside of the Church? Of course, it could be said that in so far as theology serves the Church in the ways already described, it indirectly serves the larger needs of the world by contributing to the witness which the Church bears in its preaching and in its life. Theology has its part in that prophetic ministry in which the Church speaks forth to the world. But is there not a more direct way in which theology may serve those who are outside of the Church?

There is such a way, and it lies in that branch of theology which is usually called "apologetics." Yet here again the boundary-line between the several theological activities is not a hard and fast one. Dogmatics and apologetics cannot be sharply separated. Indeed, there is good theological precedent for the view that the Church and the world cannot be sharply separated, for the Church on earth is always a *corpus permixtum*, and the boundaries between the Church and the world are blurred. In so far as those within the Church are never sealed off from the prevalent secular thought of the age, they need an apologetic if they are to hold the faith firmly and intelligently in their generation. And in so far as there are many outside of the Church who are asking the kind of questions to which the Christian faith gives answers, they have that minimum of participation which is necessary to an understanding of the faith, if it is put to them in language the meaning of which they can grasp. While remaining true to the faith once delivered to the saints, theology must in its apologetic function find new terms, new ideas intelligible to the contemporary world, new cultural forms capable of making impact. It may borrow ideas from the current philosophy, and indeed theologians have done so from New Testament times onward. This does not imply a secularizing of Christian thought, though no doubt there is always the danger of distortion. What is aimed at is rather the Christianizing of current language and culture, and the dangers have to be faced. If theology shrinks from this wider service, then Christianity will increasingly become not a proclamation any more but a museum piece.

For there is a real danger that in our day Christianity may find itself not so much rejected as merely disregarded. This danger seems to me far more serious than the alleged danger of having Christian faith corrupted through alliances with modern philosophies. Since theology rediscovered its kerygmatic character a generation or so ago, it has tended to remain within the charmed circle of its own ideas. In the process, it has become more and more isolated. While this essay has fully conceded the difference between theology and other studies, it has also stressed that theology stands in relation to them. In the end, truth is one and our knowledge should be one. The theologian must step out of his circle. Surely we believe that the modern man to whom the Gospel is addressed should not be asked just to take a leap in the dark. He deserves to be shown, so far as it can be shown, that Christianity is a faith which can be reasonably held in the twentieth century. And who is to perform this service for him, unless it be the theologian? Admittedly there are difficulties which can only be solved *ambulando*, as one moves along in the life of faith, and admittedly there are mysteries which can never be fully penetrated. As has been fully recognized, understanding demands here some participation, and cannot be given in advance. But this by no means relieves the Church of removing preliminary obstacles to faith, by showing that the Christian message is not just a tissue of absurdities.

If I have in any way rightly described some of the tasks of the theologian, then he should be the last man to become arrogant or dogmatic, in the bad sense. He must rather be frightened by the responsibility that is laid upon him. He can only turn to his fellow-servants in the Church and say: "Pray for me too, that I may be given words to speak my mind boldly, in making known the Gospel revelation."[5] His is no privileged position. Sometimes he will be tempted to pervert it. Often he will fall down on his task. But a genuine Christian theology, seeking as it does to interpret the revelation given in him who took the nature of a servant, is itself an essential service both to the Church of Christ and to mankind. Still more, it is a service to God, for the true science of God, as more than an intellectual discipline, leads to the love of God and is inseparable from it.

[5]Eph. 6: 19.

Some Philosophical Presuppositions PART II

Feeling and Understanding

3

Schleiermacher's theology, which has been under a cloud in recent years, seems to be claiming attention once more. In several passages[1] Paul Tillich has called for a renewed examination of the thought of Schleiermacher who, he thinks, has been the victim of mistaken interpretation. Schleiermacher's famous definition of religion as the "feeling of absolute dependence" has been rejected as romanticism or sentimentalism or irrationalism, because it was supposed to banish religion to the regions of subjective emotion. Apparently Tillich himself took this view at one time, for at an earlier stage of his career he declared that "Schleiermacher injured the understanding of religion by delivering it to emotional subjectivity."[2] But now, we are told, all such criticism is beside the point. Feeling, as Schleiermacher understood it, is not merely subjective emotion but includes awareness and is therefore not without a cognitive function. We misinterpret Schleiermacher unless we see that for him feeling refers, in Tillich's words, "to the awareness of that

[1]*Systematic Theology*, I, 18, 47, 170.
[2]"The Two Types of Philosophy of Religion" in *Union Seminary Quarterly Review*, vol. I/4, p. 10. This passage has been revised in the reprint of the essay in *Theology of Culture* (London: Oxford University Press, 1959), pp. 23-24.

which transcends intellect and will, subject and object."[3] It is to be compared with Rudolf Otto's "creaturely feeling" or with Tillich's own concept of "ultimate concern." Admittedly these remarks call for a good deal of elucidation, but clearly they are putting forward the suggestion that feeling, or at least some kinds of feeling, is much more than the "mere feeling" or subjective emotion that it is often supposed to be. If this suggestion is correct, then much of our suspicion of feeling may be unfounded, and the theologian has a duty to seek a clearer understanding of what feeling really is, and of its place in the structure of religion.

Tillich's remarks are timely from another point of view, because there are a number of influential contemporary philosophers who assert that religion is a matter of feeling, and they understand this as "mere feeling." Alfred J. Ayer, for instance, has contended that both ethical and religious statements are not genuine propositions but pseudo-propositions; and by this he means that they do not make any significant assertions but simply evince feeling, so that they can be neither true nor false but are strictly meaningless.[4] Of course, there has been a reaction against the extreme point of view which Ayer represented, and there are many philosophers of the analytical school who would not follow him on these points. Stephen Toulmin rejects Ayer's view of ethics, and he says further that it is only if we mistakenly regard religious questions as being of the same nature as scientific questions that "we have any grounds for concluding with Ayer that all utterances about the nature of God are nonsensical."[5] The older view that simply swept ethical, religious, esthetic and other types of utterance into the comprehensive categories of the "emotive" and the "nonsensical" is no longer widely held, and it is recognized that the various kinds of statements may have their own meanings and their own uses, and that they may have to be judged by criteria other than those which apply in the case of the state-

[3]*Systematic Theology*, I, p. 47.
[4]*Language, Truth and Logic* (2nd ed.; London: V. Gollancz, 1946), pp. 102-20.
[5]*Reason in Ethics* (Cambridge: Cambridge University Press, 1950), p. 212.

ments of empirical science. This broader outlook surely represents an advance. Yet there are still many who would be inclined to retain the more extreme view in the case of religious utterances, and to say that these refer to nothing in reality, but simply serve to express subjective feelings which some people happen to have while other people do not. This view remains plausible because feeling obviously does play a part in religion. So we are pointed again to the task to which Tillich's remarks had also directed us—that of asking about the place of feeling in religion and in religious assertions.

It is an error to attempt to reply to the positivist's attack on the meaningfulness of religious statements by seeking to minimize the element of feeling which is bound up with them, or by representing them as rational objective judgments pronounced in the absence of feeling. The mistake consists precisely in this, that it is a tacit acceptance of the false presupposition on which the attack itself is based, namely that feeling is "mere feeling," a subjective emotion divorced from any cognitive function. The correct procedure is not to fall over backward in an attempt to get away from feeling, but to show that the opposition between feeling and understanding, on which the emotive theory's denial of meaning to religious statements rests, is false and misleading. We have to look anew at feeling in religion and its relation to understanding.

H. H. Farmer has correctly pointed out[6] that feelings are highly specific. Pure feeling is an abstraction, and when we do experience a feeling, it is a feeling of some definite kind. There are moral feelings and religious feelings, while on a more mundane level there are feelings like fear and boredom. Even within such groupings, feelings differ in kind, and it may be worth recalling that most languages seem to possess very rich vocabularies for naming the various shades of feeling. When we inquire about differences of feeling, we see that feelings differ according to the different situations which evoke them. For every feeling includes a reference to a situation in the world (it is, in Brentano's expression, "intentional"), and it arises in the interaction of the self and the world.

[6]*Revelation and Religion* (London: Nisbet, 1954), pp. 74-75.

Furthermore, every feeling carries with it an awareness, an understanding however vague, of the situation to which it refers in its intentionality. At least implicitly, it asserts that the situation has a certain character. A feeling of fear, for example, carries an awareness of some threat, and asserts that something has a menacing character. Of course, the awareness which belongs to feeling may be only rarely put into words or raised to the level of an explicit understanding. No doubt man feared before he had a term for or a concept of the menacing. But already the understanding was implicit in his fear as a preconceptual awareness of the menacing. And so it is with all other feelings. Whether or not what they give us to understand is put into words, it is always in principle capable of being made explicit as a statement which expresses what the feeling itself implicitly asserts about the situation which has evoked it. In other words, there are no "mere feelings," but only feelings which give us to understand something and which, as "intentional," make assertions.

Thus when Ayer says that a sentence of the form "Your going to London last week was wrong" asserts no more than "You went to London last week," conjoined with a feeling of disapproval, he has by no means shown that "wrong" is a meaningless symbol and merely an interjection expressive of subjective emotion. For the feeling of disapproval is no mere emotion but, when it is evoked by a particular situation, it carries the implicit assertion, "This is wrong." As Sir David Ross has put it, "It is impossible to disapprove without *thinking* [italics mine] that whatever you disapprove is *worthy of disapproval* [italics his]."[7] All that Ayer has shown is that the original sentence can be broken up into two shorter sentences: "You went to London last week" and "That was wrong." This is of course very useful, since it draws attention to the fact that the two sentences seem to be making assertions of very different kinds. The first is a plain factual proposition, easily verifiable by some empirical test or other. The second is an ethical judgment which does not seem to be so obviously verifiable, and yet, as we

[7]*The Foundations of Ethics* (London: Oxford University Press, 1939), p. 34.

have seen, it makes an assertion and does not just evince a subjective emotion. Ayer has not explained away its meaning, but he has certainly made the problem of its meaning more urgent.

At this point we may receive some help from certain of the existentialist philosophers, whose investigations will confirm that to every feeling belongs its own understanding, and will throw further light on the nature of this understanding. We find Sartre writing a book round the feeling of disgust.[8] The book consists largely of a description from day to day of passing moods, and the reader is left with the impression that Sartre has tried to convey to him through the description of changeable feelings an understanding of human existence that perhaps could not have been so well communicated in any other way. However, let us turn to the more exact and philosophical analyses of feeling carried out by Martin Heidegger.[9] He does not use the term "feeling" but rejects it, as he does with so many other traditional terms, because of the misleading associations that have gathered round them; and of these misleading associations in the case of "feeling," the chief is the notion of "mere feeling" or subjective emotion. Heidegger does indeed allude to theories of the "affects," but he prefers to speak of "state" or "condition" in the sense of the "way one finds oneself" (*Befindlichkeit*), or alternatively of "mood" (*Stimmung, Gestimmtheit*), the way one is "attuned" to one's situation. As a typical illustration of such a state or mood, he carries out an analysis of fear.

Leaving aside the details of this particular analysis, there are three points which we may notice in Heidegger's treatment of feeling-states. The first has already been sufficiently stressed—it is that to every such state there belongs its own understanding. Such a state, in Heidegger's terminology, "discloses" something to us. Clearly this disclosure is different from the perception of an object through the senses. Yet the disclosure makes us aware of something, gives us to understand something, asserts that to something there belongs a certain character; and although

[8] *La Nausée* (Paris: Gallimard, 1938).

[9] *Sein und Zeit* (6th ed.; Tübingen: Niemeyer, 1949), pp. 134ff.

the understanding may be only implicit in a passing mood, it is always in principle capable of being made explicit through the reflective analysis of the mood.

A second point is that what is disclosed is a structure or pattern—something like the *Gestalt* of which some psychologists speak. It has already been said that a feeling is evoked by a situation, and this is a more accurate way of speaking than to say that it is evoked by an object, even if it has a special reference to some object in the situation. Considered purely as an object, nothing can have ascribed to it any other properties than those perceptible by the senses or at any rate deducible from sense perception. Your going to London, as mere observable occurrence, has no moral character. It can only evoke a feeling of disapproval when it is disclosed in a structural context which gives it its character of being wrong. Again, the same tiger which would be disclosed as menacing were I to meet him in my back garden would evoke no fear and would not have a menacing character were I to view him suitably restrained at the zoo.

Thirdly, the structures thus disclosed, together with the characters to which they give meaning and which we are given to understand in the disclosure, cannot be described as either subjective or objective. They belong to the situation in which we are ourselves involved. They embrace both the self and the world, that is, they belong to existence, and the understanding of them may be called "existential." Such understanding is prior to the separation of subject and object. A purely subjective and a purely objective understanding are alike abstractions from the self-world correlation which alone makes possible any understanding whatsoever. Such purely subjective or purely objective understandings are therefore fragmentary. This is why Heidegger is led to claim that the disclosure implicit in a mood or feeling-state is more *primordial* or *original* than the disclosure yielded by any purely objective understanding. Again, he points out that even the most penetrating objective understanding could never disclose anything like the menacing. Also, we are now in a position to understand Tillich's remark, quoted earlier, in a clearer way. He asserted that feeling, as Schleiermacher understood it, refers to "the awareness of that which transcends intellect and will, subject and object." The mention of intellect and will is, of course, an allusion to Schleiermacher's discourse *On Religion*, where religion is distinguished from these and located in feeling; while the transcending of subject and object arises from the way in which feeling operates in a situation already involving the self.

Heidegger recognizes a fundamental feeling-state (*Grundbefindlichkeit*) which, he claims, yields a disclosure of a unique kind. This fundamental state he identifies with an ontological anxiety.[10] Such anxiety, unlike other moods such as fear with which it is explicitly contrasted, is evoked not by any particular situation but by man's total situation as a being thrown into existence, knowing neither his whence nor his whither, but simply that he is in the world. It discloses man to himself in his finitude, as limited possibility, and we may call it an "ontological" state of mind because it lights up man in his being. This description of anxiety immediately invites comparison with the religious feelings already mentioned, not only with Otto's "creaturely feeling" but also with Schleiermacher's "feeling of absolute dependence" and Tillich's "ultimate concern." In the last two, the adjectives "absolute" and "ultimate" indicate the same reference to a total situation. It may well be, of course, that in any given case religious feeling will be stirred by some particular object, but this will happen only in so far as the object (let us say, a crucifix) has acquired the character of a religious symbol and points beyond itself to the total situation.

Elsewhere in his writings Heidegger seems to imply that feelings other than anxiety may light up the total situation and have some ontological import. He mentions both joy and boredom in this connection.[11] But this does not take away from the special place given to anxiety in his philosophy, and it would seem to be anxiety that most easily links up with specifically religious feeling-states, such as awe.

[10] *Sein und Zeit*, p. 184.
[11] *Einführing in die Metaphysik* (Tübingen: Niemeyer, 1953), p. 1.

Curiously enough, we find in Ayer too a tacit recognition that religious feeling is not "mere feeling" but carries some significant assertion. Having denied that there can be any quarrel between science and religion (on the ground that there can be no logical relation between the propositions of science and the nonsensical pseudo-propositions of religion!), he goes on to say that there may be antagonism between the two for another reason. This is that "science tends to destroy the feeling of awe."[12] It holds out to man the prospect of increasing mastery over natural phenomena, and so weakens the sense of his finitude and of his inability to determine his own destiny. It is therefore not strictly science, but a dogma (for one could scarcely call it an empirical hypothesis) of human self-sufficiency and perfectibility born of scientific and technical advance–it is this which is alleged to destroy the feeling of awe. But what does "to destroy the feeling of awe" mean, except to contradict the understanding implicit in that feeling, namely, that man is not self-sufficient but a finite creature before God? There is a logical relation here, one of contradiction, between an assertion about man implicit in the religious feeling of awe and a secular theory of man such as one would expect to be popular in a period of unparalleled technical advance. And since there is a logical relation, then religious statements have a meaning after all. Actually, in this passage Ayer has put his finger on a main source of irreligion, but the phenomenon which he describes has been known at least since the writers of Genesis set down the story of the tower of Babel. But our concern is to note that here we have a tacit recognition that to a religious feeling similar to those that have been described, there belongs an implicit understanding which is capable of being significantly asserted.

Let us now pause to see where the argument has led us. We began with the reaction among many theologians against Schleiermacher's view of the place of feeling in religion, and we widened the argument to take in views that religious utterances are nothing but expressions of subjective emotion, so that they make no meaningful assertions. But

[12]*Language, Truth and Logic*, p. 178.

noting Tillich's change of mind on Schleiermacher, we endeavoured to show that both the hostility of some theologians to Schleiermacher and the positivists' emotive theory of religious language arise from a misunderstanding of the nature of feeling. For feeling is never divorced from cognition, and always conceals in itself an implicit assertion. We acknowledged that what is asserted in this way is different from what is asserted in a factual proposition, and making use of Heidegger's analyses, we found that the meaning of the assertions which are implicit in feeling is to be sought in structures in which both the self and the world participate, that is to say, they come before the separation of subject and object. So the position now reached is that we have found that the assertions that arise out of our feeling-states are meaningful, and are presumably capable of being either true or false.

The next problem is to find a criterion for judging the truth of such assertions, for our feelings are notoriously misleading, and while I certainly want to reduce the sharp opposition between feeling and cognition, I do not wish for a moment to give the impression of suggesting that we must always rely upon our feelings. Even if the understanding which belongs to feeling is, as Heidegger claims, a primordial or original one, it is also a fallible one. I can fear something which is not in the very least menacing, as when I am the victim of a phobia; and I can reverence something which has no claim to be holy, as when I lapse into idolatry. The very fact that we can think of feelings being misplaced in such ways as these is itself evidence that we are not dealing only with subjective states of mind. The feeling does not create the character which is asserted of the situation, but discloses it, since the character is no more subjective than it is purely objective. No doubt there are many possibilities of error, at least three of which are clearly described by Heidegger.[13] There may be failure to recognize a character, or the character may be buried over, or—the commonest and most dangerous case —the character is misplaced or put in the place of another. How then are we to sift and criticize the understandings that belong to feeling,

[13] *Sein und Zeit*, p. 36.

and especially to religious feeling, which is our main concern here?

It should be obvious at once that those methods of logical procedure which are applicable to the objective statements of science have no relevance here since, as we have seen, religious statements are of a different kind from scientific propositions, and require a different criterion. But the trouble is, to quote a picturesque sentence of Toulmin, that "the question of God's existence is often discussed by philosophers in a way which would only be appropriate, if it were the literal counterpart of the question, 'Are there any one-eyed cats?' "[14] It is little wonder that, when such methods of discussion are used, religious assertions come to appear as either false or quite meaningless. Tillich says bluntly that attempts to prove the existence of God as an object are bound to lead to negative conclusions, because God is not an object.[15] Dom Illtyd Trethowan has done useful work in helping to dispel some of the misunderstandings which encourage this false approach to the question of the meaning and validity of religious statements.[16]

The difficulty in setting aside the ordinary logical procedures is this, that the theologian seems to be saying that he is not going to submit his statements to the same kind of tests that are applied in most other branches of inquiry, and at once he becomes suspect as the dogmatist who lays claim to a private store of authoritative information, access to which is denied to ordinary people. But this difficulty ought to be set aside when it is understood that religious statements (at least, of the kind we have been considering here) are of quite a different order from factual propositions.

The obvious criterion for religious statements would be some form of phenomenology. Heidegger expounds a method of phenomenology which is a modification of Husserl's, but it will be sufficient here to quote a few sentences of Tillich: "Theology must apply the phenomenological approach to all its basic concepts, forcing its critics first

[14]*Reason in Ethics*, p. 213.
[15]*Theology of Culture*, p. 25.
[16]See *An Essay in Christian Philosophy* (London: Longman, 1954).

of all to see what the criticized concepts mean and also forcing itself to make careful descriptions of its concepts and to use them with logical consistency, thus avoiding the danger of trying to fill in logical gaps with devotional material. The test of a phenomenological description is that the picture given by it is convincing, that it can be seen by anyone who is willing to look in the same direction, that the description illuminates other related ideas, and that it makes the reality which these ideas are supposed to reflect understandable. Phenomenology is a way of pointing to phenomena as they 'give themselves,' without the interference of negative or positive prejudices and explanations."[17] If, as we have seen reason to believe, religious statements point to the fundamental structures of man's existence and are not factual propositions about objects in the world, then the method which Tillich describes would seem to be the appropriate one for sifting and criticizing what these statements give us to understand.

We conclude that the basic religious feelings should be neither ignored by the theologian nor dismissed as irrelevant by the philosopher, as though they had nothing to tell us. The existentialist analysis of the disclosive character of affective states seems to me an important contribution, and a corrective to a one-sided reliance on the objective, detached thinking that is characteristic of the sciences. Indeed, if it is denied that there are disclosive moods of the kind described by Heidegger and others, I find it hard to see how one could avoid positivism, or claim for religion any cognitive element whatever. Disclosive feeling-states seem to be a presupposition of religion, and one part of philosophical theology would consist in the explication of the disclosures which belong to these states and in the analysis and clarification of what they give us to understand.

There is another consideration which shows that this task has more than theoretical importance, and that it has also apologetic possibilities. Tillich has remarked that in his experience the most impressive way of introducing people into the meaning of religion has been to begin with

[17]*Systematic Theology*, I, 118.

such affective experiences as anxiety, care and the like. The person accustomed to matter-of-fact ways of thinking, to whom even the simplest statement of Christian doctrine may seem puzzling and irrelevant, is nevertheless likely to be acquainted with feelings such as anxiety, and perhaps even awe. These offer a point of departure for the attempt to make religion meaningful to such a person, if he can be shown that such feelings are not mere emotions without significance but that they arise from and disclose the very structures of human existence, which can only rest in God.

Death and Its Existential Significance

4

To claim that death may provide an important clue to the understanding of human existence may strike us as paradoxical. Death—or so it would seem at first sight—is not so much a factor that constitutes existence and makes it what it is, as rather simply the end of existence, the purely negative phenomenon of ceasing to exist. No doubt we would all acknowledge that the way in which a man meets his death sometimes reveals more clearly than anything that has taken place before in his life what kind of man he really is. Occasionally we may even revise our judgment of someone in the light of the way he died, as if somehow death could have a certain redemptive character. "Nothing in his life became him like the leaving of it," says Malcolm, alluding to the executed thane of Cawdor, and we cannot help feeling some respect for the dead man who "died as one that had been studied in his death," even though most of his life seems to have been one of treachery and cruelty. Yet such cases seem to be exceptional, and we would need much more persuasion to convince us that death has a major role to play in elucidating the character of human existence in general, and still more to establish the claim that death is a phenomenon of basic philosophical importance. These however are precisely the ideas that we meet in Martin Heidegger. Death occupies such a central place in his exposition of human existence that he can describe this existence as a being-towards-death; and when he moves from the consideration of human existence to the wider philosophical question of Being, it is still the phenomenon of death that marks out the way into this inquiry.

There is about Heidegger's philosophy, even for his admirers, something disturbing and at times a little irritating. He seems to take us into a strange new world, so that no matter how widely we may have read in the traditional Western philosophy from Plato and Aristotle down to the moderns, we look in vain for the familiar landmarks. The terminology is different, the very problems seem to be different, and perhaps we are puzzled to know where he is taking us and whether what he is saying is very important or merely very mystifying. To some extent, of course, this is due to Heidegger's deliberate attempt to shake us out of the traditional approaches to philosophy into new ways of thinking, or possibly into ways that were lost long ago. As he sees it, Western philosophy has been dominated by what he calls a "forgetting of Being," and this is not just an accidental characteristic but one which arises out of the way in which our own being is constituted, so that we human beings who alone do the philosophizing have an inherent tendency to cover up Being and to disguise its genuine character. For this reason, Heidegger visualizes one of his tasks to be the "destruction" of the traditional ontology.

Such a destruction is not to be understood as a purely negative undertaking. It is rather an attempt to exhibit how the traditional approaches have gone astray in virtue of tendencies that belong to our very existence, so that it may become possible to reach back behind the tradition to the primordial sources of philosophizing and to find a new and more adequate approach. The first step in any such enterprise would therefore lie in bringing to light the basic structure of human existence itself, since it is out of human existence that all philosophizing arises. So Heidegger built up his impressive analysis of human existence in terms of care, with its threefold structure of possibility, facticity and falling; and in turn care is shown to be made possible by a temporality which is bounded by death. Thus death receives a key position in the existential analytic; and since this analytic is offered to us not as a philosophical anthropology for its own sake, but as a "fundamental ontology" which is to provide a bridgehead into the question of Being in general, the importance of the phenomenon of death extends into Heidegger's entire ontology. It is death indeed that summons us back from the "forgetting" of Being and makes possible something like a confrontation with Being.

Heidegger's approach is a novel one, taken as a whole, but perhaps what will strike most of us as strangest of all in it is just this extraordinary focusing of attention upon death. It is true that many philosophers have touched upon death in one way or another, as have also theologians and literary men. But it could not be said that death has been a central idea in Western philosophy. This, of course, could be a symptom of the alleged "forgetting" of Being, for with Heidegger death would seem to be an indispensable clue in investigating the riddle of Being. It may be of interest to recall what Richard Kroner, a former colleague of Heidegger, has to say about the impression which *Sein und Zeit* created in German philosophical circles when it appeared in 1927. After speaking about the "baffling new insights" of Heidegger's book, and acknowledging that he himself had read it with "a breathless tension," Kroner goes on to say: "What was most fascinating and startling to me was not so much his metaphysical conception of Being, but rather his thoughts about death and mortality. These thoughts seemed to be in the very centre of his whole discussion." Kroner then recalls that in his own student days, there had been much talk in Germany of the "philosophy of life" (*Lebensphilosophie*), popularized by Nietzsche and others. It had widely established itself in literary circles, but according to Kroner it was suspect in the eyes of professional philosophers, who thought of it as romantic and emotional, but unscientific and easily refutable by a serious analysis. "Heidegger, however," continues Kroner, "had transformed this philosophy of life into a philosophy of death and had furnished it with the solid defence of a critical method, thus giving it academic respectability. In this new attire, the formerly rejected philosophy of life demanded the greatest attention and the most careful study. Was this philosophy that dared to make death the dominant problem of a new ontology still philosophy in the traditional sense, or was it merely the manifestation of a revolutionary feeling, aimed at arousing people?'"[1]

This question is still being debated. Can death have for philosophical understanding the importance that Heidegger claims for it? Or is it the case that in spite of the apparently strict and systematic character of his phenomenological analyses, Heidegger is just as much a romantic as the exponents of the philosophies of life, to be read perhaps as a poet or a seer rather than as a philosopher? And if so, can we then set aside his puzzling and disquieting utterances about death and existence and Being as the expression, which may be interesting to some people, of one man's subjective and emotional reactions to the human situation, but not to be accepted as a statement of any philosophical consequence?

How we answer these questions will depend on where we consider the sources of philosophizing to lie. Is philosophy a purely intellectual procedure, so that it must be carried out in abstraction from the affective and volitional sides of our humanity by techniques of reasoning alone? Or does philosophizing have a broader basis—at least, such philosophizing as can take for its theme the question of Being? Must this kind of philosophy be rooted in the total human existence, and not on any single abstract factor in that existence, so that we take account of the insights and disclosures that may arise in affective and volitional experience as well as of the generalizing judgments of discursive thought? Or to put the matter in another way: are we disclosed to ourselves as existents who are always already in a world—a world with which we are concerned and involved in all kinds of ways—so that it is

[1]"Heidegger's Private Religion" in *Union Seminary Quarterly Review*, XI/4, p. 24.

out of this total situation that we must seek after whatever understanding of Being may be possible for us; or are we, as the traditional Western philosophy has been inclined to regard us, primarily thinking subjects, before whom there is spread out for our inspection a world, and this world is to be understood in a genuine way only along the lines of detached theoretical inquiry?

If we give our assent to the second of these alternatives, then we may as well proceed no further with Heidegger. He has nothing to say to us, or at least, nothing of philosophical interest. However, Heidegger would not be perturbed to hear that what he has said, especially about death, amounts to nothing. For as he tries to show in *Was ist Metaphysik?*, this very "nothing" raises a question of its own: "How does it stand with the nothing?" It may be that what our common-sense empiricism sets contemptuously aside as "nothing" is, after all, not just nothing. Heidegger on his side would tell us that even the most penetrating theoretical investigation of the world, of man, and of his behaviour would miss (regard as nothing) aspects of basic significance in these phenomena. This significance is disclosed only in our participation as total existents who are affectively and conatively involved in the world, as well as being able to behold it in a theoretical way.

In the light of these remarks, then, we may understand that Heidegger does not propose to discuss death when considered as a natural phenomenon. It is of course not denied that death can be considered in this way, and indeed this is how the biologist looks upon it. Even to biological science, it would seem, natural death remains something of a mystery. It is a phenomenon which does not occur among some of the simpler living things, and it is not clear why the higher organisms should be subject to senescence and eventually to death. But this natural phenomenon of the ending of a life, a fate which man shares with many other living things and which Heidegger calls "perishing" (*Verenden*), is something much less than is intended by the expression "death." Physiology, zoology and related sciences can investigate the termination of life from their own point of view as natural sciences, but this does not tell us about death as it interests Heidegger—namely, death as an existential phenomenon.

It must be pointed out also that just as Heidegger is not interested in death as a natural phenomenon such as one might discuss from the point of view of the biological sciences, he is equally careful to leave aside any speculative questions which might be raised in a metaphysical discussion of death—the very questions which philosophers have traditionally raised in connection with death. Whether, for instance, man has a life after death or whether he can have another kind of being in another world, these are questions that Heidegger does not raise. "The this-worldly ontological interpretation of death," he tells us, "takes precedence over any ontical other-worldly speculation."[2] That is to say, it is only after the character of death as a phenomenon that is immanent in human existence has been fully explored that one can see whether it makes sense to ask about what may be after death, and how such a question can be raised. Likewise the question of the origin of death and its significance as an evil which afflicts mankind is not one which Heidegger proposes to consider, for to answer such a question, or even to formulate it properly with an understanding of what it entails, would imply not only that we had already grasped the existential phenomenon of death but also that we had arrived at a wide understanding of Being in general, and in particular of negativity and evil.

Distinct from both the naturalistic and the metaphysical approaches to the question of death is the existential one. This existential question inquires about the significance of death as something belonging to human existence, as one of the constitutive factors in the structure of such an existence. But does this idea not contradict the common-sense view mentioned at the beginning of this essay, the view that death is not a factor that goes to constitute existence, but simply the end of existence, ceasing to exist? We find this common-sense view coming to expression in another contemporary philosopher, Ludwig Wittgenstein, who declared: "Death is not an event of life. Death is not lived through

[2]*Sein und Zeit*, p. 248.

(*erlebt*)."[3] Wittgenstein's second sentence raises a further difficulty. For even if we could accept that death is an event of life, or a factor in existence, how could it be investigated phenomenologically if it is not "lived through" or experienced? An existential understanding of death, one might suppose, could only come out of the total existence that was itself involved in death and dying. If death is to be investigated by the same method of phenomenological analysis that Heidegger employs in the rest of the existential analytic, there are clearly difficulties here that do not attend any of the other phenomena analysed. Understanding, moods, speech, anxiety, concern, solicitude—these are all phenomena of existence that undoubtedly go to constitute our daily living. We know them from experience and from continuous participation in them, and from reflection upon them it is in principle possible to describe their structures and lay bare the conditions which enable such existential attitudes to come into play. All this is possible because our experience of these matters is a "living through" them, so that we are then able to reflect upon them and describe them.

But how about death? Death is precisely the kind of experience (if indeed this word may be used) which we do *not* live through, or if in some sense we do, at least we do not live through it as the beings that we were before death. Death can be described ontologically as "loss of being." Hence, since death is the loss of his being, anyone who undergoes death seems by that very fact to be robbed of any possibility of understanding and analysing what it was to undergo death. He has ceased to be, therefore he has ceased to be disclosed to himself; his being is no longer lit up to himself in the only way that would seem to make anything like an existential analysis possible, and so it appears that he cannot by any means understand what the undergoing of death may be like, as an existential phenomenon.

Heidegger of course is aware of these difficulties. His own conviction is that death does indeed enter into the structure of existence, for existence itself is a being-towards-death. Existence is dying, and death is

[3]*Tractatus Logico-Philosophicus* (London: Kegan Paul, 1922), p. 185.

present to us and, in a way, accessible to us, although we normally turn our attention away from it. But to see how he leads into this understanding of the matter, let us follow the skilful way in which he narrows down the existential question of death.

His first move, when he is confronted with the difficulty of how anyone can understand his own death, is to ask whether it might be the case that we can learn about death by observing the deaths of others. We can see them ceasing to exist, going out of the world, so to speak. But clearly this vicarious experience of death is not adequate for grasping it as an existential phenomenon. The death of the other is experienced as the loss sustained by those who are left behind, but what is really of interest to us is the loss of being sustained by the deceased himself, and this remains completely inaccessible to us. And he cannot any longer communicate with us to describe this loss of being. So it would seem that an inquiry into the death of others, while it might teach us much about the natural phenomenon of coming to the termination of life and much too about social customs connected with death, psychological reactions in the face of death, and so on, can never disclose death as an existential phenomenon. Yet even from this seemingly negative result, one positive characteristic of death has emerged—namely, that death is always someone's own death, and cannot be experienced vicariously. There are innumerably many ways in which one person can represent or stand in for another, and we utilize these ways every day. But nothing of the kind is possible in the case of death. Death shares one of the characteristics that Heidegger recognizes as belonging fundamentally to all human existence; it is always *someone's own* (*jemeinig*). No one, Heidegger maintains, can die for another, in the sense of taking the other's dying away from him and performing his death for him. It is true of course that one man can go to his death for another, and in this way perhaps save the other's life in a definite situation and for a longer or shorter time. "Such 'dying for'," however, "can never signify that the other has thus had his death taken away in even the slightest degree."[4]

[4]*Sein und Zeit*, p. 240.

So the unsuccessful attempt to reach an understanding of death by observing the deaths of others does at least conduce to the recognition that death is untransferable.

Heidegger also considers the possibility whether there are any analogies that might throw light on the character of death. We could think of what remains of life as something still outstanding, such as a sum of money that has still to be paid to make up a certain amount. Is death something like the payment of the final instalment, which settles the account? This analogy is not a good one. Human life has a unity which does not allow it to be usefully compared to a procedure in which separate instalments get added on until a sum is reached. Or we may think of death as an end—the end of the existent as a being-in-the-world. But the word "end" has many meanings, from just stopping or breaking off, to reaching a goal. From a consideration of these unsatisfactory analogies, it is argued that death is a kind of end that is not just added on, so to speak, but an end that somehow belongs to the very being of man. This suggests another possible analogy. If death, as an end, is somehow intrinsic to the existence which it terminates, could we liken it to the ripeness of a fruit? This is not something that gets added on to the fruit in its state of immaturity; it is rather a specific way in which the fruit itself *is* or comes to be. But this particular analogy cannot be pressed too far, for whereas ripeness is the fulfilment of the fruit, the end may come for man while his powers are still undeveloped or it may delay until he is broken down and exhausted, with his fulfilment long past. Here again, however, something positive emerges from these unsuccessful attempts to comprehend death. The very lack of suitable analogies drawn from the level of things or even of living organisms points us to existence itself as the level on which we must look for further understanding. So the analysis is carried out in terms of that which constitutes existence—care with its threefold structure of possibility, facticity and falling.

As possibility, death lies in the future. Indeed, it lies at the very boundary of the future, closing it off. Death is the uttermost possibility, the possibility that cannot be outstripped, in the sense that there is no further possibility beyond death. We cannot get behind or beyond it, and all the other possibilities of existence are, so to speak, spread out in front of it. We must notice that by a "possibility," Heidegger does not mean just something that may happen to us at a future time. To exist is to stand before possibilities in the sense that these are the various ways of being and acting that are open to us in any particular situation, and for one or other of which we may decide. Now it is clear that if we think of death as a possibility, it is a possibility of a quite unique kind. It is the possibility of ceasing to be, the possibility of not having any further possibilities, and hence the uttermost possibility. It may seem very odd to talk of death as a possibility at all—and indeed Sartre sees it rather as the cancellation of all possibility and the final absurdity. But Heidegger's point is that death must be reckoned in with my possibilities. It need not be left as a loose end, an arbitrary and contingent happening that will one day befall me. It can be taken up into existence as the capital possibility before which all the others are stretched out and in the light of which they are to be evaluated. But what does it mean to take up death in this way? To take up any possibility, in the sense of deciding for it, is to cut off other possibilities; but to take up death, as the possibility of the impossibility of further existing, might seem to mean cutting oneself off from possibilities altogether. Heidegger, of course, does not mean that one rushes suicidally into death, or even that one broods upon death. But what is required is to be free for death, to anticipate it in such a way that it is brought into existence and one lives now in the face of it as one's uttermost and untransferable possibility.

If death relates to the future as possibility, it also relates to what has been, that is to say, it belongs to the facticity of existence. It is not something accidental or occasional in human existence, but something into which every existent is already thrown. To be born is already to be on the way to death, so that existence, as a being towards the end, is also a dying. Thus death is handed down to us along with our being as part of our heritage. We can take it over passively or we can actively appropriate it. Under no circumstance, however, can we get away from it. It is the one certain factor in our existence, and yet along with its certainty there goes an indefinite character—it can happen at any moment.

Thus death is also, in a sense, already in the present. It is already accessible, as thrown possibility, to the investigation of the existential analytic. But here we come to the parting of the ways. A "fallen" or "inauthentic" existence, which is characterized precisely by its tendency to dwell in the present, nevertheless covers up from itself the present possibility of death. It interprets the indefiniteness of death to mean "some time—but not now." We all know how in everyday talking the theme of death is made harmless and anonymous. It is a question too whether ceremonies for the dead, from those of ancient Egypt down to the controversial funeral customs of contemporary America, are not motivated at least in part by the flight from the finality of death. At least, one rarely finds death recognized as Heidegger understands it: as one's very own, present, certain, untransferable, uttermost possibility.

If it is characteristic of an inauthentic mode of existing to cover up death or to relegate it to an indefinite future as something that will happen "one day," an authentic existence is characterized by its freedom for death. In such freedom, there is the frank acceptance that our human existence is a being-towards-death. The man who exists authentically resolutely anticipates death, orders his day-to-day possibilities in the light of this capital possibility and finds, Heidegger tells us, joy in this mode of life.

Death is the mark of human finitude. Our existence is temporal, and our temporality is bounded. But even traditional Western philosophy has assisted in the process of disguising the finite and temporal character of existence. Heidegger criticizes, for instance, Hegel's theory of time as an inauthentic way of taking time, because it visualizes man as caught up out of his finite temporality into an immortal and unending process. Thus not only on the unreflective but also on the philosophical level is there operative the tendency to concealment that is, according to Heidegger, inherent in all human existence. So we now begin to see how his understanding of death is to play a part in the "destruction" of traditional ontology, while at the same time it will shape the new "fundamental ontology."

Is Heidegger himself then the advocate of a kind of nihilism? Is this the final meaning of his exaltation of death and his "destruction" of ontology? Does the insistence on death as the uttermost possibility, and on the nullity that enters into the very constitution of human existence, lead us to a point of view where everything has been levelled down to the nothing?

At first sight, one might think so. But Heidegger himself insists that he is no nihilist, and indeed believes that his philosophy may rather be able to provide us with a living option to that true nihilism towards which, in his view, the Western philosophical tradition has been inexorably moving. This true nihilism is the subjective will-to-power, culminating in the age of technology; this is the true levelling down to nothing, where man is dehumanized, the gods are absent and Being is forgotten. Admittedly, Heidegger's own philosophy frankly accepts death, transience and finitude. Yet we have already seen enough of his concept of death to be impressed with the positive significance that it comes to have, and that points us beyond any merely nihilistic interpretation. This positive significance appears to be twofold.

In the first place, death becomes integrative rather than destructive for existence. An authentic existence which resolutely anticipates death and understands all living to be also dying transcends the triviality of everyday existence and achieves meaning and unity. Death makes this possible; it becomes, we must say, creative of selfhood. For it is through laying hold of and appropriating this untransferable and intrinsic possibility of the self that genuine unified selfhood is attained. In such an existence as a being-towards-death, the anticipation of death plays something like the part which the eschatological expectation played in primitive Christianity, and perhaps Heidegger is no more a nihilist than was St. Paul. Both see human existence as lying before the imminent end, in the face of which responsible decisions have to be made, and in the light of which all the possibilities that lie before the end have to be evaluated. Both let us see how futile and baseless are many of the things on which men expend their efforts, and they point the way to an attitude that can bring new seriousness, resolution and power into life.

In the second place, death or, to speak more accurately, anxiety in the face of death, has the positive role of recalling man from the forgetting of Being, and awakening him to the wonder of Being. It is the experience of nullity that brings awareness of Being and prepares the way for that "primordial" thinking which Heidegger has come to stress in his later writing, a meditative thinking in which man receives the communication of Being. From this stems the whole mystical side of Heidegger's thought. Once again, the parallel with Christian theology is fairly clear. Perhaps the closest parallel is with the thought of Paul Tillich who speaks of the shock of non-being as the prelude to the revelatory experience. It is probably the case, however, that Tillich's way of describing this owes a good deal to what he has learned from the philosophy of Heidegger.

Thus the positive religious dimensions of Heidegger's thought become clear, and these can be traced back to their origin in his concept of what is generally taken to be the negative phenomenon of death. Although I have mentioned parallels with Christian theology by way of illustration, it should be said that Heidegger's philosophy seems to offer a natural religion or natural theology which deserves to be considered in its own right and which is no doubt satisfying to some persons who are not attracted to institutional religion. Certainly we should not read the religious elements in his work through the eyes of Bultmann or Tillich or Ott or other theologians who have learned from him. But the fact that so many theologians have learned from him indicates that his philosophy is important for all religion and theology, and may well be able to provide what Christian theology seems most badly to need today—a sound and contemporary philosophical basis on which to rear its theological superstructure.

Selfhood and Temporality

5

One of the most serious problems confronting philosophical theology today is that of finding an adequate conception of selfhood. There are many areas of dogmatic theology, such as the doctrines of salvation, of grace, of judgment and of a life to come, which assume that man has, or perhaps rather is, a self or soul, and that this self or soul is somehow unitary, responsible and abiding. The business of philosophical theology is to bring into the open such a hidden assumption, to set out in a philosophically intelligible language the idea of which dogmatic theology is already implicitly making use, and to show, if possible, that this idea is a coherent and defensible one.

The problem has become serious in the case of the self because the traditional philosophical description has broken down in the face of mounting criticism. This traditional philosophical description of the self provided Christian theologians with an idea of which they have made use for centuries—the idea, namely, of the self as substance. Admittedly, it is no ordinary substance; it is said to be an immaterial substance. And it has often been supposed that only by positing such a substantial self can we find an adequate basis for such ideas as those of the unity and abidingness of the self, and above all, for any belief in the immortality of the soul. Beginning from Plato, or probably earlier still from the Orphic mysteries, the doctrine of a substantial self continued on through Hellenistic and medieval thought, and enters the modern period through the work of Descartes, who gave to the doctrine perhaps its most typical and widely influential formulation. On his view, as is well known, man has a kind of dual being. He is body and soul, and these are described as *res extensa* and *res cogitans* respectively. The *res extensa* is the material substance, whose basic characteristic is to occupy space; while the *res cogitans* is the immaterial substance of the soul, and its distinguishing characteristic is the activity of thinking. Descartes' theory is of interest not only because of the influence which it has exerted but also because of his use of the world *res* to describe both body and soul. The use of this word shows us that the underlying analogy or, so to speak, the explanatory model for the self is "thinghood." It may, I think, be fairly said that most Christian theologians from the Fathers onward have either explicitly or implicitly availed themselves of the concept of a substantial self, that is to say, of a reified self, a self which Descartes frankly designated by the word *res*. So deeply has this idea of the self as a substance become intertwined with Christian dogma that an attack on this philosophical way of conceiving the self has come to look, in the eyes of Christian theologians, like an attack on a basic conviction of the Christian faith itself.

Yet we cannot ignore the fact that such attacks have been pressed in the modern period, and that the venerable idea of the substantial self or soul is now labouring in serious difficulties, if indeed it has not been completely discredited. A notable example of such an attack is Gilbert Ryle's book, *The Concept of Mind*. His attempt to "rectify the logical geography" of mental concepts exposes the "category mistake," as Ryle calls it, of supposing that such a word as "mind" stands for some strange kind of substantial entity. Perhaps we are misled by the fact that the word is a noun, and so we suppose that there must be some "thing" corresponding to it. But such words function simply as descriptions of human behaviour. Ryle's doctrine is sometimes interpreted as a neo-behaviourism, and although this is not the only possible interpretation and while he explicitly disclaims a reductionist view of man, there is no doubt that he firmly intends to drive out the ghost from the machine and has presented a persuasive case.

Even philosophers who are perhaps more sympathetic to traditional points of view than Ryle is, are just as unhappy as he about conceiving the self in a substantial way. John Macmurray, for example, rightly sees that when we think of the self as a substance, we are trying to elucidate it on the analogy of a material thing, since this is what provides us with our normative concept of substantiality; and Macmurray's argument is that thinghood cannot be an illuminating analogy for selfhood, for a self is a far more complex mode of being than a thing, or even than a living organism.

Furthermore, theologians themselves have been joining in the attack on the traditional doctrine. The revival in recent years of biblical theology has led to the rediscovery that the Bible itself does not usually think of man in terms of two different but interacting substances, soul and body, but talks of him rather as a unity—nowadays we would say, a "psychosomatic" unity. This is nowhere clearer than in the doctrine of a resurrection of the body, which visualizes not the survival of an indestructible soul-substance on its escape from the imprisoning body, but rather the attainment of new life by the whole man.

Thus the old idea of a substantial soul is fast crumbling away, but so far we seem to have little in the way of a positive idea of the self to put in its place. To many people, it will no doubt seem that these developments are just one more nail in the coffin of the Christian faith, one more step towards the dispelling of theological superstition, and that deprived of the idea of a substantial self or soul, Christianity must abandon those traditional doctrines which seem to imply the existence of such a soul. It is just here, however, that I think that we must pay attention to some other developments in contemporary philosophy, and particularly in German philosophy of existence. Martin Heidegger has been no less severe than most of his contemporaries in criticizing the traditional (and especially the Cartesian) idea of a substantial self, but perhaps to a greater extent than most of his contemporaries he has given us something like a positive account of selfhood which might replace the traditional one; and this new account is, I believe, one that should be of great interest to the Christian theologian.

Three preliminary points may be made about this existentialist doctrine of the self. These will show us the general orientation of this style of thought, and the direction in which we must look for an alternative to the old idea of a substantial soul. They will also serve to remind us that no matter how novel some of the formulations of Heidegger and other existentialists may seem, they too have their roots in the tradition of Western philosophy.

The first point is that from the existentialist point of view, selfhood is not something that is given ready-made in human existence, but something that has to be won, indeed, even hammered out in the course of life. We are not to think of the self as some "thing" that is implanted in us at birth or at conception or whenever, but rather as a possibility before which we stand and which we either realize or let slip as we go along the way from birth to death. True selfhood is not something that is ours by nature; it is something to be gained, or perhaps lost (never gained). Here I think is our first link with the philosophies of the past, for Aristotle, it will be remembered, thought of the self or soul differently from Plato. According to Aristotle, the self or soul is to the body as form is to matter, that is to say, the self is the actualization of the potentiality of the body, where the body can be understood, if you like, as the raw material of existence in the world. To use his technical term, the soul is the "entelechy" of the body, the bringing to fulfilment of those potentialities provided by an embodied existence in the world.

The second preliminary point is that in Heidegger's account of selfhood, the basic elucidatory category is not thinghood (substantiality)—which has in any case been pretty well ruled out by our first point—but time or, better, temporality. Heidegger claims, as is well known, that the being of man is to be understood as care, and by "care" he means precisely what many of our poets have taken to be characteristic of man, namely, that what distinguishes him from the animals is that "he looks before and after" (Shelley) or that whereas in the case of the animal, "the present only touches thee," man has to say: "I backward cast my eye on prospects drear; and forward, though I canna' see, I guess and fear" (Burns). What constitutes a self is a strange and complex time-relationship in which past, present and future are somehow brought into a unity. And since nothing of the sort is conceivable in the case of a mere thing, thinghood is an utterly inadequate concept by which to explain selfhood. This second point establishes a further link with the history of philosophy, for it recalls St. Augustine's view of the temporal character of our human existence, a moving process which yet constitutes a whole, reaching back into the past by memory, judging in the present by intellect, and directed into the future by will.

A third preliminary point may be made. Whereas the idealist tradition stressed the thinking subject as the centre of selfhood, existentialism looks rather to the whole man in his active concerns with the world. It conceives the self as agent rather than as subject, although of course to be an agent implies that one must also be a thinking subject. This suggests that selfhood manifests itself most typically in what we commonly call "will" or "willing," that is to say, in the initiation of chosen courses of action in the world. Such willing has to be distinguished on the one side from mere urges or drives, and indeed one obvious measure of the attainment of selfhood is precisely the extent to which biological drives have been subjected to the intelligent will. On the other side, willing is to be distinguished from mere wishing. The latter is only a kind of hankering, a flickering of the will, as it were, so that it does not get beyond thinking of action and remains a mere velleity.

In view of what has been said already, it need hardly be added that the will is not a special faculty of the self, or a ghostly phenomenon that operates somehow behind our outward acts—though again the noun form is misleading, and we may need some of Ryle's "logical rectification" to keep us from going astray. The will is simply our way of describing the whole self in action, or as Austin Farrer expresses it, " 'will' is action itself, in the full and personal sense of the verb to 'act.' "[1] Existentialist philosophers may have little to say about "will" and "willing" in so many words (Heidegger, for instance, rarely uses these expressions, just as he avoids other traditional philosophical terms) but they have much to say in their own terminology about the phenomena which were usually called "will" and "willing" in the past, and we shall see how important these phenomena are in the existential conception of selfhood, and also how this bears on the theological notion of a faith-commitment and its place in the structure of a stable unified self.

But now let us consider in more detail the existentialist conception of selfhood. We may take our departure from Heidegger's doctrine that the being of man is care, and that care exhibits the threefold structure of possibility, facticity and falling. This, however, is not Heidegger's final analysis of human existence. He goes on to ask what it is that makes care possible; and the answer to this question is: temporality (*Zeitlichkeit*).[2] Man is possibility because he stands before a future, he is always on his way and incomplete in his being, he has always to make himself and is not provided with a ready-made nature like a stone or an iceberg. Man is facticity because he never stands before a world of virgin possibility. He always is already in a world, and more than that, he is in a particular situation in the world. In other words, he always *is* as something that *has been*, so that if possibility relates to the temporal dimension of what is to come, facticity relates to that of what has been. A man's whole past, what he has already done, what others have done before him, the whole situation into which he is "thrown"—these all narrow down the range of possibility before which he stands at any given moment. The third factor in care, falling, relates to the present.

[1]*The Freedom of the Will* (New York: Scribner, 1958), p. 109.
[2]*Sein und Zeit*, pp. 323ff.

It arises from our natural tendency to shrink on the one hand from responsibility towards the future and on the other from acceptance of what has been, and so to become merged and absorbed in the concerns of the present.

It is against this background of the temporal structure of existence that one must look for an existential interpretation of the self. At this point it may be useful to call to mind some of the standard ways in which in ordinary language we talk about certain experiences of the self. We can say: "I was not myself when I did that"; or, "He mastered himself with an effort"; or, "He came to himself"; or even, "He is at war with himself." There is nothing specially strained about these expressions, we all have a tolerably clear understanding of what is meant by them, and yet if we reflect on them for even a moment, we see that the kind of language used here is very puzzling indeed. Who is this "I" that gets distinguished from "myself"? If we follow the traditional point of view and think of the self as a "substance" or even as a "subject," this kind of talk seems to be quite unintelligible. For the notion of "substance" has as its explanatory model "thinghood," and how can a thing be anything other than itself? Is this not demanded even by the very logic of talking about things, by the so-called "law of identity"? Yet we have agreed that we do have some understanding of what is meant by such an expression as "He mastered himself," and if we think that this kind of language is saying something, and maybe even something of importance, then we have to look around for a more adequate explanatory model of selfhood than the traditional one in terms of substantiality. It is such a different model that Heidegger offers us in his explication of selfhood, and the new model is in temporal terms. The structure of selfhood is to be conceived in terms of the three dimensions or ecstases of temporality—the future or what is to come, what has been, and the present.

We can think of a thing as enduring through a series of "nows," each of which can be regarded as a discrete instant in the stretch of time through which the thing endures. It is true that what the thing is now is determined by what it has been, and that what it will be in some future instant is in turn dependent on what it is now. Yet past, present and future are here related only as successive instants, each one of which stands outside of every other one; and we think of only the instant which is now as "real," while those which are no longer now or which are not yet now are "unreal." Even an animal, we may suppose, lives "in the present," and its life-story can be conceived in terms of a succession of "nows." On the other hand, man, or more accurately, the human *Dasein* or being-there, has an openness to what has been and to what is to come in such a way that these are somehow brought into the present. Man exists in what Heidegger calls the three "ecstases" of temporality, he does not just "hop," as it were, from one "now" to the next "now," but "temporalizes" as something that always *is* in the way of *having been* and in the way of projecting itself upon what *is to come.*

We have to remember, of course, that Heidegger distinguishes between what he calls "authentic" and "inauthentic" modes of existence. These words are not meant to express some moral valuation, but to indicate whether or to what degree the complex temporal structure of selfhood has actualized itself, though it should be added that this always will be a matter of degree and may vary in different situations. We shall see, I think, that something like what has traditionally been called "willing"—though Heidegger employs a different terminology—is the decisive factor in the attainment of authentic existence.

Inauthentic existence is characterized precisely by lack of will or, to use Heidegger's language, by "irresoluteness." In temporal terms, this irresoluteness is a dwelling in the present, and could be considered as a declination from a distinctively human existence in the direction of a merely animal or even thinglike mode of being. For such irresolute existence consists in a hopping from one immediate concern to the next, from one "now" to another. And in such an existence, it is not really the *Dasein* that in any way controls the course of its existence, but rather the chance circumstances that present it with its objects of concern. Even in such concerns, the inauthentic *Dasein* has, as we commonly say, no will of its own or no mind of its own, for its preferences and judgments are imposed on it by the collective standards of the group to which it belongs. As Heidegger expresses it, "the way things have been interpreted by the 'they' has already restricted the possible options of choice to what lies within the range of the familiar, the attainable, the respectable—that which is fitting and proper. This levelling off of *Dasein's* possibilities to what is proximally at its everyday disposal also results in a dimming down of the possible as such. The average everydayness of concern becomes blind to its possibilities and tranquillizes itself with that which is merely 'actual.' "[3] Of course, this does not mean any "unreality" in the person who lives this way, any diminution of his diligence or activity, nor does the so-called "tranquillized willing" under the influence of the "they" or depersonalized collective mass mean the extinction of a genuine potentiality for being a self, but only its modification and arrestment. But this is inauthentic existence, a preoccupation with the present which screens off the future and also what has been, and so restricts the temporal dimensions of existence.

One can also recognize the case of an inauthentic preoccupation with the future, the case which fails to relate the future to the factical situation of the present and of what has been, and so tends to dwell in possibilities that are not genuinely open in the situation. Day-dreaming, utopianism and the like illustrate what I am alluding to here. This brings us back to our earlier distinction between willing and wishing, for the wish-world is a realm of unrealistic possibilities with which, so to speak, one can toy but which present no living option for decision and action. Similarly it would be possible to dwell in the past, to surround oneself with the security of familiar routines and rituals, so as never to expose oneself to the future and to the possibility of novelty and radical change.

By way of summary, we may say then that the inauthentic modes of existence are characterized by the absence of anything like will, decision or resoluteness; and that this condition can be described in

[3]*Sein und Zeit*, pp. 194-95.

temporal terms as an imbalance among the ecstases of temporality. In such imbalance, there is preoccupation with one of the three ecstases to the exclusion or at least the dimming down of the others, and the typical case is a dwelling in the present, which modifies existence in the direction of the kind of being belonging to things or animals, conceived as enduring through a succession of mutually exclusive "nows."

The idea of an authentic existence is reached by reversing the conditions which hold good in the inauthentic mode. On the one side, authentic existence is characterized precisely by resoluteness, by the exercise of will and decision; while in terms of the temporal structure of existence, this means that the imbalance among the ecstases is overcome, so that future, present and what has been are held together in their unity. This is the authentic present, the "moment" (*Augenblick*) in existentialist terminology from Kierkegaard to Heidegger. The root-meaning of the German word *Augenblick* should be borne in mind—it is a moment of vision, in which are disclosed the three dimensions of temporality, and in this respect it contrasts with the inauthentic present, which dwells in the present alone. It is indeed this possibility of the disclosure of the threefold temporal horizon that makes human existence possible, together with distinctively human activities.

To explicate further the phenomenon of selfhood in terms of the temporal structure of human existence, it will be convenient to discuss four specific topics—the unity of the self; the acceptance of the self; the self in relation to conscience, guilt and grace; and finally the immortality of the self. The discussion of these themes will orient the discussion back to the problems of philosophical theology from which we set out.

1. How is it possible to conceive of the unity of the self? We all assume that there is such a unity—I am today the same person that I was yesterday, I cannot disclaim the things that I did yesterday or the opinions that I expressed yesterday. Of course, this unity is a matter of degree. If the fact that we hold people responsible today for what they did yesterday is one of the chief evidences for our common-sense belief

in the unity of the self, it is also true that we sometimes do not hold a person accountable for a past action because, let us say, he may have been in an abnormal state of mind. I mentioned before some of the puzzling ways in which we talk about the self in ordinary language, and we may recall that one of the examples was: "I was not myself when I did that." We likewise talk of one person's being "better integrated" than another, though this is not so much an example of ordinary language as of popular psychological jargon.

Traditionally, as has been noted, the unity of the self was accounted for in terms of an enduring soul-substance (and it matters little if philosophers preferred to talk of a "subject"). Just as a table, possessed of solid enduring thinghood, persists through successive instants and remains in some way the same table, so, it might be supposed, there is some mysterious thing called the "self" or "soul" which in a similar fashion maintains its identity through time. However, we have already seen something of the difficulties in such a view of the self. Here another objection may be mentioned, one that was expressed long ago by John Locke. Let us suppose that there are soul-substances, and let us also suppose, for a moment, that the same soul might be joined to successive and different bodies, as in the theory of transmigration of souls. Then, as Locke points out, one might be driven to the absurd belief that Seth, Ishmael, Socrates, Pilate, St. Augustine and Caesar Borgia were all the same man![4] This seems to be a sufficient refutation of the view that an underlying "substance" is necessary to personal identity. Locke goes on to argue that it is consciousness that constitutes the unity of the self, so that if, let us say, I remember an action as my own action, then the same "I" is involved, and the question about a "substance" is beside the point. Locke's argument would presumably have to be modified to allow for modern theories of the unconscious, but in principle this would not be difficult. What he makes clear is that the kind of unity exhibited by a table or any other thing (substance) as it persists through time is quite different from that remarkable unity in diversity which con-

[4]*An Essay concerning Human Understanding* (London: Ward Lock), p. 244.

stitutes a self and which exhibits itself in such phenomena as memory. How then can we think of the unity of the self if the self is conceived in terms of temporality rather than of substantiality?

In the inauthentic mode of existence, we may think of the degree of unity as being at a low level. We have seen that it is precisely characteristic of such an inauthentic existence to "hop," as it were, from one concern to another, these being dictated by chance circumstances or compulsive drives or social pressures. The unity may be little more than that each concern is associated with the same physical body which we can recognize as possessing the kind of persistent identity that belongs to thinghood; and presumably the limiting case is the pathological one where personal being breaks down and there is neither responsibility nor any coherent pattern of behaviour. The unity of selfhood is to be sought elsewhere. What is characteristic of authentic selfhood is resoluteness, that is to say, that total action of the self which we call "willing." Unity is brought about where there is the steady projection of the self upon a master possibility to which all other concerns have been subordinated and in the light of which they are evaluated.

In Heidegger's philosophy, this master possibility is death, conceived as the possibility which is nearest to an absolute in human existence. Whatever the content may be, the master possibility is of the kind which Tillich calls "ultimate concern." A religious faith, considered as a commitment or engagement of the whole being of the believer, is a good example (perhaps even the paradigmatic case) of such a concern or master possibility. This resolute commitment is not an attitude taken up once for all, but rather a course or policy of action (or perhaps better, a way of being) into which the existent must keep on projecting himself in various situations. In this sense it is "willing," that is to say, personal action in which one lays hold of a possibility and throws or projects onself into it. The resultant existential unity (the attainment of which will, of course, be only a matter of degree) is not the unity of a persisting self-identical substance, of which one can say "A is A," but a unity of form. This is a different kind of unity, but it is the kind of unity which is appropriate when one tries to conceive the unity of authentic selfhood. To express it somewhat differently, it is a unity like that of a perspective where the various concerns of the existent, which are scattered in the inauthentic mode of existence, converge together upon the ultimate concern. In so far as we can conceive a religious faith-commitment as playing the part of the integrating master possibility, then we can understand also how it can be claimed that faith makes a man whole.

2. When we turn to the question of the acceptance of the self, we have to raise more precisely the question about the content of the master possibility or ultimate concern. Would any possibility serve for this purpose, and lead to a unity of the self, so that perhaps a Nazi fanatic wholeheartedly devoted to his cause would be just as good an illustration of authentic selfhood as a sincere Christian? Or have we in any case assumed too lightly that a religious faith can serve as the required master possibility?

Here we must recall our earlier distinction between willing and wishing. What was characteristic of wish was its neglect of the *factical* possibilities. It closes off an important dimension of temporality, namely, what has been, and deludes itself into thinking that all possibilities are open. This leads to a toying with unrealistic possibilities, to inaction, and, at worst, to becoming lost in a world of fantasy. If, for instance, as Sartre tells us, the ultimate concern of the *pour-soi* is to become God, like the moth aiming at the star, then man is indeed an absurd creature, foredoomed to frustration because he aims at the impossible.

Heidegger's view that death is the master possibility is not, as is sometimes supposed, an expression of nihilism. Rather it is the recognition in the fullest degree that any resoluteness that can unify the self in more than an illusory way, and that is to say, anything that can properly be called "willing" rather than mere "wish," must have regard to the full temporalizing of existence in all three of its ecstases. When we discussed the unity of the self, although memory was mentioned, our attention was chiefly on the master possibility which introduces the unifying perspective into the dimension that lies ahead. Now we must come back to what has been, the facticity of human existence, the situation into which we are already thrown and from which alone our possibilities are available. Death is the supreme "given" in human existence, although there are many other givens besides, all that man has not chosen, yet makes him what he is, all that makes any particular man what he in particular is, such as his race, his intelligence, his physical powers and so on. These all constitute facticity, the finite pole of human existence.

In exalting the supreme given, death, to the rank of master possibility, Heidegger is, among other things, drawing our attention to the fact that any authentic resoluteness, any genuine act of commitment, must take up and accept into itself that which is factically given in the situation. Magda King suggests[5] that the expressions "*eigentlich*" and "*uneigentlich*," usually translated as "authentic" and "inauthentic," might be better rendered as "owned" and "disowned." This proposal might have some disadvantages, but it has an obvious relevance to the questions we are presently discussing. An act of authentic commitment is not just self-projection into a possibility, it is the appropriation of a *factical* possibility; that is to say, it is open to the dimension of what has been as well as to the future. Otherwise it may degenerate into mere wish, fanaticism, superstition and the like. These considerations serve to remind us of the importance of the historical dimension in Christianity. Its faith-commitment is not drawn from sheer speculative possibility, but from a possibility drawn from a factical situation which was, significantly enough, the death of a man on a cross.

3. In considering the relation of the self to conscience, we must once more try to see this in temporal terms. As commonly understood, conscience is an ethical phenomenon—a superego or a kind of built-in mechanism which reflects the ethical standards of the society within

[5]*Heidegger's Philosophy: A Guide to his Basic Thought* (New York: Macmillan, 1964), p. 56.

which one lives, and regulates one's conduct accordingly. But if this were an exhaustive conception of conscience, then it would be very difficult, if not impossible, to explain why any individual's conscience should ever lead him to oppose the standards of his group, or how there could be such a thing as moral progress. The very word "conscience" (*conscientia*, συνειδήσις) points beyond the ethical phenomenon to its wider ontological foundation—to some synoptic kind of knowing, to the disclosedness in their togetherness of a number of phenomena. After all that has been said, we can say without further ado what this co-disclosedness is—it relates to the distinctive structure of human existence which moves in the three temporal ecstases of future, present and what has been, and has these disclosed in their togetherness. The authentic conscience is nothing other than the call or address of the authentic self (the unified self) to the actual self (scattered in its inauthentic immediate concerns). In ordinary language we recognize this character by talking of the "voice of conscience," and there is no need to think of this voice either in theological terms as the address of God or in naturalistic terms as the veiled utterance of society, though presumably these and other influences may play their part in shaping conscience. But our ordinary language which distinguishes the "I" from "myself" has its sufficient justification in the temporal structure of human existence.

This kind of language is justified because the self does not have a fixed essence like a thing, but is always ahead of itself, already in its potentiality for being. It is this potentiality which can, so to speak, address the actual self and so present the occasion for a commitment by holding out a possibility which we can either appropriate or let slip. This also justifies the traditional language to the effect that vice is slavery and virtue alone is free. For vice—if we may use the term—is behaviour not subjected to any authentic commitment. It must in the end be self-destructive and disintegrative. But although in a sense slavery, it need not be considered irresponsible, for this is a kind of behaviour that has not become free rather than one that is absolutely determined; in other words, we have failed to act with authentic resoluteness.

But what then is to be said of the self in relation to guilt? We seem to have recognized a good will, but no evil will. We might, of course, take comfort from the fact that there have been many philosophers, and some very famous ones among them, who have taught that men do not wilfully do evil. Certainly, if the account just given of selfhood and conscience has any truth in it, it is hard to see how anyone could wilfully do evil, since such action would be self-destructive. Yet to claim that there is no evil will is so paradoxical that we instinctively feel that there is something wrong with any theory that takes up such a point of view.

There could be several ways out of the difficulty. It might be said that strange as it may seem, men do sometimes will their own destruction and disintegration, and psychoanalysis would lend some support to the view that a subtle death-wish operates in human behaviour. However, this would be different from a wilful choice of self-destruction. A second solution then might be to follow the Socratic line, and say that the bad choices are made through ignorance. No doubt, ignorance does play its part, but it hardly allows for all the cases that have to be taken into account. It seems to me that the only way out is to take a third way—let us call it the Augustinian as distinct from the Freudian and the Socratic. This way is the frank recognition that will, resoluteness, decision and the like are constantly attended by failure and carry the seeds of guilt within themselves. The conscience summons to authentic selfhood, but the openness of the future (the potentiality which summons) is already to a greater or lesser extent closed off by what has been (the facticity of the situation). It seems that the finite self cannot escape guilt, and perhaps this is what is intended by the traditional doctrine of original sin. And here we seem to have come once more to a position where we are driven in the direction of Sartre's thought, and compelled to say that human existence is a self-frustrating absurdity; or where we must look for a religious solution in terms of a divine grace which can accomplish what will and resoluteness of themselves cannot do. It may be noted here that if we attend only to the earlier writings of Heidegger, we might think that his views on these matters are Pelagian or even Promethean, and that if man can accomplish anything in the way of selfhood or wholeness, he can do so only through his own efforts. But as Heidegger's thought has unfolded, more and more stress has been laid on the initiative of Being, which must give itself to man if he in turn is to gain his true humanity.

4. Something must finally be said about the difficult question of the self and immortality. Does not the rejection of a substantial soul rule out a belief in a continuation of the individual's life beyond death? If indeed "immortality" is conceived as the unending existence in time of an imperishable soul-substance, conceived on the analogy of the indestructibility of matter, then this does seem to be ruled out. Our very starting-point, when it was said that selfhood is not given ready-made but has to be won, already departed from any belief in "natural" immortality. It is doubtful, however, whether Christian belief requires any natural immortality of the soul. The view of selfhood developed in this essay might permit a "conditional" immortality, as theologians have called it, and perhaps this is more in line with the spirit of Christian belief, for it would not require the embarrassing conception of an everlasting hell, since a life of utter wickedness (if there could be such a life) would lead simply to annihilation or total disintegration.

But what kind of conditional immortality would be possible? If we stand by the rejection of Cartesian dualism, we can hardly think of the self outliving the body and continuing indefinitely in time—a very difficult view in any case; nor can we think of immortality as timeless, for it has been argued that the self is to be conceived in temporal terms, so that a timeless self is a contradiction. Timelessness would be the annihilation of selfhood. It may be suggested, however, that "immortality" means simply that transcending of transience, that rising above the succession of "nows" which constitutes authentic selfhood itself; so that immortality, or perhaps better, eternal life or resurrection life is, as in the Fourth Gospel, the achievement of selfhood here in this world. It will be urged that the Christian hope means more than this, and probably it does. Can we suppose, then, that Being or God, in a way which must go beyond anything that we can understand, though we may find a dim analogy in authentic human selfhood, gathers up all time in a vaster unity? Then in so far as human existents had themselves been close to Being and caught up in the grace of Being, they would have their place in Being's overcoming of transience? Such might be the Christian hope, though it would be founded rather on the commitment to the grace of Being than on any confidence that we could penetrate to an understanding of these matters, still less "prove" them. For we have now reached or even trespassed the limits of existential phenomenology, and our further speculation can be only very tentative.

The Language of Being

6

One of the commonest objections brought against existentialist theologies or philosophies of religion is that they give an entirely subjective account of the matter. They are, so it is said, contemporary counterparts of the nineteenth-century *Bewusstseinstheologie* or theology of consciousness; they describe the inner attitudes of the religious man, and however useful such a description may be, it tells us nothing about the validity of the religious experience, that is to say, whether such an experience does indeed establish a relation between some transhuman reality and man, or whether it is all accountable in terms of factors that are immanent within human experience itself.

In some respects, the kind of objections that we have in mind are surprising, for the existentialist often insists that existence is encounter and that the starting-point for his philosophy is never a bare subject but a self that is already involved with a world. But even if we concede this, and agree that an existent self is inconceivable except as it is in interaction with a real world and with other real selves, we might think that the reality of God cannot be so easily conceded. The supposed analogy between an encounter or confrontation with God or Being and an encounter with another embodied self breaks down at several points, and it is hard indeed to know what can be meant by an "encounter" with God, or whatever expression may be used. It would seem that the only reply which the existentialist can make to such criticism is to describe as clearly as he can what he means by a religious confrontation with a supposedly transhuman reality, and to show us how he uses expressions like "Being," "existence" and the like in his description. Then we may find ourselves in a better position to judge how probable or improbable are the claims which he makes for the validity of his experience.

We ought to notice that the leaders of *Existenzphilosophie* in Germany, though they are often called "existentialists," are very unhappy about this label and regard it as more appropriate to some of the French philosophers whose approach is indeed more subjective and egocentric. Heidegger's interest has always lain in the problem of Being, not merely in the problem of man's being; and his detailed investigations of human existence were carried out only in the hope that they might provide a "fundamental ontology" and open a way into the question of Being itself. It would be equally inadequate to characterize Karl Jaspers as an "existentialist," for although he too has had much to say about human existence, this is for him only one of several modes of being, and like Heidegger he is interested in moving from the study of existence to that of Being in the broadest sense.

Both philosophers claim that in human existence we come into situations where, so to speak, we find ourselves at the very boundary of existence and strike against Being–Being which in some sense can be called "transcendent," though we should be on our guard against reading into this word in too facile a way its traditional connotations. The situations of which these philosophers speak have in them an absolute or total dimension that differentiates them from the relative situations in which we find ourselves in everyday existence. But this total dimension, strangely enough, gets opened up in a negative way. It is when existence itself has been reduced to nothing that the confrontation with Being takes place. Jaspers calls such experiences "limit-situations." In them, existence comes up against a wall or, to vary the metaphors, makes shipwreck, falls to pieces, comes to the end of its resources. It is then, so it is claimed, that man becomes open to the transcendence that meets him in this situation. We should notice, of course, that Jaspers does not think of this as a kind of automatic process. It is quite possible to find oneself in an extremity without in the least recognizing it as a limit-situation. We have a tendency to level down everything that happens so that it appears as the familiar and the manageable, and a limit-situation can also be treated in this way so that its "transcendent" dimension does not show. For such a situation is not a mere misfortune that befalls us, but includes our response; thus it takes place in what Jaspers calls the "comprehensive," a region that lies on both sides of the subject-object split. The common disjunction between "subjective" and "objective" has to be overcome by the recognition that there are experiences which cannot properly be described as merely "subjective" or merely "objective." Jaspers remarks, however: "The great danger is that what has happened may pass without anything happening to us men as men, without our hearing the voice of transcendence, without our attaining to any insight and acting with insight."[1]

I propose now to follow in greater detail Heidegger's account of the patterns of such experiences as bring us to the limit of existence and so to the alleged confrontation with Being. As is well known, he accords a paramount place to death in his analysis of human existence. Of all the possibilities before which man stands, death is the capital one in the light of which all the others are to be evaluated; and the man who exists authentically is the man who resolutely anticipates death. Such a man is saved from the kind of existence that may be trivial and irresponsible, for he has seized on the possibility that represents his own uttermost potentiality for being, and the way is opened to bringing into existence an integrity and even a certain absolute character that could not be achieved in any other way. Thus death, though from one point of view

[1]*The Perennial Scope of Philosophy* (London: Routledge & Kegan Paul, 1950), p. 162.

a negative phenomenon, can be taken up into existence so as to become a unifying factor. If this seems a somewhat grim doctrine, it may be understood as rather like the eschatological outlook of the primitive Church. In both cases, life is lived in expectation of the imminent end, and this in turn means a transvaluation of values; the things which up till now had been regarded as of most value appear trivial in the light of the end. The general effect of such an outlook is to introduce a new sense of urgency and responsibility. It is no longer possible to take refuge in illusory securities or distracting concerns, or to hide oneself away in the anonymous mass that is responsible to no one. Each one is asked to accept answerability for his individual existence or, to put it more briefly, he has to *exist*, in the fullest sense as a human being.

Now the state of mind that discloses human existence as a Being-towards-death is anxiety. This is called by Heidegger the "basic" state-of-mind (*Grundbefindlichkeit*), for unlike those relative states of mind that light up this or that particular situation, anxiety lights up man's total situation in the world. It discloses him as thrown into an existence, of which the ultimate *rationale*, if any, is concealed from him, but the finite and transient character of which is disclosed to him. Anxiety discloses the precariousness of human existence which is, so to speak, poised all the time over the void of non-existence. Anxiety makes manifest the nullity, the possibility of ceasing to be, that enters into the very constitution of man's being. We can say then that anxiety in the face of death and finitude brings man to confront nothing.

But as soon as this word "nothing" has been uttered, we must pause to ask how Heidegger makes use of it. Is it possible to make sense of this language about "being" and "nothing" into which we have allowed ourselves to be manoeuvred in the two preceding paragraphs? Is this kind of talk not merely nonsensical? Does talking about "nothing" just mean that nothing is said? Or when it is said that man is brought to "confront nothing," does not this mean that there is no confrontation? Is Heidegger, together with others who talk like him, making the elementary mistake of supposing that because in our language we have a word "nothing," there must be "something" corresponding to this word in the world? And this is an obvious absurdity, since "nothing" means simply the absence of anything. Surely an "encounter with nothing" or an "experience of nothing" can mean only that there was no encounter, no experience, unless once more it is foolishly supposed that "nothing" really is "something."

No doubt the logical analyst can have some excellent sport in shooting down the kind of talk we meet in Heidegger and others, and in fact many analysts have engaged in the pastime, beginning with Rudolf Carnap as long ago as 1932. Heidegger is not much perturbed by their criticisms, and surely he is right about this. For the language of "nothing" and "being" that we meet in Heidegger is not one that could possibly be assessd in any merely syntactical analysis which treated it in abstraction from the discourse-situation in which the language arises. The language must be put into the existential situation which it expresses, but in this situation—the situation in which human existence knows itself to be given over to finitude, death and anxiety—this talk not only makes sense, but very good sense indeed. Obviously it can never be as straightforward as the kind of talk in which we discuss ordinary empirical matters of fact, and since our language is designed for such everyday matters, it is bound to be stretched if one wishes to express something different. Heidegger is well aware of the peculiarities of his language. He points out that the traditional logic was based on the "ontology of the present-at-hand," and that grammar in turn reflects this logic. "It is one thing," he remarks, "to give a report in which we tell about *entities*, but another to grasp entities in their *Being*. For the latter task, we lack not only most of the words but, above all, the 'grammar.' " However, he also visualizes the task of "liberating" grammar from the traditional logic, and of "reestablishing the science of language on foundations which are ontologically more primordial."[2] It may be added that only through such stretching of "grammar," by poets, philosophers and others, could language have developed.

[2]*Sein und Zeit*, pp. 39, 165.

But now let us study more closely what this ontological language, and especially, to begin with, this talk about "nothing" can mean. First we must note that Heidegger's ontological language is not an abstract metaphysical language. Hence when there is talk of "nothing," this word cannot stand for a purely general idea of negativity. Indeed Heidegger holds that the logical idea of negation presupposes the ontological confrontation with the nullity that belongs to existence itself, and is derived from it. His polemics against "logic" should not be misunderstood, for by "logic" he understands the traditional logic, stemming as he believes from the way in which the Greeks experienced the world. If the signification of the word "logic" were widened, Heidegger would have no quarrel with the statement often heard nowadays that "every language has its logic." His complaint about (traditional) logic is precisely that it gives the rules for only one "language-game" and cannot be legitimately extended to others.[3] What he is doing is not abandoning logic, but drawing attention to a "logic" that has broader ontological foundations than the traditional logic. Heidegger's language is rooted in and grows out of the language of existence, but it provides a bridge from a merely existential language to an ontological language, so overcoming the subjectivism which, as we have seen, is often urged as an objection against the language of existence. The bridge is this strange talk of "nothing," and if we are to make sense of the language, it is to this "nothing" that we must pay attention—and we can at least pay attention to the *idea* of "nothing" or to the *word* "nothing" without falling into obvious absurdity. Whether we can make sense of the language depends on whether we can find an appropriate meaning for "nothing," once the language is placed in the discourse-situation where it belongs. Heidegger has already told us that by "nothing" we are not to understand sheer negativity. He also remarks that "nothing" has more than one meaning (*mehrdeutig*). What then can we make of it?

I believe that a careful examination of Heidegger's usage makes it possible to distinguish at least four shades of meaning in his talk about

[3] *Was ist Metaphysik?*, p. 47.

"nothing," over and above the rejected meaning of sheer negativity. (1) "Nothing" is used first of all to designate the nullity which we find within our own existence. As finite and thrown into death, our existence has in it the possibility of ceasing to be, a possibility which is disclosed to us in the mood of anxiety. "Nothing" stands for the disclosure in our experience as existents of this possibility of ceasing to be. This is presumably the fundamental significance of the word, and gives it something like an empirical anchor. (2) Another strand of meaning appears in Heidegger's description of the mood of anxiety. In this mood, it is said that the world of entities sinks to "nothing." This is because of the transvaluation of values that takes place in the face of the end. "Nothing" is used here for the wilting away of the familiar world which, though it normally preoccupies us and absorbs our attention, becomes nugatory in the face of death. (3) In a further sense, "nothing" becomes the foil for Being, and with this something like a positive sense is being given to the word, just as a positive significance is brought into the notion of death when Heidegger exhibits it as the unifying factor in existence. "Nothing" makes it possible for us to recognize entities as entities, that is to say, as things that *are*. It is only when the things that are are seen against the background or rather the abyss of nothing that for the first time we notice what Heidegger calls the "wonder" of Being—that is to say, for the first time we find ourselves asking Leibniz's famous question, "Why is there anything at all, and not just nothing?" (4) Finally, "nothing" is in some sense paradoxically equated with Being itself. When Heidegger claims that Western philosophy has been forgetful of Being, so that it has concerned itself with entities and nothing else, and then goes on to inquire about this "nothing else," he is not being merely rhetorical (and much less, of course, stupid, as some naive analysts seem to imagine), though no doubt he has deliberately chosen a way of speaking which, he hopes, will shock his readers out of their forgetting of Being into those new ways of thinking about Being which he wishes to put in place of the traditional metaphysics. For this Being, by which is meant the "is-hood" in virtue of which anything that is, *is*, cannot itself be regarded as another entity, as something else that is. However we may try to conceive it, it is a non-entity, and so from the point of view of the metaphysical thinking that concerns itself with what is and "nothing else," this Being has to be relegated to the "nothing else."

Perhaps this discussion of the meanings (or some of the meanings) of the word "nothing" in Heidegger is sufficiently complex to justify our dwelling on it a little longer for the purpose of further elucidation. It is always helpful in such cases to look around for parallels. Could we perhaps find some parallels or near-parallels in traditional philosophy and theology that would enable us to see what Heidegger is driving at in his admittedly difficult language?

Christian theology supplies a parallel to the first of the four meanings of "nothing." The Christian doctrine of creation was interpreted as *creatio ex nihilo*. Since man too is a creature, then he is made out of nothing. It is true that he was sometimes conceived as having an immortal or imperishable soul by nature, but this could also be understood as an added gift superimposed upon his creatureliness. Thus St. Athanasius could write that "man is by nature mortal, inasmuch as he is made out of what is not."[4] He depicts man as continually threatened with the possibility of ceasing to be, of lapsing back into the "nothing" from which he comes. Thus in his very being man has an experience of "nothing," and this certainly cannot be equated with no experience at all. On the other hand, it gives him an empirical understanding of "nothing," at once more fundamental and more concrete than any abstract concept of the nothing as sheer negativity. To Christian theology we can turn again for some illumination of the second phase of meaning in "nothing"—the case where the world and everything that is sinks to the level of nothing in the face of the end. Let us recall the earlier comparison between Heidegger's thought of death and early Christian eschatology. If we think of the transvaluation of values which takes place in such situations as a kind of nihilism in which that which was formerly

[4]*De Incarnatione,* IV, 6.

prized sinks to nothing and is held of no account, then there is something of the sort in St. Paul's advice that because the time is very short, those who deal with the world should live as if they had no dealings with it.[5] Neither St. Paul nor Heidegger would be called a "nihilist" in the sense of one who denies worth or meaning or existence to everything. But both describe the experience of the world's sinking to nothing, so that things which are commonly prized appear to be nothing worth. Coming to the third point, that nothing is the foil against which we notice the things that are as things that *are*, we may recall Hegel's teaching that pure undifferentiated Being is the same as nothing; and it seems more appropriate to take Hegel's teaching here than in relation to the fourth point, still to be discussed. For it is only in concrete, particular, determinate things that Being can stand out from nothing, so that for the first time we can become aware of the "wonder" of Being, that there are entities and not just nothing.

The fourth point, that in some way "Being" is to be understood as a "nothing," requires a somewhat fuller discussion. According to St. Thomas Aquinas, "being" is the first idea to fall under our minds; for whatever we perceive or talk about, we already think of as something which is. We do this, however, quite implicitly, and it might escape notice altogether were it not that occasionally we explicitly *deny* that what we are talking about has being, as in recounting a dream or a fairy-tale. Because of the very universality of Being, we hardly ever pay any attention to it. More likely we shall be entirely forgetful of Being and cencern ourselves only with the things that are, and nothing else—as indeed Heidegger believes to be the case in Western thinking generally. F. C. Copleston, taking cognizance of our normal inadvertence of Being, suggests that the distinction between "seeing" and "noticing" is useful here. We all see the same things—the things that are, entities. Only when some experience shakes us out of our normal taking-for-granted attitude do we notice that these entities *are*, and become explicitly aware of Being.

[5]I Cor. 7: 31.

One of the most lucid passages that does not, indeed, *explain* the meaning of the word "Being" but that *awakens* us to it is in a novel of Sartre. The passage is too long to quote here in full. But it shows us someone noticing Being for the first time. "Ordinarily it conceals itself. It is there, around us, within us, it is us, we cannot say anything without speaking of it, and yet we don't touch it. When I believed I was thinking of it, I had to believe I was thinking of nothing, my head was empty or rather there was just one word in my head, the word 'being.' "[6] In the experience of Sartre's hero, every particular thing loses its identity, fades away to nothing, and he is left confronted only with the brute fact of Being.

These parallels help us to see more clearly what Heidegger is saying when he argues that it is only through confrontation with the nothing that for the first time we become seized of the wonder of Being. But how can this Being, which can be contrasted with nothing as the foil against which it stands out, come to be regarded at the same time as itself a nothing? In the first place, it should not require much reflection to see that Being cannot possibly be itself regarded as an entity, as something which is. We cannot say "Being is." One can enumerate the contents of a room, such as tables, chairs, people and so on, and these are all things that are, or entities, and presumably we implicity think "being" with all of them, but it would be absurd to say that there is also Being in the room. In the second place, it is easily seen that it is equally wrong to regard "Being" as a predicate, or a property which can characterize an entity, though perhaps this mistake has sometimes been made, as in some versions of the ontological argument for the existence of God. If we take any entity in the room, let us say the table, then we can say that it is metal, that it is green, that it is polished, and so on, but nothing is added to the description by saying that it is existent; for if it did not exist, it could have none of the properties mentioned.

The word "Being," in that usage which corresponds to the German *das Sein* or the Greek τὸ εἶναι, stands neither for an entity nor for a

[6]*La Nausée*, p. 180.

property, but points rather to the condition that there should be any entities or properties at all. Being does not fall under any of the familiar categories, and indeed it could not. It is "incomparable," to use one of Heidegger's expressions, and we talk also of the "mystery" of Being, the "wonder" of being. Yet these words do not mean just blank incomprehensibility, so that the word "Being" in turn would be just a sound. For we already have some understanding of Being. We ourselves are and know that we are, and, as was remarked already, it can be claimed that the idea of Being is the first idea to fall under our minds.

Heidegger has many ways of talking about Being. Being is said to be the *transcendens* pure and simple,[7] where a medieval term has been pressed into service. Elsewhere "transcendence" is defined as the relation between entities and Being.[8] Again, Heidegger can talk of "being" as the "wholly other" to all entities,[9] an expression which recognizes the incomparable and transcendent character of Being. Yet he can also say that although Being "is" not an entity but a non-entity, and so from the point of view of the thinking that confines itself to entities, nothing at all, this non-entity is in a sense "more beingful" (*seiender*) than any possible entity, since indeed it is the condition that there should be any entities whatsoever.

The talk of Being as a *transcendens* must not mislead us into thinking that Being is transcendent in the traditional metaphysical sense, as standing somehow above or beyond the world. For Heidegger, Being is also immanent, and it would be senseless to talk of Being apart from the things that are. Among the things that are, Heidegger of course assigns a special place to man, whose mode of being is *Dasein*, being-there. For whereas mountains, stars, tables and so on all are and participate in Being or manifest Being, man not only is but has his being disclosed to himself. He *exists*, he can as it were stand out from the world of entities and become aware of his being and of his responsibility for his being.

[7]*Sein und Zeit*, p. 38.
[8]*The Question of Being* (New York: Twayne, 1958), pp. 56-57.
[9]*Was ist Metaphysik?*, p. 45.

To use one of Heidegger's favourite expressions, man is the clearing (*Lichtung*) in Being, the place where Being becomes transparent to itself. Man exists in the truth of Being, where truth is understood in the original sense of ἀλήθεια, the unhiddenness of Being. Yet because man is essentially finite, his understanding is subject to error and concealment, and his standing in the truth of Being is at the same time a wandering in untruth.

The awareness of Being cannot properly be described as either "subjective" or "objective" but, like Jaspers' "comprehensive," transcends this distinction. A statement in *Sein und Zeit* that "only as long as *Dasein is*, 'is there' Being"[10] has been taken by some interpreters to mean that for Heidegger, Being itself is a creation of the human existent. The German expression translated above as " 'is there' Being" is " '*gibt es*' *Sein*." (The quotation marks are in the original, presumably to draw attention to a special usage). Although one would normally translate "*es gibt*" as "there is," it literally means "it gives." As is so often (if not invariably) the case with Heidegger, one has to take account of the original meaning of the expression, or go astray in one's interpretation. He has himself exegeted[11] this passage, and insists that "*es gibt*" is to be taken in the literal sense of "it gives," and also points out that strictly speaking one cannot say "There is Being," for such an expression implies that Being is an entity, and of course this is precisely what Heidegger is never tired of denying. But if we say, "It gives Being," it seems fair to ask, "What gives Being?" To this Heidegger replies that the "it" must be taken as Being itself. The statement in *Sein und Zeit* is not to be taken in a subjectivizing sense, but it means that man is the only entity (so far as we know) to which Being gives itself, makes itself open, manifests itself. So man becomes the guardian of Being, the entity to which Being entrust itself.

It is unfortunate that the subjective misinterpretation of Heidegger has been reinforced by one of the few English books devoted to an ex-

[10]*Sein und Zeit*, p. 212.
[11]*Über den Humanismus* (Frankfurt: Klostermann, 1947), p. 22.

position of his thought, that of Thomas Langan.[12] He makes the extraordinary mistake of misquoting Heidegger to say, "*Dasein ist Transcendenz schlechthin*" ("Dasein is transcendence pure and simple") whereas Heidegger actually wrote "*Sein ist das transcendens schlechthin*" ("Being is the *transcendens* pure and simple").[13] On the strength of this very careless misquotation, Langan attributes to Heidegger the view that Dasein is the "fundamental source of the light of significance which endows the *Seienden* with Being." The mistake is the less excusable since Heidegger himself, in refuting such subjectivist interpretations, has specifically drawn attention to the passage in which he makes his assertion that Being is the *transcendens*: "In the introduction to *Sein und Zeit*," he writes, "stands simply, clearly and even in spaced type [the sentence], 'Being is the *transcendens* pure and simple.' "[14]

Since Being gives itself to man, so that Heidegger can even speak of its grace and favour towards man, the understanding of Being is in the nature of a gift. Heidegger recognizes a thinking about Being which has a meditative character and differs from the probing analytical thought whereby we investigate the properties of the things that are. In the earlier writings, he speaks of a thinking that "repeats" the great historical insights of the past such as those of the pre-Socratics, so that by thinking their thoughts after them and with them, one might get back to the original sources of philosophizing before misleading ontologies had made their influence felt. But then Heidegger speaks of a thinking which is more direct. One of his most acute interpreters, Werner Marx, comments: "In spite of all similarities, 'essential' thinking is distinguished from the historical inquiring and interpreting of 'repetitive' thinking by the fact that it no longer 'justifies' itself in terms of the historicity and temporality of *Dasein*, but in terms of Being itself which prevails and permits (*vermögend-mögend*). According to Heidegger, this thinking is an 'occurrence' of Being itself, Being itself shows itself

[12]*The Meaning of Heidegger* (New York: Columbia University Press, 1959), p. 212.

[13]*Sein und Zeit*, p. 38.

[14]*Über den Humanismus*, p. 24.

or conceals itself in it, 'transmits' itself or 'withdraws' itself, and is to this extent a Being with a fate or history.'"[15] The initiative seems to have passed from man to Being, and this primordial thinking about Being is variously said to be a thinking that is submissive to Being, a thinking that hears the quiet word of Being, a thinking that stands in sharpest opposition to the kind of thinking that goes on in the sciences. The essential submissive thinking is the kind of thinking that arises out of the wonder of Being when we have been brought to experience this through becoming aware of the nothing.

This kind of talk enables us to see clearly the mystical, religious dimension of Heidegger's philosophy. With his usual fondness for etymologies and his eye for real or alleged connections between the roots of words, he sees a connection among the three German verbs: *denken*, "to think"; *danken*, "to thank"; and *dichten*, "to compose poetry." The essential thinking (*denken*) of the philosopher is akin to religious devotion (*danken*) or to the poet's mode of expression (*dichten*).

Of course, this thinking is never more than fragmentary. While Being is to be understood as giving itself to man in such thinking, rather than as a product of human thought, it is also to be understood as vaster than our thinking of it, for our thinking moves in untruth and concealment as well as in truth and openness. Being has its mysterious unfathomable character—it is, after all, the "incomparable." The question "Why are there entities rather than just nothing at all?" is not a question that we can set about answering as if it were a question of empirical fact, or even that we can set about answering along the lines of traditional metaphysics. This is rather the question to excite the wonder about Being, to make us open to Being. As Heidegger sees it, this question does not get answered in metaphysics but leads rather to the overcoming of metaphysics, so that we can only await such answers to the question as Being may grant in its self-manifestation.

Heidegger is not unaware that this style of philosophizing is not one

[15]*Heidegger und die Tradition* (Tübingen, Niemeyer, 1962), p. 123.

that is likely to commend itself to the temper of our time. The Western tradition as a whole has been characterized by the forgetting of Being, and this has led to an increasing preoccupation with entities, the things that are. This preoccupation reaches its peak in the modern technological age, when all things are progressively subjected to manipulation and utility. The primordial thinking that is submissive to Being and which constitutes man the guardian of Being has been almost entirely replaced by what Heidegger calls "calculative" thinking, the thinking that concerns itself with the mastering of entities. But he also seems to believe that the experience of the emptiness of a purely technological culture, the forgetting of Being, the closing off of the dimension of the holy, the absence of the gods, all the characteristics which mark such an era as the one in which the West presently finds itself, will of themselves reawaken the quest for Being. The purpose of *Sein und Zeit* was to rekindle the question of Being, to reawaken an understanding for it. Heidegger believes that men are perhaps "grazed at least once by the hidden power of this question"[16] in moods like anxiety, joy, boredom, though perhaps without being aware of what is happening. Maybe he thinks of himself as the prophet of a new age and the bearer of a mission, the aim of which is to recall men to Being.

It must at this point be frankly acknowledged that there are many obscurities in Heidegger's idea of Being, some of them due to the fact that the idea has developed in the course of his writings, some of them due to conflicting interpretations offered by his critics. Certainly, Being is not for him a static and eternal Absolute, nor is it anything apart from the particular beings which manifest it.

Here however we are not concerned with the further exegesis of Being in Heidegger's writings. We have followed him thus far in the hope that he might furnish us with some sort of paradigm on which we could found a pattern for theological discourse, and especially find what procedures can lead from the language of existence into ontological language, and so take us at least some way toward overcoming

[16]*Einführung in die Metaphysik*, p. 1.

complaints against subjectivism. I believe that Heidegger does provide us with such a paradigm. His language, however strange it may seem at first sight, does make sense when it is set in the concrete situation which he seeks to describe. Furthermore, it advances from being a language about man's being to becoming a language about that wider Being in which man lives and moves and has his being.

In particular, the road which Heidegger describes may be claimed as illuminating what the theologian calls the "revelatory" situation. In this situation too, man moves through the awareness of finitude and guilt to confrontation with the Being which the religious man calls "God." This involves too a transition from the kind of thinking in which we objectify and thus to some extent master that which confronts us, to the kind of thinking in which that which confronts us masters us, yet in such a way that it also communicates itself to us.

Can we, however, think of the God of Christian faith and theology as in any way like the "Being" of which Heidegger speaks? If we cannot, then is not the whole attempt to find in Heidegger's philosophy something like a natural theology, and especially a model for religious thinking and talking, doomed to failure? As Heidegger himself sees it, Being cannot be equated with God, for traditional Christian theology has always conceived of God not as Being but as a being or entity, albeit the supreme entity, the entity which has most being, the *ens realissimum.* Theology has suffered from the same defect as Western metaphysics—it has concerned itself exclusively with entities, and has sought to ground entities in another entity (God) without asking about the Being of entities.

I think that such criticisms are well taken, and that theology has shared with philosophy the forgetting of Being. But does not this simply mean that theology too must be recalled to Being? And do we not already see this happening in some of our contemporary theology, where the traditional idea of God as *another* being, albeit a transcendent one, has been called in question, and we are being asked to reconceive God in terms of Being itself? And just as Heidegger in reaching back to the pre-Socratic philosophers and to the primordial sources of philosophizing claims to be resuming, in a sense, the oldest tradition of all, so the theologian can point out that one of the oldest revelations of God is in terms of Being, in that dramatic moment when he is said to have revealed his name to Moses: I AM THAT I AM.[17] Something of this understanding of God as Being has, of course, persisted ever since through many variations. We can trace it in patristic writers and again in the medieval idea that the essence of God is to be. One could visualize the possibility of a critical rethinking of the history of theology as a parallel enterprise to Heidegger's own critical rethinking of the story of Western ontology.

The fundamental difference between the believer and the atheist is not therefore over the question of whether or not a certain entity called "God" exists. It is a difference in the ways of experiencing Being, or of interpreting such experience. The believer is convinced that Being has revealed itself as such that he cannot withhold the response of worship and commitment, which is the recognition of Being as "God." The atheist cannot acknowledge this.

We can now see also how existential and ontological languages converge in theology. In the existential language, God is talked of in terms of the goals and ideals of existence, as *summum bonum*, ultimate concern, absolute love or whatever the expression may be. In ontological language, he is talked of as Being. One way of saying what religion is would be simply to assert that it affirms the ultimate convergence of these two kinds of language.

It may seem that talk about existence and Being is a far cry from Christian theology as it is ordinarily expressed, and a still farther cry from the language of Christian faith and devotion. No doubt it is. In any actual theology, the bare language of existence and Being becomes clothed, so to speak, in the concrete symbolism of a particular religious faith. This is possible because every entity, as something that *is*, is a bearer of or a participant in Being. It can therefore function as a

[17]Ex. 3: 14.

symbol of Being. Obviously some entities manifest Being more than others, and on more levels, and can therefore function more adequately as symbols. In the Christian religion, with its symbol of the Christ, it is the being of man, this very entity which exists in the light of Being, that becomes the symbol for Being itself. But while any actual theology must thus clothe itself in a concrete symbolism, it is necessary for us sometimes to investigate the foundations of theology and of its procedures of thinking and discoursing. The present investigation has been designed to do this, and to show what help may be had in this task from contemporary philosophy.

Existential Method in Theology PART III

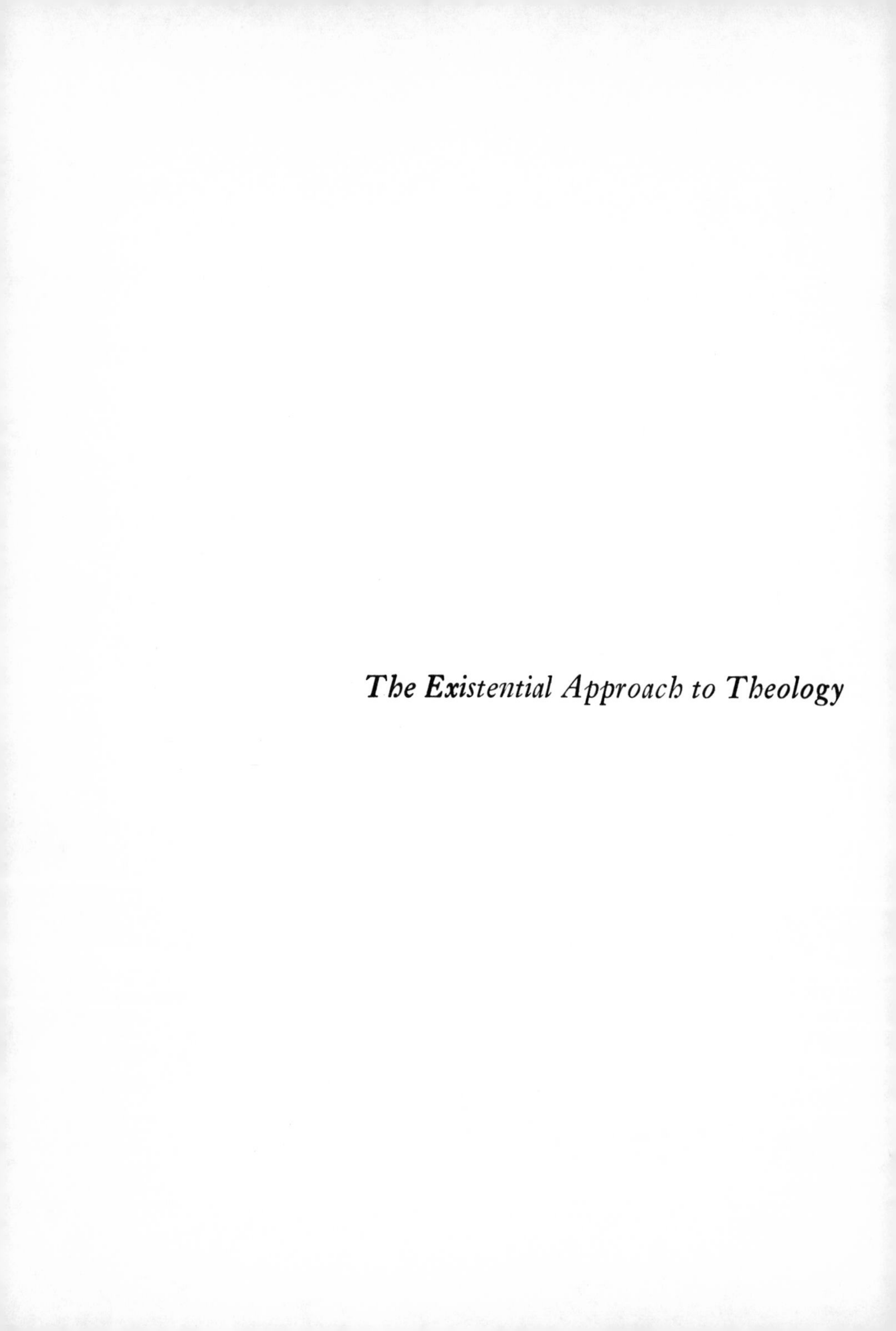

The Existential Approach to Theology

7

Theology has the never-ending task of exploring and elucidating the Christian faith, and of seeking to arrive at a fuller understanding of it. It is impossible to believe anything without having some understanding of that which is believed. If a belief is to be firmly and intelligently held, there must be a clear grasp of the content of that belief. Now, every contemporary theologian and preacher knows that in this sophisticated age of ours it is difficult to awaken a genuine *understanding* for the Christian faith, apart altogether from awakening a *belief* in it. Not only those who are outside of the Church but even many of the members of the Church themselves are puzzled, and find it difficult to see what the Christian message really is. The primary problem of contemporary theology may therefore be stated quite simply. It is the problem of the intelligibility of this Christian message, of presenting it in a way that the modern mind can understand.

The problem becomes specially acute if we consider the New Testament, the fountainhead of all Christian belief and theology. Can the New Testament make sense for people of our time? There are some parts of it, certainly, where no one has any special difficulty in understanding what is meant. There are fairly straightforward narratives, like that of the trial and crucifixion of Jesus, and these presumably will never cease to move men. There are simple parables, like that of the prodigal son, and these will continue to throw light on both the realities and the possibilities in men's relations with each other. There are moral injunctions, like the command to love our neighbour, and these will remain to call forth our best aspirations and endeavours. These things we can grasp and appreciate readily enough.

But we soon discover that even those passages which seem to be readily intelligible are closely entangled in other passages with which the case is very different. The general picture which the New Testament offers is a strange and almost fantastic one to anybody with a modern outlook. What do we make of the stories of wonders and miracles, of voices from heaven and angels sent from God? How do we understand the mysterious "principalities and powers," those demonic forces of darkness under which the world is said to be held in subjection? What does it mean to speak of the death of Jesus as a "ransom for many," or as a "propitiation" for the sins of the world? Can we attach any significance to the story of Christ's descent into the underworld, where he preached to the "spirits in prison"? Can we make sense of the strange incidents that are recounted in connection with his resurrection? With our ideas of the universe, can we understand his ascension into heaven, where he is exalted at the right hand of the Father? And what are we to say of those pictures of the coming end, when the Son of Man will return on the clouds, and the faithful will meet him in the air?

The illustrations could be multiplied, but enough has been said. The matters mentioned, and others like them, take us into a realm where we of the twentieth century are no longer at home, and one which indeed must seem to us a realm of fantasy. It is rather as if we found ourselves in a museum of strange objects, but a museum in which the exhibits are not the material possessions of a past race of men, but their ideas, their language, their outlook. These ideas are just as remote from our modern world as the objects which we might see in a museum of classical antiquities, let us say, the domestic oil-lamps of a Roman citizen, or the equipment of a Roman soldier. It is not so much that we judge the ideas to be false; it is just that they seem to have nothing to do with us, they are no longer meaningful or relevant.

The reason for this loss of relevance is not far to seek. It lies in the fact that we today have quite a different way of looking at the world from that which belonged to the writers of the New Testament. Their ideas and ways of speaking are so foreign to us because they come out of a different world from our world. The world of the New Testament was essentially the world whose creation is described in the Hebrew scriptures, and ultimately reflects the world of the old Babylonian cosmology. It was a compact universe in three stories, with the earth in the middle, heaven above, and the underworld beneath men's feet. It is true that at least some of the New Testament writers had presumably advanced beyond this conception to a more advanced cosmology, in which the earth is surrounded by a series of concentric spherical heavens. In any case, it was a geocentric universe, with man and his concerns at its focus, heaven above, and hell below. Furthermore, in that world those events the causes of which were not understood were referred to the direct agency of good spirits—perhaps even God himself—from above, or evil spirits from below, as the case might be. We would say nowadays that these men had a mythical picture of the world.

Our own way of looking at the world is completely different. It is true that long before the New Testament was written the Ionian philosophers had already begun to grope towards a rational rather than a mythical way of looking at things, but it is only in our modern Western culture that something like a scientific understanding of the world has replaced the older pictures in the minds of ordinary people. This is not to say that we all understand science. A real grasp of science belongs only to a few, and scientists themselves frequently complain that among the general public there is too little in the way of a genuine understanding of the principles of their investigations, and too much in the way of a superstitious reverence for their more spectacular achievements. But however this may be, it cannot be denied that everyone nowadays grows up in a world in which science plays a leading part, and no one can help having his outlook moulded to some extent by the spirit and achievements of science. Everyone understands that the old compact universe has vanished away; that man and his earth have been dethroned from the centre of things; that we look out on vistas of time and space that make us dizzy when we try to contemplate them. Everyone understands too that when an event is not understood, we do not assign it to the agency of the supernatural, but set about looking for an explanation in terms of natural causes. It is this changed outlook upon the world that makes the New Testament so remote. The story of Christ's ascension, for instance, was perfectly intelligible to men who entertained the old picture of the world, but it has become unintelligible to us in the post-Copernican era.

Are we then to eliminate and reject as of no further consequence the mythical elements in the New Testament, and retain only the moral and religious teaching of Jesus, together with the example of his life of service and his self-sacrificing death? Some such conclusion was reached by liberal theologians such as Adolf Harnack at the end of the nineteenth century, for the problem of myth in the New Testament is not, of course, a new one. But such a drastic solution is hardly satisfactory. Apart from the almost insuperable difficulties involved in trying to separate out the non-mythical from the mythical, the New Testament writings would be so mutilated and impoverished by such treatment that we would have to ask very seriously whether what was left could possibly be regarded as the authentic teaching of their authors.

Harnack's attempt to strip away the veil of myth so as to lay bare the actual Jesus of history and his ethical ideal of the Kingdom of God has now been for the most part abandoned, and it is the great merit of Rudolf Bultmann that he has shown us a new and better way of coming to grips with the problem of myth. Just as much as the older liberal theologians, Bultmann finds myth a stumbling-block in the way of modern man's understanding the Christian message. But his solution to the problem of what is to be done about this stumbling-block is quite different from Harnack's. Myth is not to be rejected, but interpreted, and in order that this may be done, we must first find the right key to the interpretation of myth. The problem is one in hermeneutics. The first step in the solution of any hermeneutical problem is to make sure that we are formulating our questions properly. It may be that many of our perplexities with the New Testament arise from the fact that we go to it with the wrong questions. It is very natural for us, for instance, to keep asking the question about what actually happened on this or that occasion. Now we have to remember that every question that is asked already has its own presuppositions. The presupposition of the question about what actually happened is that the document to which we address this particular question is intended to be a record of objective historical facts, so that it would make sense to seek from such a document an account of what actually happened. But if in any particular case this presupposition is a mistaken one, it need not surprise us if our way of asking the question leads us into great perplexities, and elicits from the document under consideration answers that are strange and unintelligible.

Actually, in the case of the New Testament, this particular presupposition is a mistaken one. The New Testament is not primarily intended to be a record of objective facts of history. Even the Synoptic Gospels are just what they claim to be—that is to say, gospels, documents that hold out to us certain religious truths that have to do with our way of life. No doubt the New Testament writings do indeed contain many references to facts of past history, and by patient labour and research the scientific historian may be able to disentangle some of these facts from the other matters with which they are entwined. But this is not a main concern. The interest of the writers was not to preserve a record, and not even the Synoptic Gospels are in their first intention biographies or chronicles of events. The New Testament, considered either as a whole or with respect to its constituent books, is guided by a religious interest, and what it seeks primarily to express is a religious meaning. If therefore we want to elicit this meaning, we must ask the questions that have to do with that theme which the book is intended to express. We must address to it questions guided by the same religious interest that was dominant for the writers. To do this is simply to obey a well-established principle of the science of hermeneutics.

Now, according to Bultmann, a religious document intends to present the reader with a possibility of existence for which he can decide. Alternatively, this may be stated: it intends to bring the reader into an understanding of his own being. Its essential meaning, therefore, lies not in any record of historical facts which it may contain, not in any world-view which it may reflect, but in that possibility of existence, that self-understanding, that way of life which it presents to the reader. If, therefore, we can only elucidate the authentic meaning of a document and follow a sound hermeneutic method by asking the questions appropriate to the intention of that document, in the case of a religious document such as the New Testament these appropriate questions turn out to be the questions of our own existence. What does this mean for my existence? With what possibility of existence does it present me? Into what understanding of my own being does it bring me? Here we have the core of the existential approach to the New Testament, and to the questions of theology in general.

Closely connected with this theory of interpretation is Bultmann's view of the nature of myth. A myth has usually the form of an imaginative story, but its meaning is not to be found in any literal reading of it as a record of actual happenings. A myth too—or at least, the kind of myths that we find in the Bible—has a religious intention. On the level of mythical expression, of course, everything is objectified and represented as happening in the world of space and time. The gods and demons are assigned distinct regions of space for their homes, the numinous regions of heaven and the underworld; they may appear among men in visible form, and their activities are manifested in sensible phenomena. As we have seen, this mythical way of looking at the world has, in our culture at least, long since been left behind, so that now it is only a remote curiosity into the understanding of which we can hardly enter even by a strenuous effort of imagination. But if some religious idea was once expressed in the myth, then is it possible to recover and to re-express this idea by means of an existential interpretation? Does there lie concealed in the objectifying language of myth something like a self-understanding, a possibility of existence? The idea is by no means far-fetched. We may recall that psychoanalysts also have taught us to look for the meanings of myths in terms of the desires, conflicts and aspirations of man himself. If we ask why a self-understanding should have been expressed in mythical form as a story of objective happenings, there are several answers that can be given. One is that myth-making belongs especially to the childhood of the human race. At a time when very few, if any, abstract terms were available and certainly nothing like a philosophical or psychological terminology had been developed, a self-understanding could find expression only in a concrete story. Another answer is that myth may have some permanent value in it, and tends to survive even in a more sophisticated age. That is because the concrete picture which the myth presents has more power to move men than an abstract presentation of the ideas behind the myth. It is not without significance that some contemporary philosophers such as Jean-Paul Sartre find that for the adequate expression of their philosophical ideas they have to employ not only the systematic treatise but also the play and the novel, with their concrete situations in which the reader can participate.

Let us take a simple story from the Old Testament for the purpose of illustrating the existential method of interpreting myth. We read that "the Lord God formed man of the dust of the ground, and breathed into his nostrils the breath of life."[1] Anyone who took this

[1]Gen. 2: 7.

myth as a literal statement of something that actually happened would miss the point altogether. Apart altogether from the fact that we no longer think of the human race as having come into being in such a way, there would be no religious value in a literal interpretation, and no reason for including this myth in a book that is concerned with religious ideas. It might satisfy natural curiosity to know the circumstances of human origins, but bare knowledge of an objective fact does not speak to us in any religious way. Again, we would be equally mistaken if we interpreted our myth as a primitive metaphysic, the view that man consists of an immaterial soul-substance and a material body-substance. Apart from the fact that such dubious speculations are hardly likely to have been a major interest in the remote times when myths were taking shape, this would once again be an interpretation with no specific religious value. A detached speculation about the nature of man would have no more religious significance in it than an objective understanding of human origins. But suppose we now seek an existential interpretation of the myth. Into what understanding of his own being does it bring the reader? It may be answered that the myth brings him to understand himself as a being who is at once finite and free, a being who is circumscribed, tied down, limited, yet at the same time a being of possibilities, responsible for his existence. This is not a detached understanding, but an understanding of the being which is one's own. It is an understanding of oneself that is presented in the myth, an understanding which one may accept or from which one may turn away. And as such, this is an understanding with religious significance.

Various questions might be raised at this point. It could be asked, for instance, how the writer himself understood the myth. Are we reading into it more than he intended? Did he not regard it simply as a literal account of human origins, so that we should think of it as an etiological myth? Very briefly, it may be replied that such a myth as the one we are considering had probably a manifold of meanings. It belongs to a period when mythical and non-mythical ways of thinking had not yet been sorted out. There were, as has been said already, no abstract terms which could be used to express some possible meanings of the myth in another form of discourse. No doubt men would take the myth in its literal sense, but at the same time, as a kind of overtone, so to speak, the existential meaning is there also. It is the question of man's own being—a question which, after all, comes before any merely curious question about how things began—that is trying to find expression in the myth. And it may be that when the literal meaning of a myth has long since been consigned to the museum, its genuine existential significance, if we can perceive it, still speaks home to us in our being.

Basically, the problem reduces to one of translation. It becomes an investigation into the language of religion, and an attempt to transpose statements from the mythical form of discourse into statements which concern human existence. But how does this procedure square with our earlier point that the concrete pictorial language of myth may have more power to bring home to our understanding a truth of existence than an abstract statement of the same truth in philosophical language has? The answer to this question is that sometimes in a sophisticated age the meaning of myth gets lost altogether. In our own highly technical civilization, for instance, when we are more and more pre-occupied with matters of fact, the language of myth, like the language of poetry, has ceased to be meaningful for many people. This of course is partly due to the objectifying language of myth itself—it seems to be talking about matters of fact, but these are so absurd that we dismiss the whole thing.

Bultmann is seeking to rediscover what he believes to be a meaning of permanent value concealed under the form of the myth. He is convinced that buried in the strange language of the New Testament lies a *kerygma*, as he calls it, a proclamation of a way of life by which men can understand themselves and for which they can decide. If we miss the *kerygma*, the myth is like a husk without a kernel. It is meaningless. But once the meaning has been restored and understood, we can go back to the myth with a new understanding, and may well find in its concrete imagery a more dynamic representation of the essential ideas which it contains than we find in the translation into existential statements, with which Bultmann's procedure provides us. Although his method is called "demythologizing," this is to be understood as the interpretation of myth and the re-expression of its content rather than as its simple elimination.

So far the existential approach has been exemplified only from the Old Testament but it is easy to see that the method can be extended to the New Testament and indeed to the whole system of Christian doctrine which theology has built up since New Testament times. As a further illustration, we may consider a matter which has been mentioned twice already—the ascension of Jesus. The ascension clearly implies the whole background of the first-century mythical world-picture. But what did the belief in the ascension try to express? The notion of "height" or "exaltation" is not just the idea of spatial elevation, but rather carries with it all the connotations which height possesses for human existence—the connotations of "power," "majesty," "lordship" and so on. The story of the ascension would be senseless if regarded as an account of a journey into the upper regions of the sky, but it makes sense if we regard it as expressing what had happened to Jesus in the experience of the disciples. The crucified One who had given his life in love had become the exalted Lord of their existence, the very manifestation of God. The human Jesus had become for the disciples the universal Christ of faith.

This illustration shows us how it is possible to make the bewildering language of the New Testament and of the doctrines drawn from it meaningful, if we approach them with the question of their significance for human existence in mind. But something more is needed. If our questions are to be clearly formulated with a proper understanding of what is involved in them and if they are to be asked in more than just a haphazard way, we must have some idea of what this existence of ours and its structure can be, and we must have suitable concepts in which to express such an understanding. Further, if we elicit from the

New Testament and from Christian theology answers which speak of possibilities of human existence, we must assure ourselves that these are genuine possibilities for which men can decide, lying within the horizons of existential possibility in general. Bultmann's whole enterprise therefore presupposes some understanding of human existence. From where does this come?

Unlike a stone or a table, man not only is, he also understands that he is. Along with his existence, there goes some understanding of existence. His being is open to himself or, as Martin Heidegger frequently expresses it, his being is such that this very being is an issue for him. The understanding of existence which belongs to human existence itself can be clarified by philosophical analysis and fixed conceptually. This is the kind of thing that Heidegger has carried out in his existential analytic, and it is precisely such a conceptual clarification of the understanding of human existence as Heidegger provides that the existential approach to theology needs for its interpretative work. And of course, as everyone knows, it is to Heidegger that Bultmann, as the pioneer of this theological approach, has turned.

Heidegger thinks that such categories as substance and accident, cause and effect, under which we commonly understand things in the world around us when we take a detached objective view of them are inapplicable to man's own existence as being-in-the-world. He proposes to find a new set of categories, or *existentialia* as he prefers to call them, which will be appropriate to the phenomena of human existence. These *existentialia* will describe not fixed properties but possible ways of being. The working out of these *existentialia* is one of the major tasks which Heidegger set himself in *Sein und Zeit*, where he develops an extensive and subtle vocabulary in which to talk about the phenomena of existence.

Now the New Testament also (and especially the Pauline epistles) employs a rich vocabulary in which to describe man's being, but the New Testament words belong to a prescientific, prephenomenological era, and are nowadays obsolete in varying degrees, at least as words for describing man's conscious life: flesh, heart, spirit and the like. Bultmann has seized on the possibility which a modern terminology like that of Heidegger offers of bringing to light once more the existential realities now buried in the archaic terms of the New Testament. He hopes to show that the contemporary philosopher's description of the passage from "inauthentic" to "authentic" existence can be a help to understanding what is the new life of faith which the New Testament holds out to us when we resolve "to make the cross of Christ our own."[2]

This procedure presupposes some correspondence, at least so far as their formal structures are concerned, between Heidegger's existential analytic and the New Testament understanding of man in the world. Heidegger provides the conceptual apparatus required for a systematic existential interpretation of the Christian way, and his terminology helps to refurbish and restore some of the older and obscurer elements in the Christian vocabulary.

Thus behind Bultmann's existential approach to the theology of the New Testament and of the Christian religion in general, there lies Heidegger's analysis of human existence. But we should be careful to notice that this does not mean that Bultmann is founding his theology upon Heidegger's philosophy. He uses the existential analytic purely as a hermeneutic tool. It provides conceptual clarification for the kind of problems in which Bultmann is interested. If we are asking questions about human existence, then we must seek the clearest presentation that we can find of the structure of that existence, and Bultmann believes that we find it in Heidegger's existential analytic. It is, however, to the Christian faith, and especially to the New Testament, that he goes for the answers to the concrete questions of existence. He calls in the aid of Heidegger's scheme in order to elicit the answers, but the content of the answers, so he claims, is not prejudged in any way.

The existential approach to theology is in some ways so revolutionary that it was bound to provoke hostile criticism from theologians of the more traditional schools. They may admit that Bultmann has given

[2]*Kerygma and Myth* (London: S.P.C.K., 1957), p. 36.

the New Testament a fresh relevance, but they are inclined to say that he has paid too high a price for this. Has he not subjectivized the whole matter, and destroyed any objective element in Christianity? Has he not, by regarding so much as myth, taken away the historical foundations on which Christianity has always been supposed to rest? Has he not gone far toward dissolving the whole Christian faith into a philosophy of existence in which we could speak of possible ways of Being without any reference to the New Testament at all? A century before Bultmann, Hegelian philosophers were absorbing Christianity into their system of thought. Their interest was in the Idea. They acknowledged that the Idea had first to manifest itself in concrete historical happenings, but once the Idea had been grasped in its purity, any particular representations of it become irrelevant. Is not Bultmann doing much the same thing, except that in place of the Idea he talks of a possibility of existence, and that instead of conceiving the essence of religion to lie in a world-view, he sees it in a way of life? But surely he could go on to speak of this way of life without reference to the symbolism of Christ and his cross, just as the Hegelians were able to do in the case of the idea of the unity of God and man?

Various replies can be made to such objections. An existential approach to Christianity does not deny that there are objective facts of history at its origin, but it rightly sees that a bare objective fact of past history has in itself no religious significance. Again, an existential interpretation of theology does not imagine for a moment that the Christian religion, with its institutions, its scriptures, its sacramental means of grace, can be replaced by a philosophy, and Bultmann himself is quite explicit on this point. But it is claimed, as against the almost pathological fear of philosophy that seems to prevail in some contemporary theological circles, that the essential content of the Christian religion needs to be explicated in viable philosophical concepts. It is not necessary that these should be Heidegger's concepts, though among contemporary philosophers he is perhaps the one whose ideas can be most helpful for the theologian's task.

But is it necessary to apologize for the existential approach to theology? It does indeed call for some radical reappraisals of matters that have been taken for granted in the past. But drastic measures are needed if the Christian faith is to maintain its claim to be a meaningful issue in the modern age. The existential approach will not be too drastic if it makes some contribution to this end.

Christian Existentialism in the New Testament

Before saying anything at all on the theme announced in the title of this essay, we must take a closer look at the title itself, for right away it seems to have committed us to two assumptions. One assumption is that there is a variety of existentialism which can properly be called "Christian"; the other is that this Christian existentialism is to be found in the New Testament. Both assumptions are sufficiently important to demand a few preliminary words of explanation.

Is there a Christian existentialism? Obviously some types of philosophy are more sympathetic to Christianity than others, but there is no one type that is wholly Christian. At the beginning of this century many people supposed that idealism was the philosophical ally of Christian faith. Yet, at the hands of its ablest British exponents–Bradley, Bosanquet and McTaggart–idealism turned out to be antagonistic to Christianity, or at least to its traditional formulations. It cannot be lightly assumed that any philosophy is inherently favourable to the Christian religion, and certainly this claim cannot be made in an unqualified way of existentialism. By "existentialism" is meant the type of philosophy which concerns itself with human existence and which tries to understand this existence out of the concrete experience which, as existents, we all have. As a way of philosophizing rather than a body of doctrine, existentialism as such is neither for nor against Christianity. In a writer like Jean-Paul Sartre, with his morbid egocentricity and his preoccupation with sex, we find a version of existentialism which is antagonistic to Christianity. On the other hand, if a philosopher had become convinced that the Christian life is the norm of human existence, and were to derive his conception of an authentic existence from an interrogation of Christian existence, then he would be a Christian existentialist. Thus it seems to be quite permissible to speak of a "Christian existentialism."

Is there then a Christian existentialism in the New Testament? This question is harder to answer. In one way, it is obviously anachronistic to talk of "Christian existentialism" in the New Testament, just as it is to talk, say, of "Christian socialism" in the New Testament. Words like "existentialism" and "socialism" belong to the modern world and carry with them connotations which cannot be projected back into the New Testament without distorting it. It is plain, for instance, that the New Testament authors did not take human existence as an explicit problem for philosophical analysis in the manner in which our contemporary existentialists do. In another way, however, it could be permissible to speak of existentialism in the New Testament, if what the sacred authors did was to set forth, even if not explicitly or systematically, a way of understanding this human existence that belongs to each one of us and for which each one of us is responsible. Used with proper care, the term "existentialism" could draw attention to an affinity between what the New Testament writers were doing and what modern philosophers of existence are doing.

But it may be objected that the New Testament writers, as religious writers, were concerned to tell us about God, angels, life after death, and generally about what transcends this world, rather than about human existence. If this way of stating the objection seems to load it too much in the direction of an irrelevant "other-worldiness" or a false "religiousness," then the point has been put more soberly and searchingly by Leopold Malevez, who says in a criticism of Bultmann: "The Bible is not primarily a treatise on anthropology; its whole aim is the knowledge of God and the contemplation of God."[1] This is, of course quite true, and needs to be said in the current discussions. Yet, as theologians have often reminded us, the Christian knowledge of God is not a knowledge of him as he is in himself—for this would presumably be unattainable—but a knowledge of him as he relates himself to us. This is what Bultmann tries to express in his assertion that at bottom the question of God is the same as the question of one's own existence. Certainly we are not asked to decide whether the New Testament is about God or about man—the question needs only to be put for its absurdity to be evident. The New Testament considers the two together. But this means that its message about God is always oriented to human existence, and in so far as it presents us with an understanding of this existence—even if it asks us to look beyond the confines of what is *merely* human for such an understanding—we can properly speak of something like an "existentialism" in the New Testament.

If then we are satisfied that the title of this piece is a legitimate one, the task which it sets before us would be that of setting down in an explicit or thematic way the conception of Christian existence contained in the New Testament writings. These writings, however, convey their teaching in various forms. To mention only three of these forms—and there are undoubtedly more—we may name elements of myth, of history, of dogma, and these are all interwoven together. The task would be to translate these various forms of discourse into statements which explicitly relate to our human existence. This task, in turn, must be done in accordance with definite hermeneutical principles. The main principles in this enterprise are that we should ask questions which relate to existence, and that we should seek to formulate answers in existential categories. The procedure may be briefly illustrated with respect to each of the three kinds of discourse mentioned.

[1]*The Christian Message and Myth* (London: SCM Press, 1958), p. 157.

First, let us consider *myth*, and in this context it will be sufficient to take the word to mean those religious stories which are *in principle* unverifiable as factual history. These are stories of events that are supposed to happen at remote and inaccessible times and places—"in the beginning," "at the end," "in heaven"—and to involve supernatural agents. An example is provided by the eschatological elements of the New Testament. According to modern scholarship, eschatology constitutes the framework for the whole New Testament teaching. The essence of the eschatological myth was taken over by the first Christians from Jewish apocalyptic. The belief was that the world would shortly come to an end through a supernatural intervention; that there would be a final judgment; and that, as a result of this judgment, men would be assigned their final destinies of bliss or torment. The first Christian disciples seem to have expected that these things would happen almost at once, but as time passed and they still did not happen, the Church began to relegate the eschatological cataclysm to some indefinite future period.

To modern minds the whole belief, if taken at all literally, looks like a piece of naive superstition. As Bultmann somewhat brashly puts it: "History did not come to an end, and as every schoolboy knows, it will continue to run its course."[2] Well, most schoolboys know that history might end if the sun got either too hot or too cool, or again, if men allowed themselves to be engulfed in nuclear warfare. But if history ever did come to an end through causes such as these, this would have nothing to do with the kind of end envisaged in the eschatological myth. But if we now apply the canons of existential interpretation to the myth, we can begin to make sense of it. The ideas of eschatology are to be related, in such an interpretation, to the here and now of our human existence. Every individual does indeed stand before the imminent end—his own death; in his everyday decisions about the existence for which he is responsible, he is working out his own judgment; here and now, he either lays hold on his true being or he loses it. Under-

[2]*Kerygma and Myth,* p. 5.

stood in this way, eschatology ceases to be merely a curious belief that has survived from a remote and superstitious past. It can be understood as a way of facing our own human existence, a way marked by the note of urgency and the summons to responsible decision. Whatever the outward form of its expression may have been, it had the kind of existential significance described, and as such helped to shape the existence of those who in primitive Christianity gave credence to the myth.

We pass now to those assertions about *history* which likewise form a part of the New Testament writings, though often hardly to be separated from myth because the history has been given a setting in the mythological framework. But these historical assertions differ from myths in that they are at least in principle verifiable, and may be assigned a definite placing in world-history. The historical element in the New Testament has its centre in the story of Jesus Christ, and especially in his cross and resurrection. How do these alleged happenings of nineteen centuries ago have any relevance or importance for us?

Again we may apply the methods of existential interpretation, and ask about the way in which these events could be conceived as impinging on the here and now of your existence and mine. R. G. Collingwood, whose writings are much admired by Bultmann, asks in one place: "What is history for?" He suggests as the answer: "History is for human self-knowledge."[3] The past becomes relevant and illuminating for our present existence when it is in some sense "re-enacted" in our own present history, when it is understood as disclosing a possible kind of existence for us now. We really "believe" in the cross of Christ when we ourselves "take up the cross" and in so doing experience a "rising" from the death of sin into a new life of the spirit. This constitutes atonement, reconciliation with one's true being and so with God. In this way the merely past event acquires a new dimension that makes it a contemporary and saving event.

A similar approach holds for the third kind of discourse which we distinguished—*dogma*. The New Testament is far from being a text-

[3]*The Idea of History* (London: Oxford University Press, 1946), p. 10.

book of dogmatic theology, but it contains the beginnings of dogma. For instance, we see the beginnings of christological dogma when the New Testament speaks of Jesus as the "Christ," the "Lord," the "Son of God," the "Word" that has become flesh, and so on. But are the various ways in which the New Testament asserts the divinity of Christ to be understood as objectifying statements with a metaphysical sense, later expressed in terms of the "consubstantiality" of the Son with the Father? If so, this would be the kind of belief to which one could give an intellectual assent without being involved in any kind of religious commitment. Prior to all metaphysical speculations on the natures of Christ and on his relation to the Father came the existential commitment of the believer to Christ, and this is what is expressed in the disciples' confession of his divinity. To acknowledge Christ as Lord and God, as St. Thomas the Apostle did,[4] is not only to say something about Christ but to say something about oneself, to declare one's attitude to Christ, to recognize in him one's "ultimate concern."

These remarks indicate what are the bare bones of a Christian existentialism. The point of view so designated visualizes man as responsible for a finite existence in the face of death. It finds the way to wholeness and salvation in an existential commitment to the person and work of Jesus Christ. A developed Christian existentialism would relate all Christian teaching to these central themes of existence, and would present the full conception of Christianity as man's authentic mode of existing. Such a project would take us far beyond the limits of this essay. We must rest content with the mere outline that has been given, and return to the other main aspect of our theme—Christian existentialism *in the New Testament*. Are these things that have been described really in the New Testament? Is the existentialist interpretation of myth, history and dogma one that is alien to the intentions of the New Testament writers, so that it has to be forced upon them, so to speak? Or does it have an adequate basis of support in these writers themselves —in other words, can we find them interpreting themselves in this way?

[4]John 20:28.

To determine this point, we shall go over the three topics again, paying special attention this time to certain matters in the New Testament itself.

The existentialist interpretation of the eschatological myth may claim to derive support especially from the author of the Fourth Gospel, writing, as is commonly believed, near the end of the first century when the early eschatological expectations had already faded. Bultmann goes so far as to claim that in this writing we already have the beginnings of demythologizing. I may quote a few sentences from a distinguished commentator, C. K. Barrett: "It is clear from consideration of the passages in which eternal life is mentioned that the concept retains something of its eschatological connection, but also that it may be equally thought of as a *present* gift of God." In a comparison of the synoptic and Johannine conceptions of judgment, the same writer tells us that in the Fourth Gospel "the judgment is no longer primarily future but proceeds *continuously*."[5] Barrett, of course, rightly points out that the author of the Fourth Gospel had not abandoned the common New Testament eschatology, and that he probably looked for a future judgment as well as the present one. It is, however, important that he has abandoned a *purely* future eschatology, and has begun to apply the ideas of the myth to present human existence. It was already said that it would be an anachronism to look for an explicit existentialism in the New Testament. In this teaching of the Fourth Gospel, however, we do find something like an implicit existentialism. Mythical and existential ways of thinking had not yet been fully sorted out, but already the existential significance of the myth is coming into the open. Nowadays, for us who no longer look for a supernatural cataclysmic end to the world (even if in some sense we still look for an ultimate consummation of the divine "purpose"), it is the existential significance of the myth that remains as the element of permanent value in it.

Passing to the existential interpretation of the historical events of the cross and resurrection of Christ, we find the clearest prototype of this

[5]*The Gospel according to Saint John* (London: S.P.C.K., 1955), pp. 179, 403.

in the teaching of St. Paul. It is true that already in the sayings of Jesus we are bidden to "take up the cross"[6]—and it is interesting to note that Bultmann believes that in spite of the reference to the cross, this saying may go back to Jesus rather than represent the Church's teaching after the event[7]—but the idea of dying (or being crucified), rising and living with Christ, of somehow participating in his death and resurrection, is presented with extraordinary power in the Pauline epistles. Commenting on St. Paul's use of these ideas, another notable New Testament scholar, Vincent Taylor, says: "It is to St. Paul above all others that the Church owes the idea, absolutely vital to a true apprehension of the doctrine of the atonement, of fellowship with the Redeemer in the realities of his saving ministry."[8] Of course, as Taylor makes clear in his careful analysis, St. Paul thought of the cross of Christ in several other ways besides. Not all of these ways are easily harmonized, and some would frankly be almost meaningless to the modern mind, or at the best they are evocative images. As with the author of the Fourth Gospel, the Christian existentialism of St. Paul is for the most part implicit, and mingles with other ways of thinking, including the objectifying way of myth. But here again it may well be the case that it is the existential elements in his thoughts that have permanent value; and that it is through a "dying" and "rising" with Christ that we can understand an event of nineteen centuries ago as a present atonement for us.

When we come to the question of dogma, and of christological dogma in particular, it surely needs no long argument to show that the titles given to Jesus by the earliest Christians were not attempts to define his metaphysical status. This problem arose only long afterwards. In using such titles as "Christ" or "Lord" or "Son of Man," the New Testament writers were trying to express no abstruse doctrine but the significance of the crucified and risen One for their existence, and to do this they drew upon such images and concepts as were already available

[6]Mark 8:34.

[7]*The History of the Synoptic Tradition* (Oxford: Blackwell, 1963), p. 161.

[8]*The Atonement in New Testament Teaching* (London: Epworth Press, 1940), p. 100.

to them in the religious thought of their times. All of these images and concepts, of course, had their own peculiar associations. The word κύριος, for instance, had its history both in the Septuagint and in the Hellenistic religions, and presumably in a religious context it carried the connotation of divinity. But surely the primitive confession of Jesus Christ as Lord was a declaration of the disciples' attitude to Christ before it was interpreted as an objective affirmation about Christ's nature. Bultmann remarks: "The pronouncements about Jesus' divinity are not, in fact, pronouncements on his nature, but seek to give expression to his significance."[9] When such pronouncements are objectified, we tend to run into what Luther called a mere "sophistical" knowledge of Christ, lacking in the kind of commitment that belongs to a "saving" knowledge. Luther said, whether justly or not, that the scholastics had "depicted Christ as God and man, had counted his bones and arms and mixed his natures wonderfully together." He went on to say: "Christ is not named Christ because he has two natures. What meaning has that for me? But he bears his lordly and comforting names because of the office and work he has taken on himself."[10]

Enough has been said to show that what may be fairly called an "existentialist" strain of thinking had its significant place in the New Testament. If then we have seen in outline what a Christian existentialism is, and if we have also seen that this way of presenting Christianity has its right as something which is rooted in the thought of the New Testament writers themselves, it remains to say something of the value and importance which a Christian existentialism may be judged to possess.

It should first be said that no exaggerated claims should be put forward. Any particular way of presenting Christianity begins to look merely foolish if it is presented as the *only* way. The remarkable power and vitality of the Christian faith is attested by the fact that it continues

[9]*Essays—Philosophical and Theological* (London: SCM Press, 1955), p. 280.
[10]See Sydney Cave, *The Doctrine of the Person of Christ* (London: Duckworth, 1925), p. 141.

to yield new interpretations in every age, but it seems that no single interpretation has finality or grasps the faith in its entirety. A Christian existentialism has its own gaps and unsolved problems. It runs the danger of so subjectivizing the historical element in the New Testament that the distinction between history and fiction gets blurred, and one would have to inquire about the importance of this problem. Again, while it saves dogma from a sterile intellectualism, it might seem to sweep away any ontological implications of dogma, and one would have to inquire about the importance of this problem also. It is doubtful whether existentialist philosophy in itself would be adequate for investigating either of these problems.

Yet within its proper limits, a Christian existentialism looks like one of the most promising ways of presenting the New Testament message in our time. It has made sense of some things that had become senseless, and it is firmly grounded in the New Testament itself. It is therefore difficult to understand the prejudices which seem to be so prevalent in some quarters against this theological venture. Even if its insights are no more final or complete than those of any other type of interpretation, it is surely better to explore the avenues that are being opened up by the contemporary existentialist theologians than to persist in flogging dead horses.

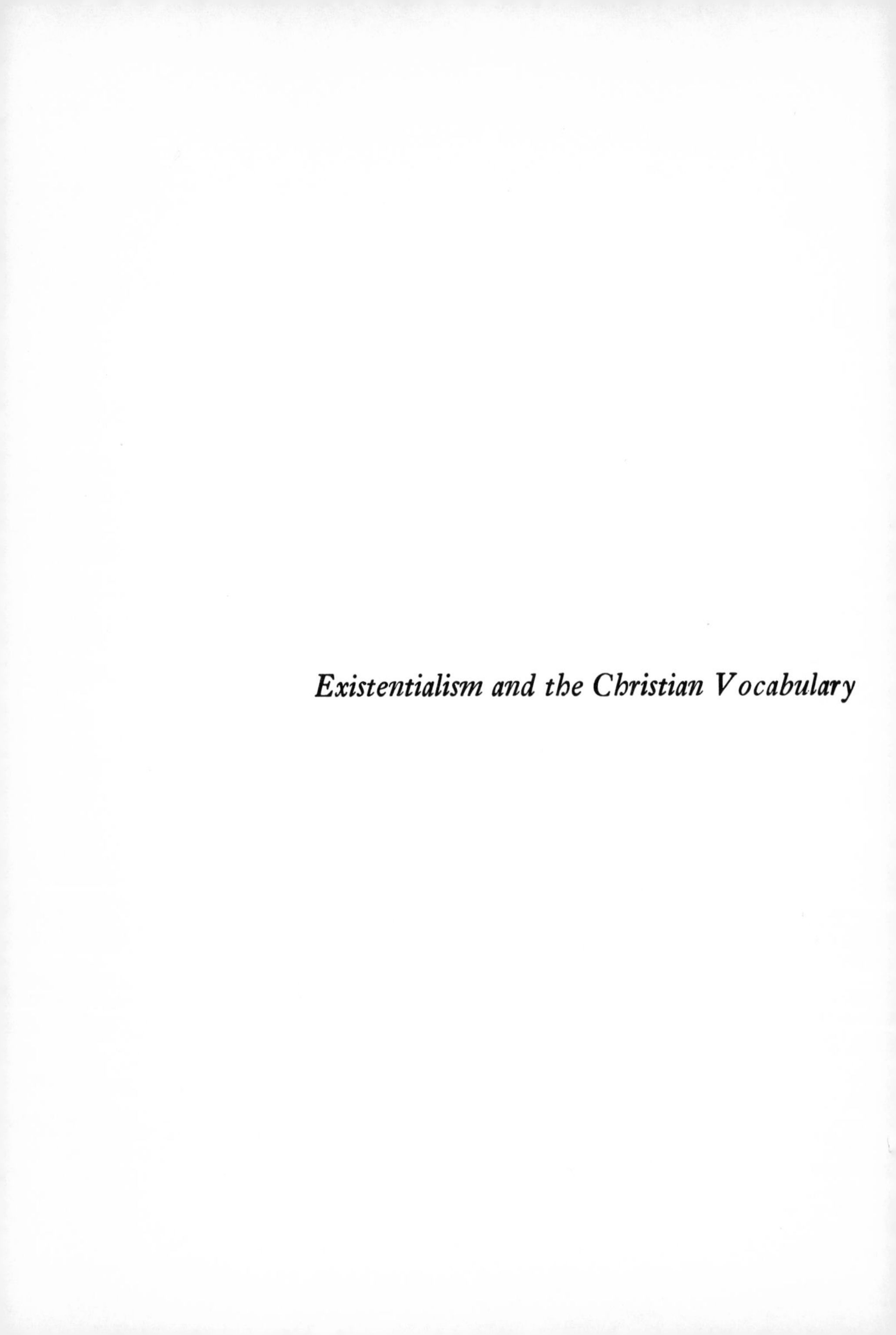

Existentialism and the Christian Vocabulary

9

Sometimes among our small change we come across an old coin which has been so thinned by long circulation that perhaps only the date of its minting, if even that, can be discerned. A comparable thinning process has gone on in some of the basic terms of the Christian vocabulary. Every preacher knows that words like "sin," "grace," "faith" have for most people lost the force and freshness which presumably they once possessed. They have become shadowy words, and to modern ears they have an archaic ring. Their meaning has been so worn down that they get understood in a superficial, harmless kind of way, if indeed they are still understood at all.

What has happened to these words? Briefly, we may say that they have been made into technical theological terms, and that they now constitute a kind of esoteric vocabulary which is still in regular use only within the Christian community and which even there is imperfectly understood. Beyond the borders of this community, the words are scarcely used at all and are even less well understood. Let us consider for a moment the word "sin." Although there is debate about the derivation, it seems probable that the English word "sin" (German:

Sünde) is connected etymologically with the verb "sunder" (German: *sondern*), so that originally talk about "sin" referred to a situation characterized by "separation." The notion of "separation" is, of course, still central to the theological understanding of the word "sin," but it has been almost entirely lost in ordinary usage. The word is commonly used in the weak sense of a "misdemeanour," and there is a tendency nowadays to contrast "sin" with "crime." "Sin" is taken to be an offence against private morality (usually sexual morality), while "crime" is a violation of public security and therefore punishable by the state. This distinction may even be held to imply that sin is a less serious matter than crime!

Is it then possible to find new words that can take the place of the old worn-out terms, and that will convey their meanings more adequately? It may be doubted whether it is either possible or desirable to replace the basic Christian vocabulary. If Christianity has something distinctive to say, it is only reasonable to suppose that Christian theologians and preachers will require some indispensable minimum of distinctive words in order to say it. It is true of course that most of the basic Christian words are shared with other religions, and there is something of a demand nowadays for a "secular" as opposed to a "religious" expression of Christianity. As a protest against a private realm of the "sacred" with a private language, the demand is justified, and if it encourages the breakdown of barriers to communication, it will accomplish something worthwhile. But Christianity, and presumably other faiths as well, possess a basic stock of words which are intended to express certain basic ideas. We cannot do without these words, or find adequate substitutes for them. Clearly, however, they stand in need of some kind of illumination that will help to restore to them a measure of their original depth and power.

It is true that in a few isolated cases some more or less adequate replacement may be available. For instance, in *The New English Bible*, the traditional word "redemption" has mostly given way to "liberation" or "release." C. H. Dodd has explained the policy of the translators in regard to this word "redemption." He tells us that it does not have the "realistic reference to common experience" which characterized its Greek equivalent, used of the manumission of a slave, and so it has become for most people a somewhat insipid word. We are however in our time familiar with the "liberation" of oppressed peoples. It is true that "liberation" is not an exact equivalent, for it leaves out the notion of a money-payment that was present in "redemption," but it is so much more relevant that the translators decided for it.[1]

Most readers will heartily approve of this decision, and think that what has been lost of the original idea is more than made good by the restoration of some power and vigour through the employment of an intelligible word. Indeed, it is a pity that the policy has not been carried further, for there are other effete words, such as "justification," that ought to be dropped even if this means losing some of the connotations, as would presumably happen if one substituted "acceptance" for "justification." But it is hard to see how even modern translations that were quite uninhibited by respect for venerable theological words could succeed in eliminating such basic terms as "sin," "faith," "grace" and the like. These words seem pretty indispensable if the distinctive Christian message is to be expressed. Yet how are we to prevent these words from lapsing into a semantic poverty in which the greater part of their original and essential meaning has been eroded away? Or how are we to keep them from becoming the words of a private language, encapsulated within the Christian community and unintelligible outside of it?

It would seem that all we can do is to look for some area of discourse in the secular world which will have sufficient affinity with what Christian theologians are talking about to permit of its terms being used in order to illumine and restore fresh life to the traditional Christian vocabulary. What is wanted is a set of terms that will light up structures or situations, once indicated by the traditional Christian

[1] "Some Problems of New Testament Translation" in *The Expository Times*, LXXII, 270-71.

words but not obscured. These terms will not be substitutes for the traditional terms, but they will help to restore lost connotations. They may be able to revivify the old language, and perhaps in the process we may come to understand the modern words better as well, for this kind of comparison of languages has frequently the result of illuminating both sides.

Some theologians of our time believe that the philosophy of existentialism is the area of secular discourse which can best serve the purpose that we have in mind. "Theology," writes Paul Tillich, "has received tremendous gifts from existentialism, gifts not dreamed of fifty years ago or even thirty years ago."[2] This sentence was written by Tillich in 1955. What he calls the "gifts" of the existentialists—though of course they were not consciously intended to be gifts to the theologian—are primarily gifts of language. In existential analysis we find ways of speaking about man's existence in the world such as light up some of the terms in the traditional Christian vocabulary, giving to them a renewed power and relevance.

Existentialism can perform this function because of certain basic affinities between its way of understanding man and the understanding of him which we find in the Bible. The existentialists, including even the most secularly minded among them, have rediscovered truths concerning man which are in many cases taught plainly enough in the Bible but which, during the past four centuries or so, have been allowed to slip out of sight in the Western world, even in the Church. Existentialism may be regarded, in one of its aspects at least, as a reaction against that optimistic post-Renaissance view of man which has dominated the West for a long time and has been closely associated with the ideas of human progress, human perfectibility and human self-sufficiency. There have of course always been isolated voices to stress the other side of the picture—voices which, if not actually pessimistic, have been at least more realistic and sober. Jacob Burckhardt and Oswald Spengler are examples of such voices from an earlier

[2]*Theology of Culture*, p. 126.

period. Today the misgivings are focused by the existentialists, who emphasize truths that had been overshadowed in the traditional Western understanding of man. The existentialists stress the finitude of man, as thrown into a world in which he has to be; the uncertainty of human life, which is all the time haunted by death as the termination of man's being in the world; the fundamental anxiety which is attendant upon such an existence, in which, however slender our resources and however uncertain our future, we are nevertheless each one responsible for the existence that is his. Ruthlessly too, do some of the existentialists expose the pathetic devices by which we continually seek to cover up some of the less agreeable and more exacting aspects of our existence. Heidegger speaks of a "tranquillizing" (*Beruhigung*) whereby we lull ourselves into a false sense of security and into the belief that everything is in the best of order. In a time when the use of so-called "tranquillizers" is widespread, this term used by Heidegger is readily intelligible. It could be maintained, however, that this is just the modern counterpart of what St. Paul called the "boasting" of Jews or Greeks who thought that they had discovered a security for their lives on the basis of a human righteousness or a human wisdom.

Theologians such as Tillich and Bultmann take this existentialist analysis of the human situation as their point of departure for their exposition of the Christian gospel as a message for our time. Tillich's method of correlation[3] begins with the existential questions that arise out of man's situation in the world, and looks for the answers in the Christian revelation. It is obvious, however, that such an orientation of the questions will determine the kind of answers that are obtained, and will also determine the kind of language in which the inquiry is to be conducted. Bultmann's method of exegesis proceeds on the assumption that "the right question to frame with regard to the Bible is the question of human existence."[4] This approach, like Tillich's, has its consequences for the kind of answers that will be obtained, and implies

[3]*Systematic Theology*, I, 67-73.
[4]*Kerygma and Myth*, pp. 191-96.

the need for an appropriate terminology in which human existence can be described—the kind of terminology which the existentialist philosophers profess to offer us.

Let us now go back to the word "sin." Does existentialism in any way illuminate or refurbish this much faded term? We find Heidegger speaking of "alienation" (*Entfremdung*). This alienation arises as one aspect or structure of man's "falling"; in his concern with and absorption in the world of things, man falls away from the possibilities of a genuine personal being. He becomes alienated or estranged from his true self. This conception recaptures something of the essential meaning that once belonged to the word "sin," but which that word has now lost for most people—"separation." "Alienation" is not simply a word that can be substituted for "sin," for the latter word has other connotations besides, and moreover, while "alienation" here means "separation from one's true self," "sin" means "separation from God." But "alienation" (or "estrangement") is undoubtedly a word that can be used to restore meaning to the traditional term "sin," and to reintroduce the word into current discussions of man. In any case, the two kinds of separation are obviously connected very closely both with each other and with a third kind of separation—separation from other human persons. In Heidegger's teaching, alienation from one's own being implies estrangement from Being as such, and a wrong kind of relation with other selves; while in the New Testament, the prodigal son had to "come to himself"[5] before he returned to the father.

Closely connected with "sin" in traditional Christian theological language is the "world." The world is understood as standing over against God, and is counted in with the "flesh" and the "devil." The world is in rebellion against God. It is the home of sin, and the sinner is indeed one who owes his allegiance to the world to which, so to speak, he has defected from God. In the New Testament, we even hear that the world is in subjection to demonic powers that are hostile to God. All this is perplexing to people who normally use the word

[5]Luke 15:17.

"world" for the physical universe. Furthermore, if they are Christian people, they also believe that the world (physical universe) was created by God and belongs to him. So why should the world be represented as evil, and hostile to God? Is it not the duty of the Christian to serve the world in what is called nowadays a "worldly" Christianity, rather than to shun the world in the escapism of "other-worldliness"? Such are the confusions that arise from our ambiguous and antiquated usages in Christian discourse.

We cannot, however, read very far in the Pauline and Johannine literature without understanding that the writers were using the word "world" in a sense very different from that to which we are nowadays accustomed. With them, the word "world" usually stands not for the physical universe, but for a social or existential phenomenon—the collective body of mankind in its fallen and sinful state, cut off from God, perverting and bringing under its domination every individual existence born into the world. This is such a staggering idea that one can hardly wonder if it has been gradually suppressed and rendered harmless over the centuries. But light is again thrown on it by the existentialists. Heidegger talks of the "they"—the depersonalized and dehumanized collective body, responsible to no one, that dictates the standards of the lowest common denominator to every individual existence. Jaspers talks likewise of the "mass" that levels everything down to the degraded mediocrity of mass-existence. Everyone is sucked into the whirlpool (perhaps this may be called "original sin") and only in and against and out of this milieu can there be any aspiration toward the stature of true selfhood.

How then can anyone rise above the level that is dictated by the world? The New Testament speaks here of "faith"—again a Christian key-word that has fared badly and been voided of its authentic sense. Most people nowadays understand faith as "belief," and more often than not they think of such a belief as a precarious one, one that is to be accepted on authority because there are no good reasons that can be given for assenting to it. If "faith" meant no more than this, then St.

Paul and many other Christians would hardly have been sustained by faith as they were. When we turn to the existentialists, we find that Heidegger speaks of a "resoluteness" which leads back from alienation to genuine selfhood. The resolve to accept one's finitude, to scatter tranquillizing concealments and false securities, to live in the steady anticipation of death itself—this unifies the self and brings wholeness. If the emphasis here seems to be Pelagian, it nevertheless throws light on a frequently forgotten or neglected element in faith, the element of commitment to a way of life, which is more fundamental than intellectual acceptance of a belief. It will not surprise us therefore that an existentialist theologian such as Bultmann lays stress on the act of decision involved in faith. Bultmann allows, of course, that there is much more to faith than this. Once again, there is no simple substitution, and one cannot put some other word such as "resoluteness," "commitment," "decision" in place of the distinctive Christian word; but all of these words illuminate an important part of the meaning of "faith," and a part which nowadays has fallen into oblivion in the common usage of the word.

Mention was made of a seemingly Pelagian bias, and perhaps someone will want to ask here whether existentialism is not a purely humanistic interpretation of existence, so that it would have nothing to say about such an important aspect of Christian experience as is designated by the word "grace." It would indeed be unfortunate if this were the case, for perhaps no term in the Christian vocabulary is more central than "grace", and perhaps none stands in greater need of illumination; for this word represents, often enough, a thoroughly confused idea, with remnants of myth and magic still stubbornly clinging to it.

Yet it is a mistake to think that existentialist philosophers are all humanists (if by this is meant that they try to found all meaning and value in man himself, making him the measure of all things, and recognizing nothing higher than human existence). This common mistake may be due to the fame of Sartre, whose existentialism is undoubtedly atheistic. It could be argued that even to Sartre the Christian owes a debt, for Sartre's honest analysis of human existence without God makes it as clear as can be found anywhere what is the difference between atheism and a religious attitude of life. Without concealment, Sartre mercilessly shows us that in the absence of grace, human existence is absurd and futile. Optimistic humanists ought to read him, to have some of their tranquillizing illusions shattered. But with the great German philosophers of existence, the case is different. Heidegger, in a work in which he explicitly differentiates his own position from that of the French atheistic school, speaks of man's subordination to Being, and in a striking utterance declares: "Man is not the lord of what is. Man is the shepherd of Being."[6] The "shepherd of Being" is the one to whom Being has entrusted itself and made itself open, and the phrase is reminiscent of St. Paul's expression: "stewards of the mysteries of God."[7] Jaspers too can talk of the gift-like character of an authentic existence, reached when man at the end of his own resources meets transcendence. In both cases the idea is that of a transhuman source of grace—Being or transcendence, beyond man and not at his disposal, *giving* itself to him. Grace, as thus understood, is the drawing near of divine Being. This is the understanding of grace that finds expression in Bultmann's description of grace as an act—the act in which God gives himself in Christ and encounters man in his need.

Running through the New Testament is the constantly recurring theme that there are two ways open to man. The theme is variously expressed. St. Paul can contrast living "according to the spirit" with living "according to the flesh," while there are also the Johannine antitheses between light and darkness, truth and falsehood, life and death. In the existentialist philosophies, these opposed possibilities are expressed in the idea that human existence can be either "authentic" or "inauthentic." In authentic existence man becomes whole, he attains the stature of genuine selfhood, he is the "shepherd of Being," the faithful guardian of the mystery of existence that has been entrusted to

[6] *Über den Humanismus,* p. 29.
[7] I Cor. 4:1.

him. In inauthentic existence, he falls apart, so to speak, he misses himself, he scatters and loses his potentiality for being. In its essentials, this kind of language is nothing but a new way of expressing the choice which confronts man in the pages of the New Testament; and when the New Testament is interpreted in the light of this fundamental choice that confronts every human existence, its relevance to our time can hardly fail to make itself apparent. It becomes indeed a decisive word of God addressed to man, and can no longer be mistaken—as so many mistake it—for a puzzling mixture of ancient history, moral insights and incredible legends, all expressed in antiquated language. David Cairns, who has been a stern critic of existentialist influences in theology and of the work of Bultmann, nevertheless acknowledges that Bultmann's use of the distinction between "authentic" and "inauthentic" existence "has in a remarkable manner made intelligible and concrete for our day an important part of the gospel."[8] And this is surely a claim that can be made for the whole range of existentialist words and ideas that we have considered.

It will be noted, however, that Cairns talks of "part of the gospel"; and also that when Tillich, in the passage quoted earlier, speaks of the "tremendous gifts" of existentialism to theology, he mentions at the same time the similar gifts of depth psychology. Both remind us that no one interpretation of Christian truth can monopolize the field, and indeed excessive concentration on a single approach could easily lead to distortion. The Christian vocabulary stands in continual need of being reinterpreted if it is to remain meaningful, but at any given time there may be several ways of doing this. At the present time, however, it may be claimed that existentialism is making a powerful contribution toward renewing some basic Christian words.

[8]*A Gospel without Myth?* (London: SCM Press, 1960), p. 179.

History and the Christ of Faith

10

"The question of whether the historical Jesus and his message are of significance for the Christian faith sounds, to anyone who is unacquainted with the debate, absurd." So writes Joachim Jeremais in an essay entitled "The Present State of the Debate about the Problem of the Historical Jesus."[1] In a moment, we shall consider more closely just what is this debate he mentions. But meantime let us hear a few more sentences from his essay. "The idea of asking such a question did not occur to anyone in the ancient Church, or in the Church of Reformation times, or in the two centuries thereafter. How is it possible that this question gets asked today in all seriousness, that it even stands at the centre of discussion of the New Testament, and that in many quarters it gets answered with a decided negative? The historical Jesus and his message, so we are told by the adherents of one widely held theological position, have no significance, or at any rate no decisive significance, for the Christian faith."

[1] "Der gegenwärtige Stand der Debatte um das Problem der historischen Jesus" in *Der historische Jesus und der kerygmatische Christus*, ed. H. Ristow and K. Matthiae (Berlin: Evangelische Verlaganstalt, 1960), p. 12.

Jeremias is not exaggerating in saying that this position must seem absurd to anyone who does not know the background of the contemporary theological debate. For is not Christianity an historical religion, inseparably bound up with Jesus of Nazareth and the events recorded about him in the New Testament? And does not Christianity stand or fall as this record is shown to be trustworthy or untrustworthy? How then can responsible theologians tell us that we know very little about the historical Jesus, that what little we do know makes it most improbable that he ever thought of himself as Messiah, and yet that these matters are irrelevant to Christian faith? An attempt to answer these questions may begin by considering three major factors that have led the theologians whom Jeremias has in mind to take up their seemingly revolutionary position that the facts about the historical Jesus are not of decisive significance for the Christian faith.

First, there is the negative result that followed from a century of intensive historical research into the facts about Jesus of Nazareth—the research described by Albert Schweitzer in *The Quest of the Historical Jesus.* No consensus of opinion emerged from this quest, such as might have been expected. On the contrary, we find a bewildering variety of portraits of the historical Jesus, many of them projecting on to him the ideals and aspirations of the biographers themselves, and some of them going so far as to deny that there ever was an historical Jesus at all. From this confusion there gradually emerged the result, now generally accepted among New Testament scholars, that to write a factually accurate biography of Jesus is an impossible task. We do not possess the kind of sources that would allow such a task to be carried out. The gospels themselves are kerygmatic documents, proclaiming a faith in which the historical Jesus and the facts about him have undergone an irreversible metamorphosis into the Church's message of a divine pre-existent being who became incarnate, died for the sins of men, was raised from the dead and returned to the heavenly places, from which, it was expected, he would shortly come again in triumph. According to Bultmann's view, even St. Mark's Gospel is thoroughly mythological, and depicts not a human figure but "the very Son of God" walking the earth.[2] It is impossible to get behind such mythological or theological presentations to the bare historical facts, and so the nineteenth-century quest of the historical Jesus came to an end in defeat.

Is it then the case that those theologians who nowadays discount the significance for faith of the historical Jesus have been driven into this position by the impossibility of getting reliable information about him, so that their new theological orientation is simply an attempt to make a virtue out of necessity? Some critics would say that this is indeed the case. But before deciding about this, we must look at a second factor.

This is the change that has come over theology itself—the change from the old-fashioned liberal theology which focused attention on the human figure of the historical Jesus to the prevailing kerygmatic theology, which shifts attention to the Christ of faith, proclaimed by the New Testament and the Church as God's Word addressed to man. One of the earliest scholars to move in this direction was Martin Kähler who, in a book which first appeared in 1892 in the heyday of Ritschlianism, maintained that "the real Christ is the preached Christ"[3] —that is to say, the kerygmatic Christ, not the so-called "historical" Jesus whom the critical scholars sought vainly to reconstruct. Faith has to do with the Christ of the *kerygma*, and those theologians who have developed Kähler's line of thought would say not only that it is impossible to get behind the kerygmatic Christ to the Jesus of history, but that even to attempt to do so reveals a misunderstanding of the nature of faith itself. Faith is a total existential commitment to the Christ proclaimed in the *kerygma*, not assent to propositions about the Jesus who lived nineteen centuries ago. If we try to bolster up faith by looking for some kind of guarantee in facts of past history, then (so

[2]*The History of the Synoptic Tradition* (New York: Harper & Row, 1963), p. 241.

[3]*Der sogenannte historische Jesus und der geschichtliche biblische Christus* (Munich: Kaiser Verlag, 1956), p. 44.

we are told) we are really departing from a genuine faith-commitment, because we are looking for a security in something outside of faith itself. Indeed, if faith were dependent on the support of historical research, then presumably it would be a kind of variable quantity, rising or falling according to the latest findings of the New Testament scholars, much as securitities rise and fall on the Stock Exchange in response to the latest news of the political or economic situation. So theologians who stress faith-commitment, so far from admitting that they are making a virtue of necessity in abandoning the quest for the facts of the historical Jesus, claim on the contrary that they are returning to a true understanding of the nature of faith. A main theme of Friedrich Gogarten's book, *Demythologizing and History*, is the continuity of the contemporary view with the teaching of Luther, and the claim that it is a return to the Lutheran principle: *sola fide*.

Moreover, a moment's reflection shows us that the most important "events" in the story of Jesus are not of the kind that any historical research could possibly confirm. For instance, the Church's belief in the resurrection of her Lord is not simply a belief that he rose from the dead, but a belief, in the words of the early preaching, that "God raised him up."[4] Historical research might possibly help to establish that someone presumed dead had been seen alive again, but no historical evidence could show that "God raised him up," for this is a judgment of faith that goes beyond bare happening to offer an interpretation of the happening—and no ordinary interpretation, either.

A third factor which should not be overlooked is the change that has taken place in the understanding of the task of the historian. In the nineteenth century, perhaps most historians understood their task to be that of making an objective reconstruction of the past fact—of exhibiting it "as it actually happened," in Ranke's famous phrase. Towards the end of the century, Dilthey was exploring the difference between the natural sciences and the human sciences (*Geisteswissenschaften*), that is to say, between the sciences having a subject-matter that can be

[4]Acts 2: 24.

objectively studied from the outside, and those whose subject-matter can be understood in a more direct way from our own participation in human experience. Dilthey's friend, the Count von Yorck, described Ranke as "a great ocularist,"[5] meaning that he viewed history as a detached spectator might view a show, without becoming involved in the life of history. On the continent, this new way of understanding history was quickened by the rise of existentialism, while in Britain related views about history have been expressed by such men as R. G. Collingwood and John Macmurray.

According to these new ways of looking at it, history is regarded not so much as an observable process that can be analysed from the spectator's point of view, as rather the course of human action which is to be properly understood only by an imaginative participation in the thoughts and decisions of the men who have made history. No doubt every historical event has its "outside," and this can be studied objectively as one might study some natural occurrence. But history, as distinctively action rather than mere process, has also its "inside," and because we are ourselves historical agents, we can seek to understand history from the inside by thinking ourselves into the situation of the agent and by, in some sense, re-enacting his conflicts and decisions in our own experience. In this way, the study of history can become the study of the possible ways of being of man himself. As in all interpretation, there is a two-way traffic here. Interpretation can take place only if we can bring to what is to be interpreted some prior understanding of the subject-matter, and in this case the historian brings to the historical phenomena the understanding of human existence which he already possesses in his own experience; but if the interpretation is to be capable of leading to new understanding, then it must also be possible for the historian to come back from his exploration of the historical phenomena to his own existence, and to perceive there possibilities and dimensions that had hitherto been hidden from him.

[5]*Briefwechsel zwischen Wilhelm Dilthey und dem Grafen Paul Yorck von Wartenburg 1877-97* (Halle-an-der-Saale: 1923), p. 60.

When this existential interpretation is applied to events described in the New Testament, say the cross and resurrection of Christ, attention is shifted from the question about actual observable facts, such as a public execution and the resuscitation of the victim, to the pattern of life and action disclosed in the events—a pattern which may be described as losing life to find it. Subsidiary stories about the blind seeing or the lame walking may be regarded as variations on this fundamental theme. The Christian life consists in the re-enactment of the pattern in present existence, in a dying and rising with Christ, as St. Paul already described it in the New Testament. In such re-enactment, the cross is experienced as reconciliation and the resurrection as new life, and in this way these events can open up new dimensions in the life of the believer. Thus the theological significance of the events is not something that gets arbitrarily added on to a bare happening of the past, not a random metaphysical or mythological framework into which the events have been fitted, but is rather the historical possibility of existence disclosed in the events and repeatable in present historical existence.

This theological orientation has become familiar to us in recent years chiefly through the work of Rudolf Bultmann. All three of the factors I have mentioned are present in his thought. His own far-reaching researches into the question of Christian origins have led him to the conclusion that we can know very little about the historical Jesus. He does indeed insist that "form-critics do not dispute the view that the Church had its origin in the works of Jesus and has preserved many of his sayings in its literary creations."[6] But we rightly understand the character of the gospels if we recognize them as "expanded cult legends."[7] Bultmann, however, made it known long ago that he is not at all embarrassed or distressed by his historical scepticism, for he understands the New Testament teaching not as a record of past happening but as *kerygma*, God's Word addressed to man and seeking

[6]*The History of the Synoptic Tradition*, p. 40.
[7]*Op. cit.*, p. 371.

the response of faith; and by existential interpretation and demythologizing, he brings the "salvation history" into the here and now of our present existence.

But this way of interpreting the New Testament raises very acutely the whole question of history and Christian theology, and especially the relation of the Jesus of history to Christian faith. Are we to think of the gospel narrative as simply a parable which delineates a way of life, so that we can neglect altogether the question of any factual truth in the story? This would be a drastic solution, but it would also be an attractive one for the theologian, for it would make him entirely independent of the historian, and the Christian faith would not be in the slightest degree vulnerable to the findings of historical research, for it would have nothing to do with the matters with which such research is concerned. A few left-wing theologians, such as Fritz Buri, have in fact chosen this solution. He thinks that the task of the theologian is to bring to light the understanding of human existence contained in the New Testament, so that in principle the theologian's work is the same as that of the philosopher of existence. The difference between the two lies only in the circumstance that the theologian has a wealth of symbolic and mythical material in which the Christian understanding of existence has found expression. This symbolic material, once we have the clue to its interpretation, can, of course, be far more effective in conveying an understanding of authentic human existence that can the abstract formulations of the philosophers. But we are told that we need not concern ourselves with the question of what history, if any, lies behind what Buri calls "the great redeemer-myth of the eschatological Christ."[8] The value of the story lies simply in its power to light up for us an authentic understanding of our own existence.

I think, however, that this solution involves an over-simplification of the issues. It puts Christ on exactly the same level as the redeemer-figures of Gnosticism and of the mystery-cults. It need not be denied

[8]*Theologie der Existenz* (Bern: Paul Haupt, 1954), p. 85.

that there are affinities between the New Testament picture of the Christ and the redeemer-figures who are portrayed in Gnostic and other literature, but it must give us pause when we remember that the Church resolutely resisted all attempts to transpose its message entirely into Gnostic terms, and it must have done so because of its belief that something quite vital is at stake here. Also, it must be said that Heidegger, Collingwood and other philosophers to whose views in the interpretation of history contemporary theologians frequently appeal, make it explicit that they do not countenance any blurring of the frontier between history and fiction. When one is confronted with so serious a question as deciding what constitutes an authentic mode of existence, does one turn to fiction for the answer? Admittedly, novels and allegories can sometimes give quite a lot of illumination about human existence, but is this not the case just so far as their authors have regard to what we call "real life" and steer away from utopian ideas, and whatever is merely fantastic or imaginary? It seems obvious that the possibilities of human existence are limited by man's own finite constitution and by the conditions of his actual historical situation. These possibilities are, as Heidegger stresses, "factical" possibilities; or again, as Collingwood teaches, to know what man can do, we must look to what he has done under the conditions of actual historical existence. Only in some such empirical way can we discover where the frontiers of human possibility lie.

Just as it would be senseless to urge an athlete to aim at the physiological impossibility of running a mile in a minute, so it might be senseless to urge a man to love his enemies, unless one could point to an actual historical instance of someone who had done this and thereby shown that it is not an existential or psychological impossibility. There must be some empirical check, if we are not to be deluded and frustrated by utopian and unrealistic ideas. If the New Testament were just as fictitious as a book of fairy-tales, could we really look to it for an understanding of the possibilities of human existence, as we have to decide about them? Does what it shows us belong to a dream-world, or to the same harsh world of actual history as we ourselves have to live in? There is no demand here for a "guarantee" of faith, but there has got to be the recognition that any faith-commitment which demands to be taken seriously must be realistic and have regard to the factical human condition.

Of course, not everyone would agree with this argument for some empirical check. Immanuel Kant, for instance, writes that "we need no empirical example to make the idea of a person morally well-pleasing to God our archetype; this idea, as an archetype, is already present in our reason."[9] Now Kant is right if this means it is on the basis of some prior understanding, whether we call it conscience, practical reason, existential self-understanding or whatever, that we recognize Jesus as the Christ and interpret him as "the archetype of a life morally well-pleasing to God," in Kant's expression. But as has already been pointed out, interpretation is a two-way traffic, and against Kant it must be claimed that it is the empirical historical example that in turn lights up hitherto unnoticed possibilities of human existence. If man were purely a rational being, perhaps he could dispense with empirical examples, but he is a being-in-the-world, a being whose possibilities are already strictly circumscribed for him by his historical situation, so that the empirical historical example cannot be irrelevant.

The fear of losing themselves in a world of myth and make-believe has caused some of Bultmann's disciples to turn again to the question of the historical Jesus. Gunther Bornkamm, for instance, thinks that there is history in the *kerygma* and that without this history "the Church would have been lost in a timeless myth."[10] He obviously thinks it would be a bad thing to get lost in such a myth, but there is little attempt to answer the question about why some factual historicity is *theologically* important. But do the investigations of Bornkamm and others mean that we must reopen the interminable arguments as to whether this incident or that argument took place as recorded? It

[9]*Religion within the Limits of Reason Alone* (New York: Harper, 1960), p. 56.
[10]*Jesus of Nazareth* (London: Hodder & Stoughton, 1960), p. 23.

cannot mean this, for the earlier quest of the historical Jesus showed that no clear answers are to be had. The new quest is intended to be different; but unfortunately it is not easy to discover precisely what is intended, or to know how this new quest bears on the questions about the relation of existential possibilities and empirical instances, as briefly discussed above.

Bultmann himself has reacted somewhat coldly to the new quest. He seems to believe that most of those who have embarked upon it are guilty of confusing existential interpretation of history with the attempt to reconstruct past facts of history. No doubt he has some grounds for this accusation, but it is also a question how these two activities are related. Bultmann himself seems content to hold that there was a Jesus who was crucified, and he sees no compelling reasons to go beyond this simple fact *that* there was a Jesus to *what* Jesus was or did. Even on the most important questions, Bultmann believes that we can arrive at no firm answers. Such a question, for example, is that of how Jesus met his death, that is to say, of how he himself understood it and comported himself toward it. About this Bultmann says: "Whether Jesus found meaning in it, and how he may have done so, we do not know. The possibility that he cracked up cannot be just set aside."[11]

In line with my earlier remarks, my own view would be that the Christian theologian seems compelled to assert what in *The Scope of Demythologizing*[12] I called a "minimal core of factuality" if the *kerygma* is to present us with a way of life that is realistic and not culled from a dream-world. But I do not think that this minimal core is simply *that* there was a Jesus who was crucified, for this in itself would seem to be a matter of no consequence whatever, unless we had some idea of *what* he was. If, for example, neither in the manner of his life nor in that of his death did he manifest the self-giving that the tradition ascribes to him, so that the association of Jesus with the

[11]"Das Verhältnis der urchristlichen Christusbotschaft zum historischen Jesus" (Heidelberg: Universitätsverlag, 1962), p. 12.
[12]London: SCM Press, 1960.

Christ of the *kerygma* is simply an accident or even a mistake, then surely a grave blow would have been struck at the Christian religion. At least, one would have to say that the real insight at the origin of Christianity did not belong to Jesus but to the disciple or disciples who first conceived the pattern of Christhood which was then associated with Jesus of Nazareth. (This has nothing to do with the relatively unimportant question of whether Jesus ever thought of himself as Messiah). And one would have to say also that these disciples (it is hard to imagine who they could have been!) thought of Christhood only as an idea, and not as a pattern of life that had been historically manifested; or, to put it otherwise, that they proclaimed a Word, but not a Word made flesh.

The "minimal core" of which I speak is not a short list of supposedly essential incidents or sayings, for there could not be such. It is simply the assertion that at the source of the Christian religion there was an actual historical instance of the pattern of life proclaimed in the *kerygma* under the notions of dying and rising. It seems to me that this is not too far from what Bultmann is saying when, conceding that individual stories in the gospels may not be historical reports of actual incidents in the life of Jesus, he nevertheless maintains that "the general character of his life is rightly portrayed in them, on the basis of historical recollections."[13] The biography of this person was quickly transformed into a mythical drama or cult legend beyond which we cannot now penetrate; but what was preserved was the actual pattern of Jesus' life, as something that had actually manifested itself in history. A parallel case is provided by Socrates. We have hardly any reliable biographical details about him, and certainly nothing like a connected account of his life; but what is more important, namely, the manner of man that he was, printed itself indelibly on the memory of mankind, and has come down to us.

This minimal core of factuality—that there was an historical instance of the pattern of life which the gospel proclaims—is not indeed some-

[13]*History of the Synoptic Tradition*, p. 50.

thing certain, but it is something that has overwhelming probability, and maintains itself as constant through all the varied findings of historical research. This core seems to be all that the theologian requires, and is sufficiently stable to allow him to get on with his work without depending on every changing estimate of the historian.

But when this has been said, it remains clear that history does not of itself settle the question about the claim of Christianity. Confronted with this way of life, stemming from Jesus himself and transmitted in the kerygmatic proclamation of the Church, one sees that contemporary theology is right in stressing that this is primarily a matter for value-judgment, existential decision, faith-commitment, or however one may care to express it. These are modern expressions for the kind of thing St. Peter meant when he said: "Thou art the Christ."[14] Historical research can give no "guarantee" for such a commitment, but we can have reasonable confidence that the commitment is to a realistic possibility of existence.

[14]Mark 8: 29.

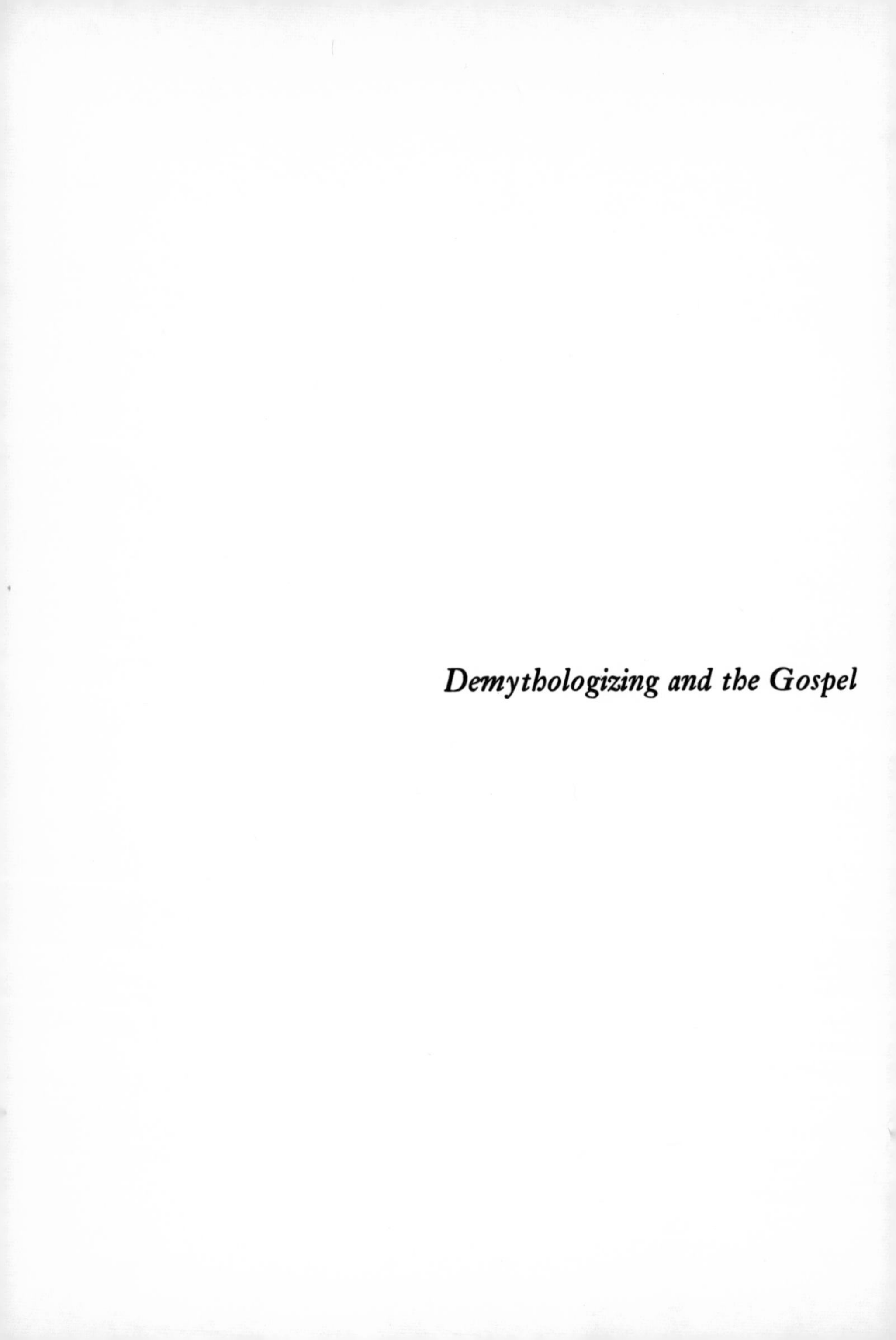

Demythologizing and the Gospel

At the end of World War II, I was serving as a chaplain with the British army in North Africa, and received an unusual and somewhat daunting assignment—that of organizing religious ministrations for the tens of thousands of German prisoners-of-war who were being held in camps throughout Egypt and the adjacent countries. About thirty German Protestant pastors from among the prisoners were available for this work, and they received as much help as possible from the British authorities. But they were facing an entirely missionary situation, and they had to begin literally from nothing. It was not just that they had to improvise churches and furnishings and the other accessories of worship in the dusty desert camps. It was rather that they were facing men who had been brought to nothing, men who had come to the end of their tethers and had begun to question everything. Many of these men had been brought up to believe fanatically in the pagan doctrines of National Socialism, but now they saw Hitler's empire laid in ruins and its idols fallen to the ground. Their own future was uncertain and unpromising. The whole framework within which they had operated had been taken away, and they found themselves asking what meaning, if any, they could attach to their lives. It was clear that no merely conventional message could get across to such men, but only one that was geared to their desperate needs, only one which was, in the jargon of today, "existentially relevant." It says much for the faith and insight of the German pastors that their ministry in the camps met with a very remarkable response.

The situation just described may be taken as mirroring in a small way the situation that characterizes Europe as a whole in our present stormy century. Old and supposedly stable structures have broken down, and often the new structures meant to replace them have also collapsed after a few years. These radical upheavals are, of course, being felt all over the world, but those of us who live in the relatively stable societies of Britain and America have not been quite so exposed to violent change as have people on the European continent itself, and we should bear this in mind. It is not surprising that in response to the needs of new situations, new theological formulations and new ways of presenting the Christian message should arise, and that these should come out of troubled Europe. Rudolf Bultmann's demythologizing has come out of this background, as did Karl Barth's crisis theology, but whereas Barth's views had perhaps their greatest influence in the period between the two World Wars—and we must never forget the part which his teaching played in strengthening the Church's resistance to Nazism—Bultmann's theology has been at the focus of attention in the period after World War II.

Of course, wars and upheavals are soon forgotten, and with them the elemental questions that men ask when they have come to the end of their resources. Philosophers like Jaspers tell us that these questions are forgotten because we want to forget them. We do not want to be disturbed by the real questions of life. We want to live complacently and securely on the surface of things, occupying ourselves with sport and television and all the trappings and trimmings of modern life, while trying to shut out the big disquieting questions of what it is all about and where we are going. Yet surely it is also true that we live nowadays in a perpetually uneasy world, and that these big questions are never very far away from us.

The kind of philosophy which occupies itself with these basic questions of human existence is existentialism, and Bultmann's theology is perhaps best understood as a Christian existentialism, for demythologizing is the existential interpretation of the Christian faith. Bultmann believes that when we go to the New Testament, the questions which we must ask of it are the fundamental questions of our own existence, and in this age of anxiety, these questions are not too far away from any one of us. So the Christian message is to be interpreted as a way of understanding ourselves and the possibilities of our existence.

However, in the working out of this approach to the Christian message, we find that Bultmann's thought moves around two basic ideas. One is the idea of demythologizing, of existential interpretation, as has already been mentioned. The other is the idea of a *kerygma*, the proclamation of a divine word addressed to men. Here Bultmann firmly retains the kerygmatic element that has been so prominent in contemporary Protestant theology since Barth. The whole aim and object of demythologizing is, indeed, to allow the *kerygma* to speak to the men of our time in a language they can understand, to set it free from the obscuring mythical setting that it has in the New Testament and in traditional formulations. As a word of God addressed to human existence, the *kerygma* should be, and indeed must be expressible in terms which relate directly to this existence of ours.

But how do these two sides of Bultmann's theology hold together? Must not a thoroughgoing demythologizing result in the dissolution of any kerygmatic element? Or if one retains the *kerygma*, does this not constitute a barrier to the carrying out of the demand for existential interpretation? Bultmann himself is well aware of this problem, and it is one of the points chiefly debated by those who have participated in the discussion sparked by Bultmann's proposals. Attempted solutions range all the way from left-wing repudiations of the *kerygma* to right-wing demands for abandoning existentialist interpretation altogether.

A consideration of this problem and of attempted solutions formed the theme of my book, *The Scope of Demythologizing*, and soon afterwards was treated by Schubert Ogden in *Christ without Myth*. He took issue with me at several points, and I want to say something about these. First of all, it should be said that the differences between us should not be exaggerated, and are probably narrower than Ogden recognizes. We have both made clear on many occasions our indebtedness to Bultmann and our conviction that his work offers a feasible approach to the theological problems of our time. However, we both criticize parts of Bultmann's view and believe that it needs some reconstruction. The differences arise partly over questions of interpreting Bultmann's meaning, partly over the fact that sometimes I criticize elements in Bultmann's teaching which Ogden wishes to defend, and *vice versa*, and partly over the ways in which we think that reconstruction ought to take place.

A general difference of orientation finds expression in the fact that Ogden several times classes me with what he calls the "camp of the right" in theology.[1] Such positioning is, of course, a matter of degree, and Ogden recognizes that there are a great many people to the right of me, for he describes my position as "quite close to Bultmann's" while he visualizes the hinterland of the right as extending to rigid positions that are "virtually antithetical" to Bultmann's.[2] I agree that I am to the right of Ogden, and indeed this is obvious from the ways in which each of us has responded to the disputes over demythologizing, Ogden looking to the left wing for the solution while my own endeavour has rather been to find a middle way and to defend Bultmann against critics of both right and left.

The difference between my middle way and Ogden's leftward tendency is well brought out in a further remark of his. He says that in views such as mine "one repeatedly meets, as a kind of distinguishing refrain, the phrase 'not only . . . but also' ";[3] and as an illustration, he

[1]*Christ without Myth* (London: Collins, 1962), p. 160.
[2]*Ibid.* [3]*Ibid.*

quotes a sentence of mine: "Theology is concerned *not only* with statements about human existence, *but* with statements about God and his activity *as well*."[4] If this is meant to be a criticism, I can only say that I welcome it. In the complicated issues of theology, the "not only . . . but also" approach is necessary if we are not to fall into vast oversimplifications. And I believe it can also be said that if one were to look for a recurring refrain in Ogden's writing, this would be the word "completely," which occurs with astonishing frequency. Within the space of half-a-dozen pages, I find these examples: "Bultmann *completely* fails to show that such a requirement has any necessary connection with what he takes to be the distinctive Christian claim"; "Bultmann's theology is shot through with an inconsistency that *completely* determines its basic structure and movement"; J. M. Robinson's "polemic (against Buri and Ogden) is *completely* lacking in force"; Bultmann "*completely* nullifies his own constructive proposal"; Macquarrie's statement is "*completely* unconvincing."[5]

This is only a small selection, but it is revealing. Where everything is completely one thing or another, then theology is no doubt much simpler and consistency is easier to achieve. But one-sided assertions like those quoted above are very dangerous. Sweeping judgments on very complicated issues are so confidently passed that many readers and probably the author himself may imagine that what has been said is self-evident. When Ogden casually remarks, to give a somewhat glaring instance, that "John *completely* eliminates the futuristic eschatology of the primitive community," a partial truth gets absolutized, difficult questions of exegesis on which New Testament commentators have spent much effort are passed over without discussion, and a simple one-sided picture is presented where there ought to be a complex one.

Ogden's very striving for consistency is suspect. It is true that theology cannot be content to contradict itself, but if we aim at getting away from an objectifying language to a language that somehow trans-

[4]*An Existentialist Theology* (London: SCM Press, 1955), p. 243.
[5]*Christ without Myth*, pp. 144-49. Italics mine.

cends the subject-object way of thinking, we may find that the new language does not conform to the same kind of logic that operates in the case of our ordinary objectifying language. Heidegger has frequently pointed out that our everyday logic comes undone in existential and ontological inquiry. Theologians such as Donald Baillie have pointed to the inevitability of paradox when we try to express in an objectifying language a content that arises from an experience transcending the subject-object pattern, and therefore involving a polarity. A failure to recognize the kind of polarity which attends theological discourse lies at the root of Ogden's striving for categorical, unqualified assertions (illustrated by his fondness for the word "completely"), and his corresponding impatience with statements of the "not only . . . but also" form. This failure takes place on various levels, sometimes as a one-sided interpretation of what Bultmann or some other writer has said, sometimes as a one-sided presentation of the theological subject-matter itself. Incidentally, although my own sympathies lie more with Ogden's position than with that of Paul Van Buren, I believe that Van Buren has had the edge over Ogden in his criticisms[6] precisely because of the latter's failure to consider how complex the problem of theological language is.

Let me point to an example of one-sided interpretation by Ogden—perhaps a trivial example in itself, but one that shows what we must guard against. He thinks that I have missed "the basic motivation of Bultmann's theology" because "like so many other interpreters, Macquarrie takes the position that Bultmann is basically an 'apologist,' that the primary motive of his work is to recommend the Christian *kerygma* to the peculiarly modern situation"; and very typically Ogden adds: "The trouble with such a position is that it *completely* disregards Bultmann's own repeated statements as to the basis of his theology."[7] Now, in the first place, it is hard to know how Ogden could have arrived at

[6]See *The Secular Meaning of the Gospel* (New York: Macmillan, 1963), especially pp. 57-79.
[7]*Christ without Myth,* p. 201.

such mistaken opinions. Already in the Preface to *An Existentialist Theology* I had indicated that I proposed to defend Bultmann's existential approach to theology on three grounds: "the right of the apologist to make use of current philosophical concepts; the claim that there is a special relation between the philosophy of existence and the work of theology; and an affinity between the concepts of existentialism and those of biblical thought." When I came to spell this out, I even explicitly stated that Bultmann's use of the "apologetic possibilities" of existentialism was the "least important" of the three points mentioned, and that "more important" was the inner connection between existentialist concepts and the theological task of biblical interpretation.[8] I have said this kind of thing over and over again, claiming that the New Testament is authentically interpreted in terms of self-understanding; I have praised not only Bultmann but any other writer who has offered such interpretation—for instance, Robert McAfee Brown for his masterly demythologizing or existential interpretation of the story of the raising of Lazarus;[9] and I have argued that existential interpretation is demanded even where there are no special "apologetic" problems, for instance, in the case of ethical teachings which have to be understood in relation to concrete existential situations. But perhaps more serious than his failure to take note of what has explicitly been said is, in the second place, Ogden's concentration on *one* motive to the exclusion of others. Like other theologians, Bultmann presumably pursues his work from a variety of motives; and it may be that with most theologians one of the most important motives is just that of trying to solve for one's own satisfaction the problems of which one has become aware.

On similar lines I could very well defend my interpretations of such concepts as "modernity" and "exclusiveness" in Bultmann, and I believe that in his criticisms of these interpretations, Ogden has again failed to take into account all the facets of Bultmann's thought. But I do not wish to weary the reader by discussing these matters at length, or to

[8]*Op. cit.*, p. 24.
[9]*The Bible Speaks to You* (Philadelphia: Westminster Press, 1955), p. 12.

give the reader the impression that I must compulsively defend the correctness of everything I have written, especially as I have already stressed the ambiguities of the matters in question, and the undesirability of taking up categorical and one-sided positions. So I will pass to matters of more substance.

Let us then consider the tenacious way in which Ogden upholds Bultmann's definition of "myth" not only against my criticisms but against those of several other writers who have paid attention to it. In *The Scope of Demythologizing*[10] I listed four criticisms of Bultmann's definition of "myth," and suggested that this definition ought to be set aside. But at the same time, I found that Bultmann himself had made changes in his ways of talking about myth, and that these changes permit the concept to be reconstructed in a more satisfactory way; however, I claimed further that this involves a reassessment of what we mean by "demythologizing," amounting to a "limit" to demythologizing, if this process is understood as the translation without remainder of mythical language into a language about human existence. Ogden, on the other hand, thinks that Bultmann's definition of "myth" is unaffected by the criticisms and permits Bultmann to press on to unrestricted demythologizing.

Perhaps we should now remind ourselves of Bultmann's definition of "myth," and we may as well use Ogden's translation, which is a good one: " 'Mythology' is that manner of representation in which the unworldly and divine (*des Unweltliche, Göttliche*) appears as the worldly and human (*das Weltliche, Menschliche*)—or, in short, in which the transcendent appears as the immanent (*das Jenseitige als Diesseitige*)."[11] It would be tedious to go over all the possible criticisms of this definition and Bultmann's use of it, so let me come at once to the one that is most germane to the present discussion. This criticism was well put by Ronald Hepburn who maintained that Bultmann had given the word "myth" "a sense sufficiently extended to include every kind of

[10] pp. 198ff.
[11] *Kerygma and Myth*, p. 10.

oblique language."[12] Thus Hepburn argued that when Bultmann uses expressions like "God acts" or "God speaks," and claims that these are analogical rather than mythological ways of talking, his distinction between analogy and mythology is unwarranted, for what he calls "analogy" falls under his own definition of "mythology."

Ogden sharply challenges Hepburn's point, which he dismisses as "groundless" and a "fatal mistake."[13] But when he later gets around to trying to explain wherein the fatal mistake consists, it seems to me that he has no success. He argues that Hepburn has failed to notice that Bultmann uses the expression "worldly" to refer to an objectifying representation, and since an analogy drawn from human existence ("God speaks" or the like) is not objectifying, it does not fall under the category of myth. But this is another extraordinary example of Ogden's one-sidedness, for he has taken only *one* of the three points in Bultmann's definition of "myth"—the representation of the unworldly by the worldly. Bultmann also mentions in his definition the representation of the divine by the human, and of the transcendent by the immanent. Ogden conveniently ignores this, but even if we grant that "God speaks" does not represent the unworldly by the worldly in the sense of objectifying God (perhaps as a "voice from heaven"), nevertheless we undoubtedly have here a case of representing the divine by the human, the transcendent by the immanent; for speaking is a human and an immanent activity. Hence "God speaks" falls under Bultmann's definition of "myth"; but since it is certainly better to call this language "analogy" rather than "mythology," then Bultmann's definition should be amended. So long as it stands, however, it seems to me, *pace* Ogden, that Bultmann's demythologizing involves, on his own terms, an element of transmythologizing.[14] But I should much prefer to see the definition abandoned and the distinction between analogy (which Ogden

[12] *New Essays in Philosophical Theology*, ed. A. Flew and A. McIntyre (London: SCM Press, 1955), p. 229.

[13] *Christ without Myth*, p. 106.

[14] See *An Existentialist Theology*, p. 176, and Ogden's comment in *Christ without Myth*, p. 172.

admits is an unclear concept in Bultmann) and mythology clarified.

The important point is that when one uses this analogical language of "God speaks" and the like, one has abandoned the attempt to translate all the content of myth into statements about human existence. What Ogden never clearly recognizes is that there is a vast logical difference between using existential or personal language of "speaking," "loving," "acting" and so on directly in relation to man, who is the proper subject of such language, and indirectly or obliquely in relation to God, who can be only analogically the subject of such language. This has nothing to do with the question of trying to talk about God independently of human existence, or apart from his relation to us. Many theologians before Bultmann have recognized that we cannot talk of God except as he acts on us. But nevertheless, when we do talk of his acting upon us, we believe that we are talking of One who is in some way over against us, and not just an element in our experience, perhaps a focus of values or an imaginary ideal as some philosophers (including an earlier generation of Marburg thinkers) have understood by the word "God." This seems to me precisely what Ogden himself has recently expressed by saying: "Whatever else Christians have usually supposed themselves to be doing in proclaiming their faith, whether in personal confession, prayer, preaching or teaching, they have surely believed they were somehow responding cognitively to a divine reality *radically other than themselves*, in whose gracious initiative and approach alone their proclamation has its basis and object."[15]

It was for this reason that I claimed that "theology is concerned not only with statements about human existence, but with statements about God and his activity as well." The reader will remember that Ogden cited this as an example of the "not only . . . but also" talk of the right wing, to which he so strongly objected. But this statement is not to be understood as claiming anything more than what he himself says in the

[15]"Theology and Objectivity" (a paper privately circulated in connection with the Consultation on Hermeneutics at Drew University, New Jersey, 1964), p. 13. Italics mine.

words I quoted from him in the last paragraph. My motive in making a statement like this was to counter the danger I see in an unrestricted demythologizing which, if we understand it in the sense of translating the myth without remainder into statements about human existence, would seem to me to result in the elimination of God as a "radically other." He would be demythologized much as the demons are in Bultmann, becoming a creation of man's existential aspiration rather than a reality that is prior to man. In particular, it seemed to me that Buri's "dekerygmatizing" was well on the way towards a point of view where one should stop altogether talking about "God" and talk instead of "authentic existence" or something of the sort. So when Ogden wonders[16] what Buri would have to say to reassure me, my answer would be: "Plenty!" Incidentally, he has somewhat modified his position since his advocacy of "dekerygmatizing."

On the other hand, I found that Bultmann, in my way of expressing it, sets a limit to demythologizing, for he clearly wants to talk of an "act of God" and so on; and although this may be called an analogy, and incorporated in a wider conception of demythologizing, it is a departure from that unrestricted demythologizing which calls for the translation of all mythical statements into statements about human existence. If one were to hold with Ogden[17] that Bultmann's identification of the questions of God and man is to be taken quite literally as meaning that "*the two questions are in fact one and the same*," then it seems to me that "God" has become just the name for an ideal of human existence. And surely Bultmann never holds to such a view. I believe that Ogden misunderstands what Bultmann means by "radical" demythologizing, for this does not mean pushing the translation into language about human existence to the end, but rather extending existential interpretation from peripheral matters like miracles, demons and the like to the central events of the cross and resurrection of Jesus Christ, as Bultmann does in the final sections of his programmatic essay, "New Testament and Mythology."[18] He does not indeed eliminate the divine ac-

[16]*Christ without Myth*, p. 213. [17]*Op. cit.*, p. 203. [18]*Kerygma and Myth*, pp. 33ff.

tivity in these events, but he does show that they can be appreciated as "saving" events only as we get away from the notion of objective transactions *extra nos* to the existential appropriation of the events. But here again, Ogden recognizes this, for in resisting Van Buren's seeming elimination of God, Ogden says that "Bultmann, for all of his insistence on the need for thoroughgoing existentialist interpretation has stoutly resisted the kind of theological reduction that Van Buren and others hold to be required."[19] These words express very well what I have understood by the "limit" to demythologizing. It may be, of course, as Ogden says, that I have set this limit more explicitly than Bultmann does, but surely it is the business of an interpreter and commentator to make explicit what may be little more than implicit in the writer he is interpreting. But Bultmann, as indeed Ogden's expression about "stoutly resisting" implies, has not been unconscious of what he is doing. Indeed, it astonishes me that Ogden should think that Bultmann is so utterly unperceptive that his theology "is shot through with an inconsistency that completely determines its basic structure and movement."[20] Ogden rightly notes my debt to Ian Henderson, who did so much to pioneer the study of Bultmann in the English-speaking countries, and I remember that he used to say, after reading some of Bultmann's critics, "You know, there really aren't many flies on Bultmann." Considering that Bultmann has been subjected to criticisms for a generation and has himself faced the problem of how the two sides of his theology hang together, it really is rather unlikely that he should be so hopelessly inconsistent as some of his critics maintain. And for this reason my first move, whether successful or not, was to "vindicate the paradox" in his thinking.

But I cannot see that Ogden's reconstruction of Bultmann is so very different from my own suggestions. For he too is not content with a demythologizing that remains on the anthropological plane. He acknowledges some force in Heinrich Ott's criticism that the demythologizing of Bultmann is too "restrictively existentialist" and requires an

[19] "Theology and Objectivity," p. 15. [20] *Christ without Myth*, p. 145.

"ampler" philosophy to overcome its limitations.[21] This would seem to indicate that I need not take too seriously his criticisms of my demands for "supplementing" Bultmann's position, since he does the same himself. However, we differ about where to look for this supplementation, for whereas I would continue with Heidegger beyond the stage at which Bultmann has parted company with him and believe that Heidegger can provide an existentially based ontology which avoids the pitfalls of the old-style metaphysics, Ogden looks rather to the metaphysics of Hartshorne and company.

Yet in spite of Ogden's recognition that a merely existentialist interpretation is inadequate to the demands of a philosophical theology, his flirting with the extreme left wing seems to me to bring him pretty close on some occasions to what he himself calls a "truncated humanism," and in particular to the obscuring of any conception of God as a source of grace. When we are told that "man can win or lose himself by his own responsible decisions" and it is suggested that the alternative to this is a view in which man is the "irresponsible victim of fate,"[22] we are, as happens so often in Ogden, presented with a *complete* disjunction between extremes—here thoroughgoing Pelagianism at one extreme and irresistible grace (or perhaps predestination) at the other. There is no recognition of what Donald Baillie calls the "paradox of grace," though surely this comes nearest to describing Christian experience.

It is therefore rather surprising to find Ogden finally suggesting that he takes issue with me chiefly because he suspects me of departing from "the Reformation principles of *sola gratia—sola fide*"! To be sure, I am not uncritical of these principles, which have often been grossly exaggerated and distorted in Protestant thought. But the rebuke comes rather oddly from Ogden. He actually raises it in connection with my demands for "supplementing" a purely existentialist interpretation of Christianity, and especially with my call for the recognition of a "mini-

[21]"The Understanding of Theology in Ott and Bultmann" in *New Frontiers in Theology*, ed. J. M. Robinson and J. B. Cobb (New York: Harper & Row, 1963), p. 158.

[22]*Christ without Myth*, p. 139.

mal core of historical factuality." I will not reply in detail to all his remarks on this theme, for in some instances (such as what he has to say about my remarks on the resurrection)[23] I believe he has misunderstood my intention. My point in all of these discussions of the historical element in Christianity has been to plead for an empirical dimension in theology. This is also the point of my question (which is simply an echo of Collingwood) about how we can know what man *can* do, except by having regard to what he *has done*. Ogden strongly objects to this, but it seems to me to be our only safeguard against being invited to embark on utopian and unrealistic policies. And moreover, I stand here very firmly by the tradition of the Church, as against those docetic and gnostic tendencies which Ogden seems to favour by his discounting of the empirical. It is, indeed, just such a docetism that he seems to mean by his understanding of the "*sola fide*."

On the other hand, I agree with Ogden and feel just as strongly as he does that grace and revelation are not *exclusively* opened to men in the Christ-event, but that other events may have served as bearers of God's truth as well. But whereas Ogden appeals for support to the "liberal" theology of modern times, my own appeal would be rather to the unbroken tradition that goes back to the earliest Fathers, and over against which an exclusive christocentricism is an aberration, currently represented by Barthianism. In the passage that Ogden quotes[24] from F. D. Maurice, for example, it is highly probable that this good Anglican was himself recalling some strikingly similar passages in St. Justin and St. Irenaeus.

But when all this has been said, it seems to me that the differences between Ogden and myself, though sharp enough at some points, are not unbridgeable, and that indeed, if we found ourselves surrounded by Barthians or neo-Calvinists, we would be standing very much side by side—and equally so if we were surrounded by followers of Braithwaite and Van Buren at the opposite extreme! At least, I hope so, for I think

[23]See *Christ without Myth*, pp. 157, 209.
[24]*Op. cit.*, pp. 181-2.

we both believe in the need for this conjunction of demythologizing *and* the gospel, a conjunction which we learned from Bultmann and which seeks to bring together the traditional faith and the conditions for its contemporary communication. This is not just for the prisoners-of-war, from whom this essay started out; for below the surface, we all know ourselves to be "pilgrims and strangers" in the world, questing for meaning and wholeness.

Some Other Approaches Considered PART IV

A New Kind of Demythologizing?

12

When anyone who is interested in contemporary theology reads R. B. Braithwaite's Eddington Memorial Lecture,[1] the question which is likely to occur to him is whether we are being offered in this lecture a new kind of demythologizing. Before the appearance of this lecture, we had been accustomed to associate the term "demythologizing" with the efforts of Rudolf Bultmann to translate mythical statements which purport to speak of some transcendent reality into statements about human existence. But Braithwaite appears to be doing something very similar. Thus he tells us that the statement, "God is love," which he very reasonably takes to epitomize the assertions of the Christian religion, is to be interpreted as the declaration of an intention to follow what he calls an "agapastic" way of life.[2] Here a statement which most people would ingenuously assume to be about a transcendent reality called "God" is translated into the assertion of a human intention. This may lead us to suppose that Bultmann and Braithwaite are both

[1] *An Empiricist's View of the Nature of Religious Belief* (London: Cambridge University Press, 1955).
[2] *Op. cit.*, p. 18.

engaged on what is fundamentally the same endeavour, and that the difference between them arises from their different philosophical presuppositions, or, as it might be better expressed, from their different ways of doing philosophy. The former speaks as an existentialist, the latter as an empiricist, but they are at one in trying to formulate religious statements in terms of human existence or human experience.

A straightforward comparison between the two points of view would be extremely difficult. Thus, for instance, Bultmann's somewhat ill-defined category of "myth" cuts across Braithwaite's distinction between religious statements and religious stories. Religious statements appear to say something about God, but, we are told, are used to announce "allegiance to a set of moral principles," and it is this use which constitutes their meaning. On the other hand, religious stories are sets of empirical propositions which are given a meaning like any other empirical propositions. Here a further distinction arises. Some of these empirical propositions will be simple historical assertions, such as that Christ suffered under Pontius Pilate, and these may be readily believed to be true. But others, such as that Christ ascended into heaven, seem to be in a different category. This kind of statement would fall within Bultmann's notion of mythology. Both he and Braithwaite seem to be agreed that from the religious point of view, it is a matter of indifference whether such stories are believed to be literally true or not.

Certainly, believing the stories, whether historical or mythical, does not seem to make anyone a Christian. It is clear that a man could believe that Christ suffered under Pontius Pilate, and not be a Christian. A man might even believe that Christ ascended into heaven, and be a Muslim; and indeed the Muslims are nowadays the guardians of the shrine on the Mount of Olives from which the Ascension traditionally took place. Both our demythologizers are right in maintaining that a crude literalism is irrelevant to religion. But when we ask what the function of the stories is, we receive different answers. Bultmann tells us that they are to be interpreted in terms of their significance for human existence. Braithwaite's view is that they are to be entertained in association with the intention to follow an agapastic way of life, and that when they are so entertained, they can have a powerful psychological effect in helping people to carry out their intended policy. Whether these two points of view are as different as they seem at first sight, it would be hard to say. Clearly, it could not be just any set of stories that would have the effect of which Braithwaite speaks, but a set which brought the person entertaining them to understand himself as committed to a certain way of life, and here we seem to come pretty near to Bultmann's idea that a myth does not give information about objective facts but either expresses or communicates a new self-understanding.

This preliminary comparison leads to another on a more fundamental level. Both thinkers appear to have similar ideas about what constitutes the essential element in religion. They are equally emphatic in their rejection of the idea that religion is primarily acceptance of a world-view. They also agree in denying that religion is primarily emotion, though they would concede that there is an emotional factor in it. For Braithwaite, religion is primarily conative, and he can talk of "an ultimate decision to accept a way of life."[3] For Bultmann, a primary element in faith is also decision or commitment. In both cases, there is an attempt to get away from what may be called the "transcendent" element in religion, and to speak in human terms of a way of life, whether the language be that of existential self-understanding or of asserting a moral intention.

We may have grave doubts as to whether religion can be so far humanized without its ceasing to be religion. It may well be that commitment to a way of life implicitly commits us at the same time to a belief about "how things are," perhaps a metaphysical belief or at any rate some kind of ontological belief, if we allow the possibility of an ontology which is not reached by way of the traditional methods of metaphysics. As far as Bultmann is concerned, it is not hard to show

[3] *Op. cit.*, p. 34.

that even if he ever intended to carry out a thoroughgoing programme of demythologizing, such as would resolve all the utterances covered by his definition of "myth" into statements about human existence, there remain in his thinking apparently irreducible transcendent elements which may lead us to question his consistency but which nevertheless seem to be true to the nature of the Christian religion. I propose now to examine Braithwaite's position to see whether there may not also be implicit in it what we may call a "transcendent" element, in spite of the fact that such an element is supposed to be excluded by his theory.

In 1935 A. J. Ayer was contending that ethics, theology and metaphysics were alike nonsensical. This contention was made chiefly on the ground that in these subjects we can have no empirical verification of what they seem to assert, and therefore there can be no meaning in these alleged assertions. But as H. J. Paton has neatly put it, "as originally expounded, logical positivism sweeps away so much into one comprehensive rubbish heap that it is difficult not to feel there must be something wrong with it."[4] Consequently there has been a gradual withdrawal from the more extreme points of view. First, there were attempts to rehabilitate ethics. Now the salvage operations are being extended to religion. But so far as I am aware, no serious attempts have yet been made to raise the wreck of metaphysics from the still deeper water in which it went down under heavy fire.

The empiricist who seeks to rehabilitate religion must therefore attempt to do so without metaphysics. As we have already seen, Braithwaite makes a valiant effort to do just this. For the older verification principle of the positivists, there is substituted the wider, more flexible principle of use. A statement gets its meaning from the way in which we use it. Thus religious statements cease to be meaningless, though the meaning now attributed to them is not an obvious one. Who would have thought, that when the Christian says that God is love, he is really evincing an intention to follow an agapastic way of life?

[4] *The Modern Predicament* (London: Allen & Unwin, 1956), p. 114.

Braithwaite's conative interpretation of the religious statement comes very close to merging religion into morality. But it does not completely do this, because there are still the stories which provide the psychological support for the intention to act in a certain way, and it is the entertaining of these stories that distinguishes religion from simple morality. Presumably too the psychological support gained from the entertaining of the stories is a kind of secularized equivalent of what in religion is called "grace."

Among other things, one may suppose that the stories entertained in religion engender certain feelings, so that one could think of religion, in Matthew Arnold's famous phrase, as "morality touched with emotion." This would not be quite adequate to Braithwaite's view. He does not wish to make too much of emotion in religion, though he admits that it has its place. He speaks, for instance, of "feelings of joy, of consolation, of being at one with the universe."[5] I have tried to maintain in another essay[6] that religious feelings are never mere emotions, but always carry with them some kind of understanding, even if it is not explicit. Thus it seems to me that I could scarcely feel "at one with the universe" unless I understood that the universe were the kind of thing with which I could be at one–if, for instance, it were the creation of a God of love. In admitting such feelings into religion, Braithwaite appears to be acknowledging that the stories which engender such feelings are not merely edifying parables to be entertained in the mind as psychological aids to good living, but that they throw light on the ultimate questions of existence–the "metaphysical" questions, if we care to call them such, though it might be better to call them "ontological" questions, since to call them "metaphysical" seems to point not only to their ultimacy but to a particular way of approaching them, that is to say, by rational speculation. In any case, it is hard to see how religion could bring the kind of joy and consolation mentioned by Braithwaite if we had no clue to the problem of what kind of a

[5]*Op. cit.*, p. 15.
[6]See above, "Feeling and Understanding", pp. 31ff.

universe this is, or if we maintained that this is a question which cannot properly be asked.

But since Braithwaite does not lay stress on the affective element in religion, we cannot attach too much importance to these considerations, even if they provide a pointer. He could drop from his theory his feeling of "being at one with the universe," and this would result in no serious damage to his main thesis, though it would certainly impoverish his conception of religion, and perhaps make us more than ever suspicious of the adequacy of this conception.

There is, however, another line of thought to be considered. Religion may be primarily commitment to a way of life, but it can be argued that such commitment inevitably involves us in some kind of belief. We must now ask how this belief is related to the act of commitment, and what kind of belief it turns out to be.

How is the belief related to the act of resolving to follow a way of life? Braithwaite claims that "to say that it is belief in the dogmas of religion which is the cause of the believer's intending to behave as he does is to put the cart before the horse."[7] I believe that on the whole, Braithwaite is right in what he asserts here. Like the devils mentioned by St. James, I could believe Christian doctrines to be true without being committed to a Christian way of life. I might be a theist as far as philosophical theory is concerned, and yet be without any conviction that could properly be called religious. Bultmann would also be in agreement here. Religious beliefs are not theoretical but existential or even practical, and it is only in living them out that we really begin to understand them.

But there is another side to the question. The initial act of commitment is surely not just a blind leap in the dark—though some have said so. A decision, to be worthy of the name, must be taken in the light of our beliefs, and it is to be hoped that these will be reasonable beliefs which we consider ourselves to have some grounds for accepting. This is recognized by Braithwaite, who quotes with approval a sentence

[7] *Op. cit.*, p. 16.

from R. M. Hare to the effect that an ultimate decision to accept a way of life "far from being arbitrary . . . would be the most well-founded of decisions, because it would be based upon a consideration of everything upon which it could possibly be founded."[8] It may be that to begin with, the belief is not fully worked out and that it is only *ambulando* that we come to understand all that is involved in it. But the point is that a belief of some kind is present from the beginning as an essential element in the committing of oneself to a way of life. So there is a sense in which we act upon our beliefs, and as rational agents we should be able to explain why we are following the policies we have chosen, rather than others.

We now have to turn to our second and more important question. What is the nature of the belief which accompanies the commitment to a way of life? Let us approach the question in this way. Using Braithwaite's own terminology, we are entitled to ask the Christian, "Why do you intend to follow an agapastic way of life?" If his decision to follow such a way of life was (as Braithwaite says it should be) not an arbitrary one but one founded on a consideration of everything that could be accounted relevant, the Christian ought to be able to answer our question. Now surely many Christians might answer by saying: "I intend to follow an agapastic way of life because God is *agape* or love." But then, if Braithwaite's interpretation of the statement "God is love" is correct, the answer amounts to saying: "I intend to follow an agapastic way of life because I declare (evince or show forth) my intention of following an agapastic way of life." This hardly looks like the answer of a rational moral agent, and it makes the decision a purely arbitrary one. Furthermore, the very odd sentence which results when one substitutes Braithwaite's translation of "God is love" is quite certainly not what the Christian means. He believes that he is doing more than uttering a tautology, and that he is in fact affirming his faith that love is the ultimate power in the universe. And he may even go on to say, following St. Augustine, that it was the

[8] *Op. cit.*, p. 34.

experience of the love of God revealed in Christ which evoked or elicited love in himself and empowered him to resolve on an agapastic way of life.

This belief that love is at the heart of the universe is presumably a metaphysical one; or better, an ontological one. For it is not, as has been said already, a detached speculation from which we would have to make the transition somehow to an agapastic way of life. It is rather an existentially rooted belief, involved in the decision taken when a man chooses the agapastic way of life in preference to any other. It seems quite implausible to suggest, as Braithwaite does, about such a man that there is "nothing which he takes to be the fundamental truth about the universe."[9] On the contrary, the way of life which Braithwaite describes implies just such a belief. Much more plausible is the old saying that every man has a metaphysic (ontology) at the back of his mind—sometimes pretty far back. He must act *as if* the universe were of some kind or other. The Christian acts (or intends to act) *as if* love were the most real and important thing of all. His understanding of what love is will become clearer and purer through following in the way of love. But love cannot cease to be a personal quality, so that to act *as if* love were the fundamental truth about the universe is to believe in a God who is *at least* personal—perhaps more, but Christian theology will avoid getting lost in a too speculative theorizing about the nature of God as he is in himself.

That religious beliefs carry ontological implications may be seen also in what Braithwaite has to say about religions other than Christianity. He argues that Judaism and Buddhism also recommend an agapastic way of life, and that the three religions are distinguished only by the different sets of stories associated in each case with the moral intention. One might question the somewhat free use here of such a distinctively New Testament word as *agape*, but it could certainly be agreed that it is in their ethical teaching that the great religions come nearest to one another. For instance, in a well-known *sutta*, the Buddha bids his

[9] *Op. cit.*, p. 33.

disciples entertain goodwill even toward bandits who may be sawing off their limbs, and this invites comparison with the Christian injunction to love one's enemies. But we may ask the Buddhist the same question that we asked the Christian: "Why do you intend to follow a policy of goodwill toward the bandits?" His reply, it seems fair to suggest, might well be to the effect that to entertain a passion of ill-will would be a hindrance to salvation. This answer, however, implies the whole Buddhist understanding of man as entangled in the wheel of becoming and seeking release—a pessimistic view of life, according to which existence is painful. Thus the difference between Christianity and Buddhism is more than just the difference between two sets of stories. It is in fact an ontological difference.

The sets of stories which, as Braithwaite himself insists, are to be taken *as a whole*, point in each case to the fundamental difference—the implicit understanding of the universe and of man's place in it, which these stories symbolize. In the case of Buddhism, it is a pessimistic understanding, in the case of Christianity it is the understanding that the ultimate reality is love, and perhaps it is only in the latter case that the term "agapastic" may properly be used. It is only fair to add that some forms of Mahayana Buddhism approximate much more closely to the Christian point of view, and teach that love or compassion is the ultimate nature of things, the ubiquitous Buddha-nature. But in any case, the point is that the sets of stories carry with them what may be called a "transcendent" reference. They point to an understanding of man's existence in its metaphysical or ontological setting.

It is to be hoped that some time Braithwaite will give us a fuller account of his views on religion than is possible in the space of a single lecture. I began by asking whether he is offering us a new kind of demythologizing, and I think we may now say that he is. Except that they are working in different philosophical traditions, Bultmann and Braithwaite appear to be moving in the same direction. Both have a profound distrust of "world-views," both are acutely aware of the intellectual climate of the times, yet both remain convinced of the value of Christianity. They are doing a great service to religion in insisting that it does not begin with accepting a metaphysical doctrine or speculative philosophy, but with an act of decision and commitment. Yet there are limits to their respective theses, and in their desire to "make sense" of Christianity, they are inclined to overstep them, Braithwaite more than Bultmann. The Christian religion is not adequately expressed either as a mere self-understanding or as a moral intention associated with a set of stories. We have to consider not only man's religious aspirations, but also God's way to man. And while the latter may be a mystery of which we can speak only obliquely in "parables and dark sayings,"[10] it seems to me to lie at the heart of the Christian gospel.

[10]Ps. 78: 2.

The Natural Theology of Teilhard de Chardin

13

Jesuit priest and authority on evolution—the combination is sufficiently unusual to afford a partial explanation of the leap into public notice of the late Pierre Teilhard de Chardin and his most celebrated book, *The Phenomenon of Man.* Experts have been sharply divided in their estimates of his work. Julian Huxley praises it highly, and believes that "its influence on the world's thinking is bound to be important."[1] P. B. Medawar almost hysterically condemns the book as nonsense for the most part, and thinks that what sense there is in it constitutes "a feeble argument, abominably expressed."[2] Teilhard's own Church seems unable to make up its mind. He was refused permission to publish during his lifetime, and we look in vain for the *imprimatur;* but the Jesuit scholar L. J. Russell tells us after a careful analysis that if his interpretation of Teilhard's views is correct, then "there does not seem to be anything unorthodox in them."[3] We shall see indeed that more than one interpretation is possible, and that a sober estimate will avoid flying to the extremes either of adulation or of vilification.

[1]In his foreword to *The Phenomenon of Man* (London: Collins, 1959), p. 26.
[2]In *Mind,* LXX/277: 99.
[3]In *The Heythrop Journal,* II/1: 13.

Teilhard claims the naturalistic starting-point of a scientist. Quite in the manner of Mach and Pearson, he says that his aim is not to *explain*, but simply to *see* and *describe* the phenomena. Yet before he has finished, he has moved from science into the fields of philosophy and theology. Obviously the crucial stages of his argument are the points where he makes his transitions from one of these fields to another, and to these transitional points we must chiefly direct our attention.

What then does Teilhard see when he looks at the phenomena? He sees first a *process;* he takes a dynamic view of the world, of which the fundamental stuff, if we may so speak, is energy. More than this, he sees an *evolutionary* process, having a discernible direction and pattern. We see the building up of increasingly complex unities or systems out of the multiple packets of energy which constitute the matrix of things. Elemental particles build up into atoms, these into molecules, these into living cells, these into multicellular organisms.

Teilhard makes two important points about the evolutionary process. The first is his recognition of thresholds or critical moments, when complexity reaches a stage at which there occurs a change of state, and something new emerges. For instance, life appears after a sufficiently complex series of chemical substances has been built up. An analogy would be the coming of a liquid to the boiling-point, when a continuous process is interrupted by a leap into a new state. Teilhard's second point—perhaps not too easily reconciled with the first one—is that "nothing could ever burst forth as final across the different thresholds successively traversed by evolution (however critical they may be) which has not already existed in an obscure and primordial way."[4] For instance, when we look for the beginning of life, we lose sight of it in intermediate stages between the living and the non-living. This continuity leads Teilhard to a kind of panpsychism or panvitalism: life and mind reach down into the so-called inanimate world, though in very rudimentary ways which, he suggests, we may call "pre-life" and "pre-mind." With this theory goes the rejection of any dualism of mind and

[4]*The Phenomenon of Man*, p. 71.

matter, and this, of course, is entirely consonant with the view that all things have a common matrix in energy. The mental and the physical are two sides of a single energy, its "without" and its "within." This denial of dualism presumably means not only that the physical always has some degree of mentality, however rudimentary, but also that the mental is never without its physical concomitant. This conclusion seems to follow also from Teilhard's important law of complexity and consciousness, which affirms, as a general characteristic of the evolutionary process, that increasing complexity of energy-systems is correlated with advance in the directions of life and consciousness.

While Teilhard seems to hold that his evolutionary theory holds good, at least in principle, for the universe as a whole, the detailed working of the process can be seen only on our own planet. Here the major critical thresholds can be traced. First, there was the emergence of life from the non-living materials of the earth, and next, the appearance of man as the bearer of reflective thought. With this second major event—"hominization," as Teilhard calls it, evolution becomes conscious of itself and within limits able to direct itself, and man becomes its spearhead on the earth. This is perhaps the closest approach to an existential element in Teilhard's theory, for here he recognizes how man "stands out" from nature in respect of his responsibility, and how he has indeed become the guardian of Being, with a fateful responsibility for the future. But this notion of responsibility tends to get submerged in Teilhard's stress upon the all-inclusive process.

He can also describe the process of evolution on earth in a slightly different way, in terms of the building up of new concentric layers or envelopes on the earth's surface. In addition to its purely physical layers, the earth has, so to speak, clothed itself with a "biosphere," the film of interconnected life which covers its surface, and with a "noosphere," a mental envelope which includes not only men but also their fields and cities and all the products of human intelligence.

Teilhard now becomes more speculative, but we should notice that as yet there is no apparent break with his phenomenal starting-point.

What he attempts is to make an intelligent extrapolation of the observed evolutionary process into the future. He assumes that the law of complexity and consciousness will continue to operate. He visualizes this operation as taking place through the emergence of a new kind of social organic unity, accompanied by a higher suprapersonal level in the evolution of consciousness. This next stage or threshold in the evolutionary process he calls the "omega-point." It is not entirely clear to me whether he thinks of the entire cosmos as tending towards the omega-point, or only the earth. If the former is the case—as Teilhard seems sometimes to maintain—then perhaps the consummation of terrestrial evolution would be only, let us say, a sigma-point, with an indefinite number of new thresholds to follow before the true omega-point is reached.

Is the omega-point to be identified with God? This is not stated explicitly, but Teilhard certainly comes near to such an identification, and it is at least clear that at the omega-point all things are brought into a supra-personal unity in God, though it is said that this does not mean the obliteration of personality. God, on this view, would seem to be the final rather than the efficient cause of the universe, gathering all things into a perfect unity in himself.

Teilhard has already told us that no matter how critical any evolutionary threshold may be, the novelty which emerges must already have existed in some obscure and primordial way. This must be true also of the omega-point, and here we see Teilhard's link with Christian theology. The self-transcending love manifested in Christ is a reflection or foretaste within the ongoing process of the perfect unity which will be attained at the omega-point, and in the agapastic community which Christ inaugurated as his mystical Body, the end is already being realized in our midst. According to Teilhard, the central Christian doctrine that God is love is indeed manifested throughout the whole evolutionary process, for even the attractions and affinities that build up new unities on the physico-chemical level are prefigurings, however primordial, both of love and of its mystical consummation at the omega-point.

The present writer is not competent to criticize the many scientific considerations adduced by Teilhard in support of his thesis. No doubt many of these considerations could be regarded as debatable by experts, but as far as I can gather from talking with competent authorities in the biological field, the general outlines of Teilhard's account of evolution are acceptable.

Our business, however, is with the philosophical and theological aspects of his teaching, and when we turn to these, the first thing to do is to try to locate Teilhard on the map of contemporary thinking. This is not difficult, for there is nothing specially novel about his views. As far as his dynamic world-view is concerned, Teilhard stands in the closest affinity with the process philosophies, and indeed he says nothing of importance that has not already been said—less picturesquely, perhaps, but often with more philosophical rigour—by such thinkers as Samuel Alexander and A. N. Whitehead. The doctrine of emergent levels of evolution is set forth in detail by Alexander, and he too claims that complexity is the governing factor. He says: "Ascent takes place, it would seem, through complexity. But at each change of quality the complexity, as it were, gathers itself together and is expressed in a new simplicity. The emergent quality is the summing together in a new totality of the component materials."[5] The denial of dualism and the correlation of physical and mental phenomena are also in Alexander, but perhaps the closest parallel to Teilhard's way of expressing it is found in Whitehead's doctrine of the dipolarity of actual entities. According to this doctrine, all actual entities from God down to the veriest "puff of existence" have both a mental and a physical pole, though in the case of the mere "puff of existence" the mental pole is very rudimentary.[6] A doctrine of panpsychism is, of course, one of the oldest things in philosophy. According to Aristotle,[7] Thales taught in the dawn of philosophy that "everything is full of gods." Thales is

[5]*Space, Time and Deity*, II, 70.
[6]*Process and Reality*, p. 50.
[7]*De Anima*, 411 a 8.

also said to have thought of the earth as a large animal or living organism, floating on the waters from which it arose and perhaps nourishing itself on them. One is vividly reminded of this ancient teaching when Teilhard talks of the early earth as an "incredibly complex germ."[8]

To have traced some of Teilhard's philosophical relationships will provide us with some useful comparisons in assessing the value of his world-view. For it would seem that at least two quite distinct interpretations of this view are possible. The first interpretation takes seriously Teilhard's statement that he is confining himself to the observable phenomena, and if this is so, then his philosophy must be read in naturalistic terms, and would very closely resemble that of Alexander. In Alexander's scheme of emergent evolution, space-time is the matrix, and the levels ascend through matter, life and mind to deity, which lies in the future and represents the next stage after mind. If we read Teilhard in naturalistic terms—and he himself invites us to do so—then his God must lie within the phenomenal world, that is to say, within space and time, and must therefore be a natural rather than a supernatural God. This God is found (like Alexander's) at the end of the evolutionary process, not at its beginning. He is the *terminus ad quem* of all things, not their *terminus a quo*, the goal of the universe, not its Creator. This indeed seems to be implied in Teilhard's association of God with Omega rather than Alpha. Such a God, moreover, will be complete and perfect only in the future. He is a God who is "on his way," so to speak, not a God of eternal static perfection. Of course, this God, like everything else that has emerged or will emerge in the universe, must be thought of, in accordance with Teilhard's principles, as already existing in some "obscure and primordial" way. This seems to mean that at any stage in the process short of the end he exists only as a potentiality or a godward trend in things. If we may coin a word in analogy with Teilhard's "pre-life" and "pre-mind," we may say that at any given point in the evolutionary process short of the end, there

[8]*The Phenomenon of Man*, p. 72.

exists a "pre-God"—and to be consistent, Teilhard ought to say something like this.

Furthermore, if we take seriously Teilhard's rejection of dualism, we must suppose that his God, like everything else in nature, has his physical as well as his mental side. Teilhard plainly says[9] that the higher mental levels are reached only through the building up of large brains—just as Alexander maintains that mind in its developed form is found only in correlation with neural systems. We must therefore suppose that a divine intelligence would require to be correlated with a physical system of unimaginable complexity. Teilhard's law of complexity and consciousness does in fact seem to suggest that the entire material of the universe, that is to say, God's physical aspect, is building up into a single unified organic system of such complexity that a brain or electronic machine would provide only a faint analogy, but a system which would be necessary as the substratum of a divine Mind.

Is this pantheism? Teilhard indeed speaks of the goal of evolution as a state in which God will be all in all, but to the charge that the interpretation of his views which I have just sketched out is a pantheistic one, it is possible to make exactly the same reply that Alexander makes to a similar charge against his understanding of God. Alexander writes: "God is immanent in respect of his body, but transcendent in respect of his deity . . . and since his deity is what is distinctive of him, this notion of God remains predominantly theistic." The point of this remark is that while the physical aspect of God coincides with the whole spatio-temporal universe, his mind or deity belongs only to a portion of space-time—the portion namely which still lies in the future and to which the evolutionary process advances, so that we, as it were, look onward and upward toward it. To say that God is "transcendent" means that he is always ahead of us in the sense explained, and perhaps this interpretation of "transcendence" is as intelligible as either the mythological image of a God in the sky or the metaphysical notion of a God who is "outside" of space and time.

[9]*Op. cit.*, p. 154.

This first interpretation of Teilhard's natural theology is almost certainly not the one that he wants us to take himself, but it seems to me to be the one that is most consistent with his own premises and with his announced intentions. No doubt it involves some speculative assumptions, but on the whole it remains within the phenomenal orbit, and is, like Alexander's philosophy, essentially a naturalism. Assuming that evolution does not end with man but that it will continue in its observed direction, this interpretation visualizes by intelligent extrapolation the emergence at some more or less distant point of a natural God, by which is meant a higher threshold of being to which we may ascribe the quality of "deity." This is at least an intelligible hypothesis, such as might be based on the kind of evidences that Teilhard adduces. Whether his conclusions are likely to be true in fact depends on the validity of his description of the phenomena (which is a matter for the scientists to determine) and on the correctness of his extrapolation of the evolutionary process (which could at best be a matter of probability); but the important point to notice is that there seems to be no *logical* obstacle in the way of such conclusions.

The second possible interpretation of Teilhard's natural theology is a much more orthodox one. It visualizes a God who is supernatural, transcending space and time; who is purely spiritual in his being, having no physical aspect; and who is the Alpha as well as the Omega, having in the beginning created the universal process out of nothing in order to raise it to himself through successive stages. This is presumably the interpretation which Teilhard wants us to take. He argues that Omega not only ends the process but stands outside of it as transcendent; and he talks of mind as detaching itself from its material matrix at the end of the process, and continuing in a liberated independent existence.[10] But if orthodox theism is the conclusion that Teilhard wishes us to draw from his argument, we are bound to say that it does not follow at all. In the first place, such a conclusion offends against his declared intention to stay within the phenomena, for he has

[10]*Op. cit.*, pp. 270, 288-89.

now leaped beyond the phenomenal level into a transempirical supernatural region, and such a leap involves here a logical hiatus. In the second place, he has abandoned that rejection of dualism which was foundational to the earlier part of his argument, and indeed when he talks of mind as getting "liberated" from its material matrix, he seems to have swung over to a thoroughgoing dualism, for such talk is reminiscent of the ancient Gnostic and Manichaean ideas about spirit's escaping from the matter which imprisons it. In the third place, if evolution were controlled by a perfect Mind eternally subsisting in its completion outside of the process, we would expect the evolutionary process to have a different character from the one that Teilhard describes. For he frequently insists on the "groping" character of evolution, which tries everything before finding the way forward. This suggests not a transcendent Intelligence, but possibly an immanent *nisus* or directed striving; not a God who is complete, as in orthodox theism, but a God who is "on his way."

So we find ourselves in something of a dilemma. If we accept Teilhard's premises, we have to draw unorthodox theological conclusions; while if we accept Teilhard's orthodox conclusions, we have to reject his premises and the whole argument on which he bases his conclusions. The ambiguous meaning of his book may account for the suspicion with which it is regarded by some in his own Church. In Roman Catholic theology, God is pure act, but Teilhard's conception seems to bring potency into the idea of God.

But leaving aside the question of orthodoxy, let us turn to the question of whether an emerging God, the more plausible conclusion from Teilhard's argument, can be a religiously satisfying conception. Does not the religious consciousness demand a God who is eternally complete and perfect? Perhaps it does, and it can scarcely be doubted that this is how Christianity has traditionally thought of God. But we may at least allude to the arguments of an American disciple of Whitehead, the philosophical theologian Charles Hartshorne, who claims that the dynamic conception of a God who has still to complete himself is more in accord with the biblical picture of the "living" God than is the static conception of a God of unchanging perfection—an idea which Hartshorne attributes to Greek influences on Christian theology. The dynamic conception, Hartshorne urges, gives meaning to the idea that responsible human beings are in a genuine sense "co-workers" with God (and this reminds us of that part of Teilhard's theory which we considered as having an existential character). And in addition, it is maintained that the conception of a God "on his way" eases the problem of evil, which has been so intractable for traditional supernaturalistic theism.[11]

Finally, we must look at the way in which Teilhard connects his natural theology with Christianity. Here again, there is nothing new. A generation earlier, the Anglican theologian, L. S. Thornton, saw an analogy between the Christian doctrine of the incarnation and the way in which each emerging level of the evolutionary process gathers up the earlier levels into a new unity. He writes: "As the series is taken up into the human organism, so in Christ the human organism is taken up on to the level of deity."[12] Like Teilhard, Thornton thinks of the next stage of the advance in social terms—it is the emergence of a new social organism of which the bond is love, the mystical Body of Christ in which all humanity is sanctified and deified. Once again these ideas have a long history; they go back to the early days of the Church, and to the New Testament itself. The classic formulation of them was given by St. Irenaeus in the second century when he interpreted the incarnation as a "recapitulation," a gathering up of all that had gone before in a new creation, the end of which is to raise man (in some sense) to the level of God.

But in these connections of natural theology with the Christian revelation, we are dealing with beliefs of a different kind from those which had hitherto come to our notice. If any man (or community of persons) sees in Christ the supreme incarnation of love, and believes

[11]See Charles Hartshorne, *Man's Vision of God* (New York: Harper, 1946).
[12]*The Incarnate Lord* (London: Longmans, Green, 1928), p. 255.

that this incarnation is somehow a key to the enigmas of life and even of the universe, he is making a judgment of value which is quite different in its logical status from the description of a phenomenon. Such a judgment is not just assent to a proposition, but commitment to a way of life. Because we have to live and take decisions as well as think and observe, we all have to take risks and make judgments of value in the light of what knowledge we have, though this knowledge may be very incomplete. At this point, I doubt if Teilhard makes the existential dimension of Christian thought clear. On the other hand, he certainly does not imagine that he is proving Christianity true. He may claim, however, to be showing us that we live in a kind of universe in which it is not unreasonable to make Christ and the love which he manifests matters of ultimate concern. This may seem a modest result, but it is not unimportant.

We must conclude that as far as the major problems of God and religion are concerned, Teilhard has said hardly anything that is new. Huxley is probably quite wrong when he asserts that Teilhard's influence on the world's thinking is bound to be important. It is much more likely that *The Phenomenon of Man* will prove to have as ephemeral a vogue as had Ernst Haeckel's *The Riddle of the Universe* sixty years earlier. Huxley is talking much more to the point when he praises Teilhard for his effort to bring together the scientific knowledge and the religious values of our world. For the split between these two has afflicted our culture with a profound sickness, and anyone who makes even a modest contribution toward healing it is worthy of some praise.

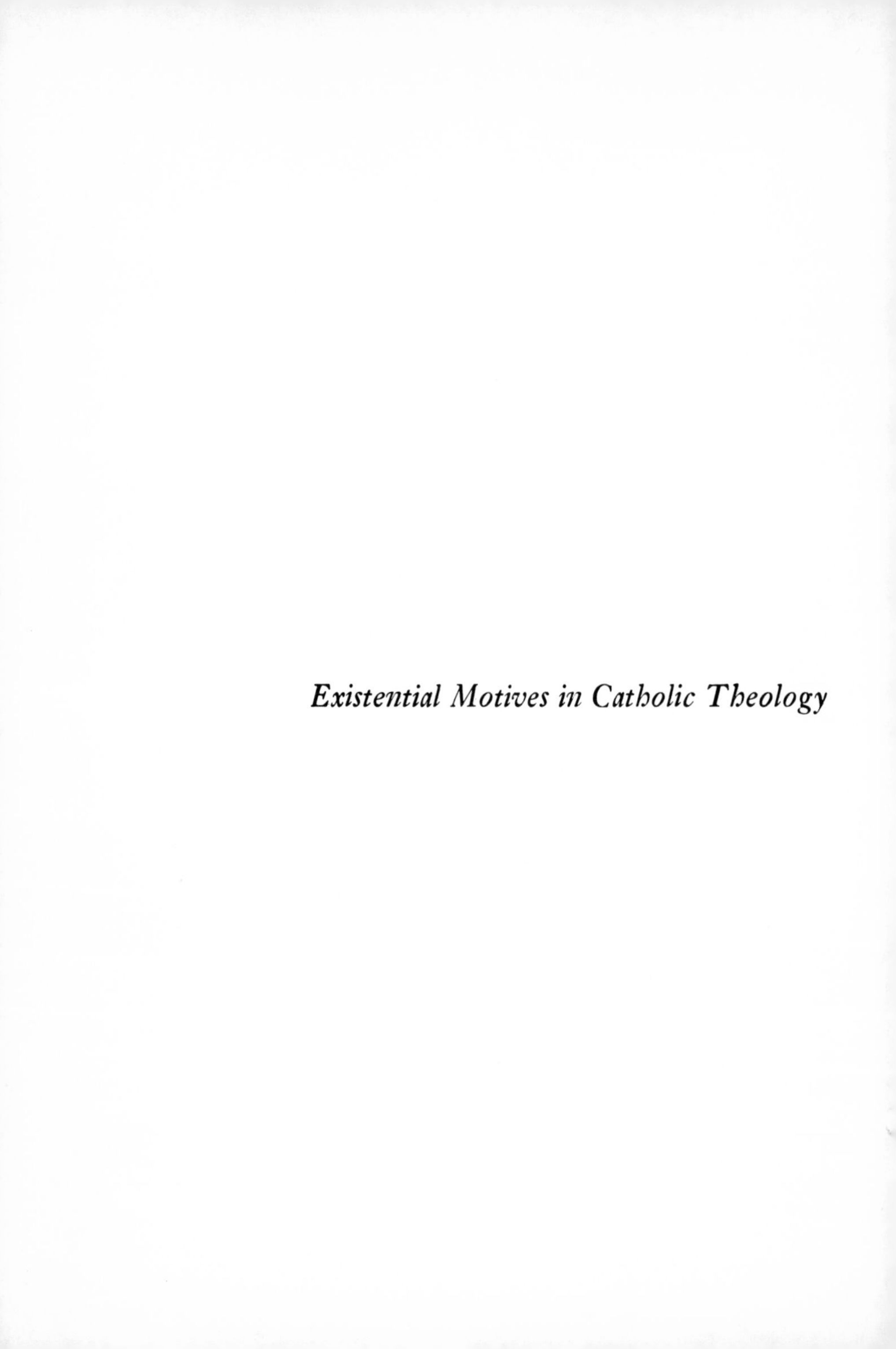

Existential Motives in Catholic Theology

14

The warmer relations between Roman Catholics and Protestants, due in such large measure to the fine spirit of charity and concern shown by the late Pope John XXIII, should result, among other things, in an increased awareness within each group of the theological work being done in the other. Such awareness has not, of course, been entirely lacking in the recent past. Especially notable are some perceptive studies by Roman Catholic scholars of some major Protestant theologians—the books by H. U. von Balthasar on Barth, L. Malevez on Bultmann, and G. H. Tavard on Tillich are well-known examples. But the awareness has been for the most part confined to professional theologians, and the studies have come mainly from the Roman Catholic side. It would surely be a good thing if the Protestant parish minister were sometimes to lay aside his Barth or Brunner and pick up a volume of contemporary Roman Catholic theology. He would find this an interesting and rewarding experience.

As good a place as any to begin is with the work of Karl Rahner. Let me at once say that this recommendation is made not because Rahner is easy, for he certainly is not, but because he is a major theological figure of our times, equal in stature to any of the leading Protestant theologians whom I mentioned in the last paragraph. This eminent Jesuit scholar is of a younger generation than Barth and company. Born in 1904, he has taught at the University of Innsbruck since 1937, and is thoroughly conversant with contemporary European philosophy, especially that of Martin Heidegger with whom he studied. The high esteem in which Rahner is held in his own communion is evidenced by the fact that he has been editor of Denzinger's standard manual, the *Enchiridion Symbolorum*, and co-editor of the *Lexikon für Theologie und Kirche;* while his growing reputation beyond his own country is shown by the increasing number of his writings that are appearing in English translation. Much of Rahner's best work has been done in the form of essays, and the German collection of these, *Schriften zur Theologie,*[1] runs to several substantial volumes. Among his many other writings, perhaps the one that has made the profoundest impression is his highly original treatise *Zur Theologie des Todes,*[2] which might be regarded as a Christian and theological answer to Heidegger's study of death and of its significance for human existence.

If the Protestant reader goes to Rahner's writings with certain preconceived ideas about Roman Catholic theology in his mind, he will find that these are speedily dispelled. If, for instance, he believes (as many seem to do) that Roman Catholic theology is purely intellectualist in its structure and that faith is conceived as the giving of assent to propositions, he will be told by Rahner that "faith is the assent of the whole man to the message of God," and that theology is the attempt to arrive at a reflective understanding of such a faith. Again, if the Protestant reader thinks that all Roman Catholic theology is drearily uniform, so that to have read one theologian is to have read

[1]Now partly available in English under the title *Theological Investigations* (London: Darton, Longman & Todd)—vol. I, God, Christ, Mary and Grace, 1961; vol. II, Man in the Church, 1964.

[2]An English version, "Towards a Theology of Death," is included in the volume *Modern Catholic Thinkers,* ed. A. R. Caponigri (London: Burns & Oates, 1960).

them all, there is no better way for him to become disillusioned than to read Rahner himself, for his own writings are the best support of his claim that there is plenty of scope for fresh thought and free discussion, even if the Catholic theologian is guided by the *magisterium* of the Church. According to the American news magazine *Time*,[3] Rahner has been one of the most influential theological advisers on the progressive side at the Vatican Council. His own essay on "Freedom in the Church"[4] argues that since the gift of freedom is brought to fulfilment in the Christian faith, the Church itself can never be a totalitarian institution but must rather be the guardian of freedom, including freedom of theological discussion.

No one could be more severe than Rahner himself in the strictures which he passes on the type of theology that allows itself to become stereotyped and stagnant. He says[5] frankly that much Roman Catholic theology in the past decades is of an unadventurous type that can be divided into three categories–textbooks of dogma, monographs in the history of dogma, and specialized studies, often on peripheral themes. As to the text books, he acknowledges that books intended to give students a grounding in dogmatic theology are not expected to be "original." He finds, however, that many of the text books produced are singularly unoriginal, repeating almost unaltered the language and formulations of earlier times, without regard to the needs and problems of our own century. One would expect, he argues, having regard to the changes that have taken place in the world in the past two hundred years, that there would be at least as much difference between a text book of dogmatics published in 1950 and one published in 1750 as there is between the writings of St. Thomas Aquinas and those of St. Augustine. But such is not usually the case. Concerning the monographs in the history of dogma, Rahner thinks that they do little to supplement the deficiencies of the text books. He finds that for the

[3]LXXX/24: 58.
[4]*Theological Investigations*, II, 89ff.
[5]In "The Prospects for Dogmatic Theology," *Theological Investigations*, I, 1ff.

most part they are entirely backward-looking (*absolut retrospektiv*), whereas such works should be providing insights for the further progress of theology. The intention which guided the theological work of the past was not to arrive at petrified results but to provide springboards for further advance in understanding. On the subject of specialized studies such as writings on mariological themes, Rahner's complaint is that too often they remain on the margin and are not adequately related to the central themes of dogmatic theology.

It is, of course, only too easy to pass sweeping judgments, and Rahner is well aware that the real problems arise when one turns to the positive tasks, and that it is easier to indicate these tasks than to accomplish them. He says himself that "pronouncements about 'how it should be done' are cheap enough," and that they "arouse the suspicion that their author is one of those people who always know better."[6] Rahner has not himself written a systematic theology, and even hints that he considers such an undertaking to be beyond the powers of a single theologian. But he has set forth in considerable detail his conception of the ground-plan for a complete dogmatic[7]—an architectural blueprint, so to speak, which visualizes an edifice no less complex and imposing than that which Karl Barth is building in his *Church Dogmatics.*

But even if Rahner has set out only the broad structure, his numerous essays give us a fair idea of how some parts of the dogmatic would look, if the formal outline were given a detailed content. In these essays, he consciously endeavours to overcome the defects which, as we have seen, he imputes to much of the Roman Catholic theology that has been done over the past few decades. Thus he believes that if theology, as the endeavour to understand salvation (*Heil*), is itself a part of the salvation-experience, it must, like salvation, be directed to where men are, in their concrete historical situations; in other words, the theology of today cannot be content just to repeat earlier formula-

[6]*Ibid.*
[7]"A Scheme for a Treatise of Dogmatic Theology" in *Theological Investigations*, I, 20ff.

tions, but must be directed to the situation of today. Furthermore, while theology will always set out from the established truths that have been handed down, it will regard these truths not as a bed on which to lie down, but as a firm point of departure from which to advance further; and this does not merely mean that the central truths are to be supplemented in various ways, but that the theologian is to work on the central truths themselves in order to gain fresh and clearer insights into their significance. Finally, while it is legitimate for a theologian to concern himself with some specialized area of his subject, such an area should not be isolated, but related to the unitary structure of Christian teaching, and seen in perspective; and presumably it is easier to do this if the theologian has before him, like Rahner, a carefully articulated scheme of the whole field of Christian dogmatics.

In order to illustrate how these principles of theological investigation govern Rahner's work, let us now turn to consider what he has to say on a central theme of dogmatic theology—the theme of christology.[8]

Here, of course, the primary datum for dogmatic theology is the Chalcedonian definition. In this definition, the Church solemnly pronounced its mind after a long period of christological controversy, and it has often been thought that this statement settled the christological question once and for all. But quite characteristically, Rahner insists that the Chalcedonian formula is not only an end but also a beginning. It was not intended to provide us with a permanent resting-place, so that we might be saved from the trouble of any further reflection on the theological problem of the person of Christ. The repetition of the formula by subsequent generations is no guarantee at all that these generations have *appropriated* or *made their own* the understanding of Christian truth which the formula enshrined. All human formulations, even those which have for their content a divinely revealed truth, are acknowledged by Rahner to be historical, in the sense that they are conditioned by an historical situation. This does not necessarily mean that a time comes when they have to be given up, but it does mean

[8]Current Problems in Christology" in *Theological Investigations,* I, 149ff.

that each new generation must *find again for itself* the truth in the formula. So we have not only a right but even a duty to consider such formulations to be as much beginnings as ends.

Failure to do this could even mean that the formula comes to obscure the truth which it was meant to express. This happens because the history of theology is not only one of advancing in the truth, but sometimes one of "forgetting." Such forgetting occurs when formulations are taken over externally, with no genuine appropriation and "making present" of the truth they contain. This results in an "average" understanding, which is a deterioration from that deeper and "more primordial" understanding of truth in which the formula was, so to speak, beaten out, and which it was meant to seize and conserve. The reader who is acquainted with Heidegger will not fail to notice at this point how even in the terminology employed, Rahner's remarks about theology approximate to the things that Heidegger has said about the philosophical quest for Being.

How then are we to find again for ourselves the truth that is at once conserved and concealed in the Church's traditional formulation of the doctrine of the person of Christ? Rahner does not think that the answer lies in any conscious endeavour to be "modern," though he does say that we shall understand matters in a way that is "theoretically more precise and existentially more alive" in so far as we grasp them in relation to the total content of our own spiritual existence. But the way lies rather through a confrontation with the matter itself—in this case christology. What Rahner seems to have in mind is something like what Heidegger calls "repetition"—a return to the sources, so that we can be addressed in the same existential manner as happened with the interpreters who devised the theological formula, and its truth made present to us. In the case of christology, this return to the sources means a new look at the biblical doctrine of Christ; and this kind of return is encouraged in the encyclical *Humani generis*.

Certainly the Chalcedonian formula itself rests upon the Bible, and brings the biblical teaching to expression in a dogmatic definition. But could it be maintained that either this definition or the subsequent expositions of it in scholastic theology represents exhaustively and without remainder all that the scriptures teach concerning Jesus as the Christ? Is it possible, then, that by allowing ourselves to be confronted with the biblical sources of christology, there may on the one hand be awakened in us a new understanding for the truth of the traditional formulation, and there may also on the other hand be given us new insights into the person of Christ that were inadequately represented in the older dogmatics, and which we have to express in language of our own?

Among contemporary Protestant theologians, the most favoured approach to christology seems to be the one that begins "from below upwards," as it were; that is to say, these theologians begin with Christ's humanity, and go on to show how we can think of him also as God. This approach is preferred to the one that begins with the Second Person of the Trinity, and then tries to show how this divine Person assumed a human nature, for the second kind of approach has tended to obscure Christ's genuine humanity and to produce in the minds of churchpeople a kind of docetic understanding, so that, as J. A. T. Robinson has claimed, Jesus is thought of not as a man but as "really God almighty walking about on earth, dressed up as a man."[9] I believe that in Rahner we can observe a similar approach to christology, motivated by a similar desire to hang on to Christ's humanity and prevent his becoming an entirely supernatural figure, far removed from the human existence we know. Thus Rahner draws attention to those passages in the New Testament which stress the humanity of Christ and his genuine participation in creaturely being. We see him praying to the Father, obeying the Father, sharing in "creature-feeling." The primitive apostolic preaching begins from below, with the human experience in Jesus for whom it is claimed that "God has made him both Lord and Christ."[10] This is called "primitive" teaching,

[9] *Honest to God* (London: SCM Press, 1960), p. 66.
[10] Acts 2: 36.

but Rahner wants to know whether it is merely primitive, or whether it has something of its own to say to us which classical christology does not say with the same clarity. The point to which Rahner is leading up is the posing of the question whether the classical christology, with its abstract metaphysical terminology ("substance," "person," "nature" and the like), can adequately express a whole area of the person of Christ that receives prominence in the New Testament. At least, as it is commonly understood, the classical terminology tends to make us think of Christ's humanity as simply an instrument for the divine action, so that we forget that this humanity is itself a centre of free, spontaneous action, thought and feeling. To do justice to this whole obscured aspect of christology, would it not be possible, without giving up the ontological categories of the traditional formulation, to bring in existential categories?

To put the matter in a more general way, Rahner thinks that if christology is to express in an adequate fashion the incarnate Lord's participation and involvement in the being of the creature, we must bring our christological discussions within the categories which can best set forth the God-creature relation. To know what this relation is, we must especially consider what man is, and of course this is the area which in our time has been opened up by the philosophy of existence, and for the description of which this philosophy has provided appropriate categories. If we think of Christ in his genuine humanity as the archetype of all humanity—the πρωτότοκος πάσης κτίσεως of the New Testament[11]—then christology may be understood as anthropology which transcends itself; or alternatively, as we shall see in a moment, anthropology may be understood as deficient christology.

It should, of course, be made perfectly clear that Rahner is not advocating a purely existential christology (if such a thing is possible). As was mentioned above, he holds that these new explorations are to be undertaken without abandoning the traditional formulation. His aim

[11]Col. 1: 15.

is not to replace the Chalcedonian definition, but to bring it alive, and also to open up hitherto neglected dimensions of christology. He explicitly criticizes those Protestant theologians—he names no one, but Friedrich Gogarten comes to mind as an example—who, through their hostility to metaphysics, abandon patristic christology and push the existential approach to extremes.

Rahner himself does not shrink from pursuing the christological theme on to the cosmic or ontological level, and in order to do this, he continues to think in terms of the God-creature relation. Taking up an idea that was common in patristic theology and is indeed rooted in the New Testament itself, he visualizes the history of creation, and especially the so-called salvation-history, as the ever clearer self-manifestation of God in the world. This history reaches its climax in the incarnation, and in the fullness of the times, the Word became flesh.

These considerations lead us back to the Chalcedonian definition. The classic christology asserts the union, without either mixture or separation, of the two natures in the one person. Can this formula be explicated and brought to life in terms of the God-creature relation? Admittedly there are many difficulties, and Rahner studies them frankly and patiently. But surely many of the difficulties are overcome when we remember (and this is something that nowadays has been chiefly stressed by the philosophies of existence) that humanity is not a fixed stock or quantity of properties. Rather, man exists in his possibility, and this means that he has an openness to what is above him. The true humanity, that is to say, the humanity in which there has been actualized its fullest potentiality, is seen in Christ; and it is of him that we affirm that he unites humanity and divinity. The fact that the ordinary humanity that we know in ourselves or in our neighbours is remote from this prototypal humanity is no valid objection to its being the true humanity. And although it is true that we learn what man is by ourselves leading human lives, we finally learn what man truly is from Christ. This is what was meant earlier when it was said that if christology can be understood as self-transcending anthropology, it is also necessary to understand anthropology as deficient christology. Thus it can be said that "christology is at once the end and the beginning of anthropology."

Rahner concludes his reflections on christology by indicating topics which might properly be followed up if our understanding of these matters is to be deepened. Among other things, he suggests a study of what he calls the "mysteries" of the life of Christ in their theological significance—the Baptism, Temptation, Transfiguration, Descent into Hell, Ascension and so on; a closer study of the relation between the doctrine of the person of Christ and soteriology; a systematic study of the historical and current misunderstandings of christology, with a view to seeing how these heterodox positions have arisen, and how the occasion for such errors can be removed through clearer and more adequate teaching on the part of the Church; and an examination of the general history of religion with special reference to the idea of incarnation.

Our purpose here is not to discuss in detail Rahner's views on christology, for these have been presented primarily as an illustration of his general approach to theological problems; and moreover, at the risk of oversimplification and even of misrepresentation, his argument has been drastically summarized in a way that passes over many of its subtleties and its anticipations of possible objections. But some comments should be made, in addition to those that suggested themselves in the course of the exposition. It is impossible not to sympathize with Rahner's endeavour to bring alive the issues of christology; and perhaps we can sympathize all the more because he does not choose the drastic but relatively easy way of abandoning the past for novel formulations, but seeks patiently to build on the tradition of the Catholic faith and to rediscover those insights which tend to get buried over as a doctrinal definition is passed along, and the primordial understanding of it grows dimmer. Rahner is able to do this by his judicious introduction of existential categories, and, as against Gogarten, he shows that these categories are not incompatible with the traditional ones. Indeed, he shows much greater wisdom than Gogarten, in avoiding the temptation of trying to formulate doctrine in purely existential terms without regard to an ontological basis.

On the other hand, it may seem to have been an omission on Rahner's part that he has not paid more attention to the Chalcedonian definition in its historical context. He does indeed recognize that all human formulations of doctrine are historically conditioned. But his argument might have been strengthened had he developed this point, and shown what existential interests and concerns were motivating the Church at the time of Chalcedon, and underlie the abstract metaphysical language in which its pronouncement was couched. Also, there are places in Rahner's argument where his success in reinstating a genuine recognition of Christ's humanity is doubtful. If the prototypal humanity of Christ is indeed so remote from our everyday humanity, has he really been brought nearer? Or must his humanity not be still further stressed, with perhaps a reconsideration of what the Church means by the doctrine of Christ's sinlessness?

However, the intention here has been to indicate Rahner's general approach to the task of theology and the existential elements in his thinking, as illustrated in his treatment of a central theological doctrine. Perhaps some hint has been given of the freshness and interest of his thought, its range and originality, and perhaps some of the Protestant readers whom I mentioned at the beginning will be encouraged to turn to Rahner's own writings.

Applications to Particular Doctrines PART V

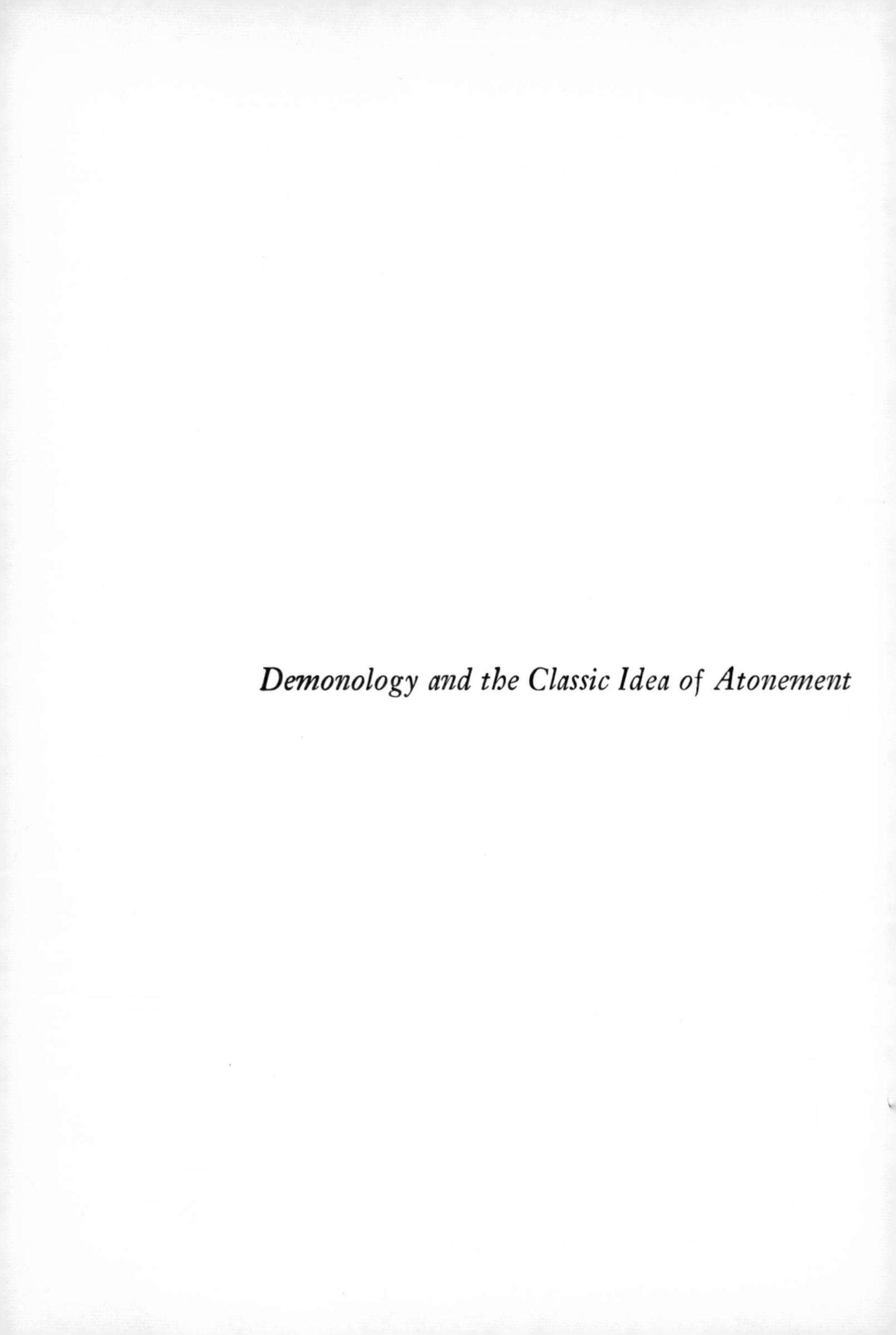

Demonology and the Classic Idea of Atonement

15

Among all ancient peoples, and among the more backward peoples of our time, we find a firmly established belief in demons, invisible and quasi-personal forces of evil which threaten the well-being of man. There are many studies in anthropology and the history of religion that show how elaborate the ramifications of such a belief could become, and how powerful its influence on the life of a people could be. Belief in demonic powers appears in the pages of the New Testament, though it certainly does not have there the overwhelming prominence that sometimes attached to it elsewhere. We are all familiar with the stories in the gospels in which Jesus is described as casting out demons. St. Paul speaks of "principalities and powers," and even of "the god of this world,"[1] cosmic beings who stand over against the true God. The demonic powers mentioned in the New Testament remain fairly shadowy. But when we come to the writings of the Fathers of the Church, we find that the demons bulk much more largely. They come forward from the background, so to speak, and practically all of the Fathers devote considerable attention to their activities, and treat them

[1]Rom. 8:38; Col. 2:15; II Cor. 4:4.

with great seriousness. Thus, to give a random example, Origen, in a reference to the study of demons, says with all earnestness that this is a subject "which is both wide in extent and difficult for human comprehension."[2]

Happenings that were once attributed to the malignant powers of darkness are in our own time explained for the most part in other ways, less appealing perhaps to the imagination, but more satisfying to the reason and less terrifying to the sufferers who once thought themselves victims of inexorable hostile powers. Plague, for instance, is now referred to a micro-organism; madness is described in terms of mental disorder; even the moral assaults of the demons in temptations and the like are differently conceived. The province of the demons has shrunk away. But *entia non sunt multiplicanda praeter necessitatem.* Occam's razor demands the excision of the demonic from the categories of modern thought. As Sir Charles Sherrington put it, "The old Walpurgis night is over; its company is disbanded; its votaries are fled . . . we can disentangle the facts of nature free from those perplexing mysteries which were in truth not there—the mystery of nature needs no superstition."[3]

The disappearance of the demons creates a problem for the Christian theologian. He goes to the ancient Christian documents to interpret the religious truths which they contain, and he finds that these truths are tied up with demonic myths to which he can no longer give credence. What is he to do? He could, of course, simply pass over references to demons with his tongue in his cheek, so to speak. He could without much difficulty eliminate the demonic element from the healing miracles of the gospels. It would not be quite so easy to eliminate the demonic from St. Paul's teaching, for there it enters into the texture of the theology. Yet the difficulty would still not be insuperable, for the concept of the demonic is surely not of such first-class importance in Pauline thought as to be quite indispensable. But in the case of the

[2]*Contra Celsum,* vii, 67.
[3]*Man on his Nature* (London: Cambridge University Press, 1940), p. 122.

Fathers, the theologian would find it quite impossible to ignore the demonic element, unless he were willing to perpetrate the most serious mutilation of their work and discard large areas of their thought. The reason for this is that in the Fathers the idea of the demonic has become closely connected with the central Christian doctrine of the atonement. The patristic teaching on the atonement is indeed a development of ideas already found in the New Testament, but whereas in the New Testament there are several images or models for representing the work of Christ, one of these tends to become predominant in the Fathers.

With variations of emphasis, the teaching of the Fathers is that the death of Christ has its meaning for faith in the victory which he won at the cross over the powers of darkness. He put to flight the demons, destroyed their dominion over man, and so rescued or liberated man from sin and death. This "Christus Victor" theme was sometimes elaborated, notably by St. Gregory of Nyssa,[4] into the idea that the death of Christ was a ransom paid to the devil as the price of man's liberation, and with this we seem to enter a completely mythological realm of thinking. Yet this way of understanding the meaning of Christ's death prevailed in the Church for about one thousand years, until St. Anselm rejected it[5] and tried to substitute a rationalistic or legalistic account of the matter for the mythological one.

We now see how serious would be the consequences if the modern theologian decided simply to ignore or discard the demonic myths in the Fathers. He would need to throw out with them much of their teaching on a central Christian doctrine—indeed, he would have to scrap one of the most important and vital elements in a millennium of theological thought. Some theologians have not hesitated to do this. Writers on the atonement have frequently prefaced their own accounts of the matter with disparaging remarks on the patristic view. But need we throw out so much? Especially if we attach importance to the classic theology of the still undivided Church, we can hardly be happy

[4]*Great Catechism*, xxii.
[5]*Cur Deus Homo*, I, 7.

about its wholesale rejection. Before we discard, should we not then pause and see if we can reinterpret? We have to reject the demonic mythology, assuredly. But have we not a duty to ask what these ideas meant to the men who made use of them, and then to see whether we cannot restate what they said in a form which will be free from outmoded mythical elements, and yet will preserve the essential meaning of the death of Christ as seen by the patristic writers, and which they were trying to bring to expression in the ideas at their disposal?

The Swedish theologian Gustaf Aulén, in his brilliant book *Christus Victor* which appeared a generation ago, attempted to vindicate the patristic understanding of the atonement as Christ's conquest of the powers of darkness. On the negative side he was undoubtedly successful in showing how shallow had been many of the criticisms of patristic teaching on the subject. The critics had taken mythical statements as statements of fact, and not surprisingly they found them childish and even repellent. About such criticisms, Aulén claims that "no serious attempt was made to penetrate behind the outward form to the underlying idea."[6] He himself did make such an attempt. He showed that the patristic view of the atonement constitutes a distinct type of interpretation of the meaning of Christ's death, differing both from the so-called objective theory of St. Anselm and from the subjective view represented by Abelard. This distinct patristic type of interpretation Aulén called the "classic" or "dramatic" view of the atonement. He held that it was already well established by the time of St. Irenaeus, and that it was the typical view of all the Fathers of both East and West, though admittedly in the West one sees the first pointers towards the Anselmian theory. Moreover, Aulén argued that the patristic view is the most natural development of the doctrine from the teaching of the New Testament itself. He also sought to interpret some of the more lurid imagery in the Fathers, and to show that in every case the essence of the dramatic view of the atonement is its assertion that the meaning of Christ's death lies in the overcoming of the enemies of mankind.

[6]*Christus Victor* (London: S.P.C.K., 1931), p. 27.

Yet it is just here, on the positive side, that we perceive the limits of Aulén's thesis. His achievement is indeed a most impressive one—he has thrown into relief the essential character of the patristic doctrine, so often in danger of being buried under the more fanciful imagery of the Fathers; he has won respect for it, as against its critics; and he has shown some of its advantages over alternative views, both "objective" theories which interpret the atonement in terms of "satisfaction" or "substitution" or something of the sort, and "subjective" theories which appeal to its "moral influence." But Aulén does not give an explicit statement of the doctrine itself in a form freed from the mythical references of the traditional dramatic idea. Yet only by so doing could he make the patristic interpretation intelligible and convincing to people who no longer think along mythical lines, and who therefore no longer see the world as dominated by demons. The reason for Aulén's failure at this point is that he lacked a satisfactory way of interpreting mythology.

It should perhaps be stated here that allegorizing is not the answer to the problem of interpreting myth. An allegory is a conscious literary device, in which the writer deliberately selects concrete imagery to express abstract notions. It is true that the Fathers could and frequently did make use of consciously figurative language when it suited their purposes, but their talk of demons is not usually of this kind. I shall have occasion later to speak in more detail of St. Antony of Egypt, the father of monasticism, and of his famous conflicts with the demons, which have been depicted for us in the most vivid terms. At this point, however, an incident from his experience can be cited to show the inadequacy of allegorizing to interpret what was in the minds of the Fathers when they talked about the demons. One of St. Antony's temptations is described in the following terms: "The demons, as if breaking the four walls of the dwelling, seemed to enter through them, coming in the likeness of beasts and creeping things. And the place was on a sudden filled with the forms of lions, bears, leopards, bulls, serpents, asps, scorpions and wolves."[7] It is tempting to try to interpret this list

[7]St. Athanasius, *Vita S. Antoni*, 9.

of animals as standing for so many vices to which the saint was tempted, but this would be to read into the text something that was present neither in the mind of St. Antony nor in that of his biographer, and so be guilty of a misinterpretation. The animals here are not literary devices. They were, on the contrary, very real to St. Antony, and his biographer obviously believed that if anyone else had been present, he too would have seen the demonic apparitions.[8]

With St. Antony's experience we may contrast a passage at the beginning of *The Divine Comedy* in which Dante tells of his encounter in the dark wood with three beasts—a leopard, a lion and a wolf[9]. Commentators quite rightly interpret the leopard, for instance, as standing for lust. They are right because they hit precisely the idea that was in Dante's mind. His thought here was consciously and deliberately allegorical. His leopard was intended to be a figure of speech, and is properly understood as such, but St. Antony's leopard was to him much more than a metaphor, even if it still fell short of the reality of that other very concrete feline of the same species which put an end to the life of St. Saturus in the arena at Carthage.[10] So we have to look further for our key to the demonic myths.

We turn to another eminent theologian of the Lutheran communion, Rudolf Bultmann, who professes to offer us just what we require and Aulén lacked. In 1941 he published his now famous essay on demythologizing, and in works such as his *Theology of the New Testament* has shown how the application of his hermeneutic principles can yield many new and valuable insights into the thought of the New Testament. It may well be that the same canons of interpretation can be extended to the patristic literature. If this is so, then we may be able to pass beyond the point at which Aulén was halted in his vindication of the dramatic view of the atonement, precisely because he lacked such canons. This is the problem to which we must now address ourselves.

[8]*Vita*, 51.
[9]Inferno, I.
[10]*The Passion of the Holy Martyrs Perpetua and Felicitas,* vi, 4.

And immediately we do find something that encourages us to go forward. Bultmann claims that it is the New Testament itself which points the way in demythologizing. Sometimes its writers seem to take the mythical elements in what they say quite seriously, but on other occasions they seek to express the same ideas in a form free from myth—in existential statements, as Bultmann would claim. Thus there is a certain ambivalence in New Testament thought, where the mythical and non-mythical have not been sharply separated out, and alternative statements of the same truth may be found side by side. So the New Testament itself may supply the clue for its own demythologizing, and this is especially the case in the writings of St. Paul and St. John. What encourages us here is that we find Aulén saying something very similar about the Fathers. Speaking of St. Irenaeus, he remarks: "By the side of sin and death, St. Irenaeus ranges the devil. But the phrase 'by the side of' scarcely does justice to his thought; it is rather that, like later Eastern theologians, he passes insensibly from the one to the other."[11] Thus there is the same kind of ambivalence in patristic thought as Bultmann claims to see in the New Testament, and it may well be that the Fathers also will supply a clue toward demythologizing what they have to say.

First of all, let us glance at Bultmann's treatment of such elements of demonic mythology as are found in St. Paul's writings. We have noted already that St. Paul can speak in mythical language of "principalities and powers" under whose domination the world lies. According to Bultmann, this terminology comes from Gnosticism or allied points of view. But St. Paul explicitly rejected such points of view, and particularly their underlying dualistic understanding of the world. So we find in St. Paul himself a tendency toward demythologizing, an alternative way of speaking in which the reference is not to cosmic powers of darkness but to man's own existence in the world. St. Paul does not trace the origin of sin to the powers of darkness, but to man himself;[12]

[11]*Christus Victor*, p. 42.
[12]Rom. 5: 12.

and in discussing the corruption of mankind, he assigns the cause of the trouble to the fact that man "worshipped and served the creature more than the Creator."[13] The suggestion is that in making the world of things his ultimate concern, man finds that it has become his master and that he is in the position of the sorcerer's apprentice. The world becomes "a hostile destroying force,"[14] as Bultmann expresses it, yet it is man who has given to it its demonic character. The myth is thus interpreted in its significance for human existence, and it is the New Testament itself which guides the interpretation.

The character of Bultmann's approach may be defined more clearly by distinguishing it from other possible approaches. In his essay entitled "The Problem of Hermeneutics"[15] he mentions four possible ways in which we may go about the interpretation of a text. In each case, the result at which we will arrive will correspond to the kind of question which we ask. The kind of question which we ask will in turn depend on the interest in our own minds, directing our attention to this particular text. The four approaches which Bultmann mentions are the historical, the psychological, the aesthetic and the existential. Let us illustrate each of these in relation to a text which I have already mentioned and which is very relevant to our discussion, the *Vita Sancti Antoni* with its luxuriant demonology.

If our interest were historical, then our approach to the text would be guided by the intention of using it to reconstruct a context of past history. We would do the same kind of thing with the mythology of the *Vita* that Edward Langton has done with the demonology of the biblical writings in his book *Essentials of Demonology*—that is to say, reconstruct the demonic beliefs, show how they arose, what influences formed them, and what influences they in turn exerted among the people who adhered to them. We could trace St. Antony's teaching that the demons have their habitat in the air to Greek sources, his animal

[13]Rom. 1: 25.
[14]*Theologie des Neuen Testaments*, p. 226.
[15]*Essays—Philosophical and Theological*, pp. 234ff.

phantoms to Egyptian mythology, perhaps to a primitive zoolatry or ultimately to the primitive feeling for the mystery of animal life, and so on. Out of the data, it would be possible to build up a coherent picture.

If our approach were psychological, we would be interested in something different. We might possibly regard St. Antony as a brainsick monk, but that would hardly be fair, since the evidence shows us that he was a kind and attractive man to whom many turned for advice, and also that he was a shrewd and even witty man who, in spite of his poor education, was able to hold his own in debate with sophisticated opponents. We would have a complex character to unravel. We would have to note that his belief in demons was not a peculiarity, but one that he shared with his contemporaries. Nevertheless, whatever our verdict on him might be, he would obviously make a very interesting psychological study. One would like to know why his visions took the form that they did, why they were so consistently visions of the demonic, what relation they may have had to some of his more eccentric habits, and so on. These are the kind of questions which a psychological approach might seek to answer.

An aesthetic approach would look upon the text as an imaginative creation of no mean power, and its attraction from this point of view may be seen from the fact that from time to time painters or literary men have found a theme in the temptations of St. Antony. Among the painters, perhaps the best known is the treatment of the temptations by Hieronymus Bosch, and presumably this strange artist who filled his pictures with demonic figures must have had some kind of mental affinity with St. Antony himself. Among literary men, one may mention Gustave Flaubert.

It will be noted, however, that in all three of these approaches, the interest of the interpreters would seem to be something different from the interest of the writer of the text. All of these approaches are legitimate, also they are both useful and interesting, not to say fascinating, but they are approaches from the outside, so to speak, and none of the meanings which they draw seems to coincide with the meaning which the writer himself was consciously trying to put across as his first priority.

In the fourth type of approach, the existential, an attempt is made to establish that identity of interest between interpreter and writer, missing in the other approaches. The writer of the *Vita* was seeking to express religious ideas (especially the ideal of monastic existence) and it is the interpreter who is asking a religious question who will hit the meaning the writer is trying to express. Now, for Bultmann a religious question is a question of man's existence, and for this reason we can call this approach "existential." The question is: "What did this mythical language mean for the existence of the men who talked in such a way?" And together with this goes the question: "What can it mean for our existence?" This is the hermeneutic approach which we must employ in our attempt to reach a demythologized version of the patristic teaching on the meaning of the death of Jesus for the Church.

We select one of the Fathers for the purpose of this investigation, and the choice is St. Athanasius. There are many reasons which make him an appropriate choice—for instance, his eminence and influence in the early Church, the moderation of his views, and the restraint of his language, compared with some of the Fathers. There is, however, one outstanding reason that makes him a particularly suitable exemplar from our point of view, and this is that he was the author of two works which are both directly relevant to our inquiry. One is the *De Incarnatione*, perhaps the best known of all the patristic treatises on the meaning of the death of Jesus. The other is the *Vita Sancti Antoni*, which draws upon St. Athanasius' own recollections of his friendship with the ascetic, together with the testimony of one of St. Antony's companions. We have already seen something of how the second of these two works gives us an account of the demonology of the time. Moreover, I shall try to show that there is a close connection between the *De Incarnatione* and the *Vita Sancti Antoni*. The doctrine taught in the former is given its practical illustration in the latter or, as we might say, is there exhibited as lived out in a concrete situation.

The first thing that may strike us in the *De Incarnatione* is once again that ambivalence of language which we have noticed elsewhere. On the one hand, there are many serious references to the demons, particularly to their deceits and illusions by which they have drawn men away from the knowledge of the true God;[16] the idea that the demons inhabit the air also appears, coupled with the argument that it was fitting for Christ to die on the cross, for in that death he was lifted into the air in order that he might drive out the demons from it.[17] Such ways of talking are unmistakably mythological. Yet alternating with them we find quite another way of speaking. We are told, without any reference to demons, that men "devised and contrived evil for themselves."[18] Sometimes we find the two modes of expression occurring side by side in the same sentence: for instance, "men . . . by the counsel of the devil turned to the things of corruption, and became the cause of their own corruption;"[19] or again, "men . . . overcome by the pleasures of the moment and by the illusions and deceits sent by demons, did not raise their heads toward the truth."[20] This ambivalence of language gives us reason to hope that, like St. Paul, St. Athanasius himself will supply us with the clue to demythologizing his own demonology.

But meantime, we must look more closely at the mythological side of his teaching. There are two ideas of special importance to be noticed here. Neither of these are peculiar to St. Athanasius, for both were common to all the Fathers. Both ideas may be illustrated by a single citation: "The evil spirits formerly used to deceive men, investing themselves with God's honour; but when the Word of God appeared in a body and made known to us his own Father, then at length the deceit of the evil spirits is done away and stopped, while men, turning their eyes to the true God, Word of the Father, are deserting the idols, and now coming to know the true God."[21]

The first idea lies in the words "the deceit of the evil spirits is done away and stopped." This is, of course, the notion with which we are

[16]xiii, 1. [17]xxv, 5-6. [18]iv, 4.
[19]v, 1. [20]xii, 6. [21]lv, 5.

already familiar, the central idea in the dramatic view of the atonement, that by his cross Christ defeated the evil powers and broke their hold upon men. As a consequence, these evil powers are now weak. This is a most important point. In spite of all the stress laid on the demonic forces, in spite of all the terrifying imagery sometimes employed, we are told again and again that the demons have no power against faith. "By the sign of the cross, though a man but use it, he drives out their deceits."[22] Exactly the same teaching appears in the *Vita*. After giving his monks a perfectly hair-raising description of the demons, St. Antony assures them that these demons are absolutely powerless against faith. Even the devil himself is represented as not only powerless but rather stupid into the bargain.[23]

The second idea appears in the words which speak of the demons as "investing themselves with God's honour" and of men as "now deserting the idols." This idea is also of first-class importance for the understanding of the myth. Its main point is the identification of the demons with the gods of the pagan world. This belief too appears in the *Vita* but it was of course common to all the Fathers, who saw in the decline of paganism a visible proof of the diminished power of the demons. To quote a random example, Minucius Felix says: "These impure spirits, the demons, consecrated under statues and images, lurk there and by their afflatus attain the authority as of a present deity."[24] The pagan gods, to these early Christians, were not just "stocks and stones" but demonic powers. St. Justin says of them: "We not only deny that they are gods, but assert that they are wicked and impious demons;" for the people who worship them "not knowing that these were demons, called them gods, and gave to each the name which each of the demons chose for himself."[25] The association of the demons with the pagan gods goes back to Jewish times, and is alluded to by St. Paul when he speaks of the Gentiles as sacrificing to demons, and not to God.[26]

These two ideas, taken in conjunction with the ambivalence of St.

[22] xlvii, 2. [23] *Vita*, 42. [24] *Octavius*, xxvii.
[25] *Apology* I, v. [26] I Cor. 10, 20.

Athanasius' language, allow us to go much of the way toward an existential interpretation of the myth. Man, in St. Athanasius' view, stands between the world of things on the one hand and God on the other, and he participates in the nature of both, in so far as he is at once part of the creation and yet possesses a reflection of the divine λόγος. He can turn to the one or the other, and, according to his choice, he either gains his being and becomes in some sense as God, or he loses his being into the world of things and falls into the condition of φθόρα, "ceasing to be," since his nature as a creature is the nothing out of which all finite things have been created. Men have in fact turned to the world of things and made that their ultimate concern. In both the *De Incarnatione* and the *Vita*, St. Athanasius quotes the significant Pauline verse (cited above) that men "worshipped and served the creature more than the Creator." This he takes to be the beginning of idolatry. But this is also the beginning of demonic domination, since, as we have seen, the pagan idols are the same as the demons. So the demons themselves turn out to be nothing other than man's own productions to which he has become enslaved. This is made perfectly explicit by St. Athanasius in the sentence, "out of wickedness men devised for themselves the worshipping of idols"[27]—and these very idols are the demons.

But once the origin of idols and therefore of demons and their tyranny is understood, the way to liberation from their power has also become clear. It lies, quite simply, in renunciation of the world to which men had become enslaved, and this is the meaning of the cross in St. Athanasius. When men cease to be attached to created things, that means an end of power for idols and demons. This understanding and this possibility of liberation have been made available to believers by Christ. He possessed or rather he was the λόγος, the reflection of which was perishing in the race of mankind. His mission was to turn men back from φθόρα to God by restoring them to participation in the λόγος. Christ's life, but above all, his death, was a negation of the power of the world and a surrender to God—or in mythological language, a

[27]*De Incarnatione*, i, 1.

victory over the demons. Faith in Christ or acceptance of his cross means sharing in his renunciation, and this is at the same time the beginning of a new life, a sharing in his resurrection. The simplest expression of this sharing in the victory of Christ is contained in the frequently repeated idea, common of course to the whole of the primitive Church, that at the sign of the cross, the demons will take flight. The cross symbolizes the act of renunciation, and when the world is renounced, its power has ceased and the demons are fled. The idea of sharing in the cross and resurrection of Christ is worked out in more detail in the *Vita*, where a favourite idea is that of the daily martyrdom of St. Antony. Each day he had to reaffirm the cross in each situation as it arose, he had to overcome temptation and conquer the demons again.

It is clear from this that St. Athanasius understood Christianity to be, in its highest form at any rate, a world-renouncing religion. There are passages in the *De Incarnatione* in praise of virginity, while the *Vita* holds up the monastic ideal for our admiration. The circumstances of St. Antony's call are of interest for the prominence which they give to the idea of renunciation. As he was entering the church one day, he heard the words of the lesson being read: "If thou wilt be perfect, go and sell all that thou hast and give to the poor." Applying this to himself or, as we might say, interpreting it existentially, he proceeded to sell his farm and distributed all his goods, except for a sum that he kept for his sister. Soon after he was moved by another passage which he heard in church: "Take no thought for the morrow." So he cut his remaining ties with the world and embarked on a life of ever-increasing austerity.

How far is St. Athanasius' interpretation of the atoning work of Christ necessarily tied up with a thoroughgoing renunciation of the world and an ascetic ideal? It seems to me that this is not really of the essence of his theory. What is essential is that things are not to be idolized, that is to say, they are to be stripped of demonic power. But as an alternative to renunciation, there is the possibility of proper use and mastery of things. Indeed, it could be argued that Christ's victory would be more complete if it not only delivered believers from the world, but at the same time delivered the world to them.

It seems undeniable, however, that St. Athanasius' ideal of Christianity was more austere than that which is current in the Western world today. Yet it is worth remembering that he himself did not become a follower of St. Antony but remained active in the world. In any case, every form of Christianity involves, in the acceptance of the cross, some measure of world-renunciation. Still, one must undoubtedly acknowledge that there has taken place what A. C. Bouquet calls "an adaptation of world-renouncing Christianity to the needs of Western nations,"[28] and it might be an interesting question to inquire how far this adaptation is correlated with the new interpretation of the meaning of Christ's death which gradually arose in the West and was fully stated by St. Anselm.

Let us now see whether we can answer some of the criticisms of the dramatic view of the atonement, as these have been directed against Aulén's presentation of it. O. C. Quick listed three objections.[29] The first was lack of precision. We may claim that this point has been answered by the employment of Bultmann's canons of interpretation for the elucidation of the meaning of mythological language, and of the ambivalent language in which the Fathers expressed their thought. The second objection was to the effect that if Christ defeated such powers as may be supposed to have held men in bondage, why do we seem to find them flourishing today with such vigour? The Fathers would have answered this objection as St. Athanasius did, by pointing to the decline of paganism and the purification of society, almost as if these were empirical proofs of Christ's triumphs over the demons. But in this twentieth century with its wars and revolutions and concentration camps, the answer of St. Athanasius will no longer meet the objection. He has, however, another answer which does seem to be adequate. This lies in

[28]*Comparative Religion* (London: Pelican Books, 1942), p. 187.
[29]*Doctrines of the Creed*, p. 225.

the idea of the daily martyrdom, or in the sign of the cross at which the demons flee. Christ's victory is not tied to a point of time but it is repeated again and again in Christian experience whenever acceptance of the cross delivers men from the tyranny of the world. This leads straight into Quick's third objection—that the theory is a subjective one and simply holds up the life and death of Christ as an edifying example, assuring us that to follow this example is to triumph over evil. But this criticism seems to arise from a confusion of ideas not uncommon when such dangerous terms as "subjective" and "objective" get used. I do not believe that there can be adequate accounts of the Christian doctrine of atonement in either "objective" or "subjective" terms, and indeed the great merit of the classic view is that it unites the objective and subjective sides, the divine grace that comes from beyond man, and man's appropriation of this grace. What is objective is the fact of Christ's cross; but this becomes a saving or atoning event only as its victory over evil is, through divine grace, repeated in the lives of the believers.

It is interesting to note that Bultmann's own understanding of the atonement might fairly be called a "demythologized" version of the view found in the Fathers, and seems to me to stand quite definitely within the classic or dramatic tradition. For him, the death of Christ is understood as "the means of liberation from the powers of this world, the law, sin and death."[30] The idea of the daily martyrdom reappears in Bultmann's assertion that to believe in the cross of Christ is to accept it as one's own, and in this sense the cross and its victory are not merely past happening, but constitute a present event. We may notice also Bultmann's emphasis on withdrawal from the world—a message not without its relevance in this gadget-ridden age—and the affinity which he claims to find between Christians on the one hand and non-Christians who have made the same kind of withdrawal, on the other. There is community between them, he says, because both, having escaped from the tyranny of things, are made free for genuine relations with one another.[31]

[30]*Kerygma and Myth*, p. 36. [31]*Essays*, pp. 301ff.

It is not necessary that one should agree with everything in Bultmann's view of the work of Christ in order to recognize that in all its main aspects his view of the atonement is a modern version of the patristic teaching, of the so-called classic idea of atonement. A rather interesting consequence follows from this. Aulén claims that "the Latin"—or Anselmian—"type of doctrine turns out to be really a side-track in the history of Christian dogma. . . . The main line in the development of doctrine is continued not by St. Anselm and the medieval scholastics but by Luther."[32] And Aulén, of course, contends that Luther revived the "classic" idea. Now if one accepts Aulén's contention, then, as far as his teaching on this central doctrine of atonement is concerned, we must conclude that Bultmann stands in the main line, the tradition of the Fathers; while some of his neo-orthodox critics, who regard him as a dangerous innovator, are themselves the people on the side-track, in so far as they are still trying to make sense of "objective" theories of the atonement.

We could from this point go on to the demythologizing of the more elaborate theory of a ransom to the devil, but this would take us beyond St. Athanasius, who makes no mention of such ideas. Essentially, however, we would still have the same point of view—that Christ's death is to be interpreted for Christian faith as meaning victory over the powers of darkness. The patristic formulation is in the ambivalent language of a period in which mythological and non-mythological ways of thinking alternated, without having been clearly sorted out. The mythological way of thinking is no longer possible for us, but we can discern what these early writers were seeking to express about a possibility of existence presented to them by the death of Christ, and we can understand it as a possibility for ourselves.

If we were to try to put this understanding of the atonement in the simplest form, with the mythological and demythologized versions side by side, it would run somewhat as follows. Acceptance of the cross of Christ (= the decision of faith, which is at once renunciation of the

[32]*Christus Victor*, p. 31.

world and surrender to God) destroys the idols and overcomes the demons (= abolishes worldly concern and so puts an end to the tyranny of things over men) and thus leads to sharing in the resurrection of Christ (= brings men into a new life in which they are open for genuine relations with one another and with God).

Aulén's impressive book, which I have had occasion to quote so frequently, ended with this sentence: "I believe that the classic idea of the atonement and of Christianity is coming back—that is to say, the genuine, authentic Christian faith."[33] Without venturing a comment on the last few provocative words of this quotation, it may at least be said that Aulén's prediction is being fulfilled, and that with Bultmann the classic idea has made a powerful come-back.

[33]*Op. cit.*, p. 176.

True Life in Death

16

The expression "true life in death" is, of course, taken from St. Ignatius, bishop of Antioch. It comes from one of the letters[1] which he wrote in the course of his journey toward martyrdom at Rome, and it is one of a series of paradoxical expressions—"fleshly and spiritual, begotten and unbegotten, God in man . . ."—in which he tries to state his understanding of the person of Jesus Christ. The particular expression "true life in death" is, however, the most typical of all those he uses, for as Rudolf Bultmann has well said, "death and life are the opposites that govern St. Ignatius' thinking."[2]

Many people have found St. Ignatius' preoccupation with death—one might almost say, his glorying in death—somewhat distasteful. Sydney Cave uses the words "boastful" and "exuberant" to describe the bishop's way of talking about his approaching martyrdom.[3] His utterances are indeed sometimes little short of lurid as he lists his expected sufferings: "grappling with wild beasts, cuttings and

[1]Eph. 7.
[2]*Existence and Faith* (New York: Meridian Books, 1960), p. 271.
[3]*The Doctrine of the Person of Christ*, p. 74.

manglings, wrenching of bones, hacking of limbs, crushings of my whole body."[4] St. Ignatius is equally inclined to dwell on the sufferings of Christ. Hastings Rashdall remarks that "references to the blood of Christ are peculiarly frequent in this writer, and he is one of the very few at all early writers who ever define the belief which saves as belief in the blood or death of Christ."[5]

In a world that is acquainted with the work of Freud, it is a temptation to see in the utterances of St. Ignatius nothing but an exaggerated manifestation of the death-wish, and to dismiss him as a pathological character. This, however, would be a very superficial judgment. Over against the adverse criticisms of St. Ignatius may be set the positive appreciation expressed by Bultmann who states his opinion that this was the only one among the Apostolic Fathers to follow St. Paul in understanding the Christian faith as an existentiell attitude.[6] Admittedly, the existentiell character of St. Ignatius' thought is obscured by the fact that it gets buried over in the mythological language which he, in common with other early Christian writers, was accustomed to use. It is the use of such language that sometimes leads modern theologians to accuse these early Christian writers of having held a "physical" conception of salvation, by which is meant that they were more concerned with salvation from death than from sin, and with the attainment of a blissful immortality than of reconciliation to God. Such charges may seem plausible if we are going to take seriously some of the mythological language that we find in these early writers. There is, for instance, a well known passage in St. Ignatius where he speaks of the Holy Eucharist as "a medicine of immortality, and the antidote that we should not die, but live for ever in Jesus Christ."[7] Here there seems to be a quasi-magical understanding of the sacrament as producing physical effects—deliverance from death and a consequent im-

[4]Rom. 5.

[5]*The Idea of Atonement in Christian Theology* (London: Macmillan, 1925), p. 190.

[6]*Existence and Faith,* p. 267.

[7]Eph. 20.

mortality. Of course, a very similar idea, though with an opposite application, is found in St. Paul, who likewise seems to attribute physical effects to the sacrament when he tells the Corinthians who have received unworthily, "That is why many of you are weak and ill, and some have died."[8] A related mythological idea was the common belief, derived from the Old Testament story of the garden of Eden, that death—that is to say, physical death—is the punishment for sin, and that death came into the world as such a punishment.

Such mythological ideas are doubly misleading. On the one hand, their objectifying language represents life and death as physical phenomena, thus lending weight to the criticism that those who talked in these mythical ways embraced a purely physical conception of salvation, one which is supposedly deficient in ethical and personal valuations, as well as being magical and superstitious. On the other hand, the mythical formulations obscure the true relation of life and death to human existence. This relation is an intrinsic one, for the issues of life and death arise out of existence itself and belong to it. In the mythical way of talking, however, life and death are represented as somehow extrinsic to existence, so that they can be thought of as a reward or a punishment that gets added on to a good or bad existence respectively.

Of course, the early Christian writers who sometimes employed mythical ways of talking had other modes of discourse at their disposal also. When we turn to these, it becomes clear that they could and sometimes did think of death as more than a physical phenomenon, and furthermore that they could understand the relation of death to sin or a sinful existence as intrinsic, and not merely that of a legal punishment that gets arbitrarily added on. Thus St. Paul can talk of "sinful passions" which are "at work" in such a way as "to bear fruit for death"; or of a "sowing to the flesh" which will "reap corruption."[9] This existential view of the relation of sin and death appears in some

[8]I Cor. 11: 20.
[9]Rom. 7: 5; Gal. 6: 8.

of the patristic writers, notably St. Athanasius, but admittedly it is not noticeably explicit in St. Ignatius, who has relatively little to say about sin. When the relation is understood as an intrinsic, existential one, death is seen as the working out of sin itself rather than as a punishment added on, and by "death" is understood not merely physical extinction but a gradual process of disintegration reaching to the entire person, a process which may be described as "loss of being." The classic statement of this point of view is surely Dante's in *The Divine Comedy*. Every so-called punishment in the living death of hell is shown by Dante as simply the progress of the sin itself in the increasing break-up of the sinner, and this means too that such a death or loss of being begins now, and is not just something threatened for the future. We may recall Dante's picture of the lustful, torn by violent winds which represent their own undisciplined passions; or the hypocrites, groaning beneath the burden of gorgeous robes that are weighted down inside by the lead of their pretences; or the great traitors, frozen solid in a block of ice, because these were men in whom all natural feelings of loyalty and affection had died. Such an understanding of the relations of sin, death and existence is already implicit, though obscurely, in the mythical formulations, but it becomes increasingly explicit as the language of myth is transcended. It is so far from being a "physical" understanding of these matters, as is sometimes alleged, that it would be better called an "ontological" understanding, since it is the notion of "loss of being" that constitutes the link between sin and death; and it is so far from being opposed to an ethical or personal understanding, that rather it must be asserted that every ethical, personal understanding presupposes an ontological basis.

Here however we must notice a remarkable ambivalence in the way in which the early Christian writers regarded death. On the one hand, as we have seen, death was conceived negatively as threat or punishment, for it is indeed "loss of being," the disintegration that may be understood as arising from sin. But on the other hand, we find that death was also conceived in a positive way. St. Paul can talk paradoxically about "dying to sin" and also about "being crucified with Christ."[10] Such dying or being crucified is not a loss of being, but rather the attainment of being. It is this positive evaluation of death that is so prominent in St. Ignatius, in his glorification of martyrdom and his intense desire to be "an imitator of the passion of my God."[11] It was not just that death was considered an unpleasant but necessary stage that must be gone through for the attainment of a future life; somehow, life is found in death, and death itself acquires a positive significance, so that it can be understood not as mere loss of being, but as possible fulfilment of being. And we must remind ourselves that what is meant here by death is once more not just physical death, for the dying with Christ belongs to the daily existence of the Christian. This holds even for St. Ignatius, despite his preoccupation with actual martyrdom, for he conceives his martyrdom as the "perfecting" of the discipleship on which he had already embarked. At a later time, the early Christian ascetics were to think of their career in terms of daily martyrdom.

Still another point that may be noted in connection with this positive valuation of death is the transition from a passive to an active attitude in the face of death. For death is not just something that will "happen" to the victim. It is something that he chooses. "I willingly die for the sake of God," writes St. Ignatius.[12] These words express no suicidal desire to be rid of existence, but rather an acceptance of death as having the possibility of becoming a positive factor in existence. A death which is somehow accepted into existence and is not just its termination gives value to that existence. When the Church worked out a belief in purgatory, it is significant that all souls were supposed to require purgation after death except those of the martyrs, whose acceptance of death, it was supposed, had already brought them to their fullest stature.

[10]Rom. 6: 2; Gal. 2: 20.
[11]Rom. 6.
[12]Rom. 4.

Secular history affords many examples of men whose deaths have been not simply the terminations of their lives, and certainly not their defeat and annihilation, but rather their fulfilment, crowning and even in some cases redeeming all that had gone before. We think especially of men who chose to die, scorning any escape or compromise, so that with them death was not just some misfortune that had overtaken them, but something that they took upon themselves to carry out. Socrates refuses to escape from prison, choosing rather to submit to laws however harsh or unjust in their operation; and by his death, he certainly loses nothing, but strikes a great blow for the human spirit. In British history, King Charles I redeemed the shortcomings of his reign by the nobility of his death; refusing to compromise with usurped military power, he chose a martyrdom that impressed even his enemies and helped to save from ruin some of the most cherished institutions of the British people.

These examples from secular history are worth recalling, for they indicate that death in itself seems to have the potentiality for becoming a positive achievement. Needless to say, what St. Paul and St. Ignatius had in mind in their estimates of death was the death of Christ, and it was because they had the thought of his death before them that they were able to think of death as fulfilment and not merely as loss of being. By a remarkable transformation, Christ's passion and death had become for the Church the manifestation of spiritual life and power, and this had made possible an altogether new understanding of the significance of death in Christian existence, a new grasp of the paradox that through losing life, men find it. Yet we should not perhaps say "altogether" new, for like everything else in the Christian revelation, this understanding is continuous with what men had known outside of Christianity. Although the new attitude to death belongs especially to the Christian faith and arises out of the revelatory experience which the disciples had of the crucified and risen Lord, we have already seen that a positive evaluation of death and an active attitude toward it is possible apart from Christian faith, as in the case of Socrates. To get a clearer understanding of the matter, whether within Christian faith or outside of it, we must first of all try to see the part which death plays in any human existence, and what attitudes it is possible to take up in the face of it.

At this point we can profitably turn to the philosopher Martin Heidegger, in whose analysis of human existence, death is assigned an important place.[13] He brings out very clearly the ambivalent character of death, considered as an existential phenomenon. On the one hand, death is the primary revelation of human finitude and transience. Every human existence is thrown into death and may indeed be characterized as a being-toward-death, a kind of being which by its very constitution already includes in itself nullity. Yet on the other hand death can make possible an integrated existence, for as the uttermost possibility in human existence, it becomes a kind of focus in the light of which other possibilities are to be ranged and evaluated. Just as the eschatological expectation gave to the early Christians a sense of urgency and responsibility, so death, as the imminent end, is able to lift human existence above the level of triviality so as to give it meaning and unity. As Richard Kroner has well said of Heidegger's teaching on death, it shows us death as "the wholesome and creative instance which presents to each one his own unique selfhood."[14]

No one could make the mistake of thinking that Heidegger is advocating nihilism. His doctrine may indeed be a species of secularism, if we understand that term to indicate an attempt to find meaning and value for human existence within the horizons of the finite and the temporal. One could also, however, interpret Heidegger's doctrine as a species of mysticism, since it is through the experience of nullity in the anticipation of death that man is set free for the encounter with Being.

But here we need not linger over a discussion as to what his ultimate

[13]See *Sein und Zeit*, pp. 235ff. See also "Death and its Existential Significance," pp. 45ff. above.

[14]"Heidegger's Private Religion" in *Union Seminary Quarterly Review*, vol. XI/4, p. 25.

meaning may be. The important point for us to notice is that his existential analytic helps to explain the ambivalent significance of death, and lets us see how he can understand the phenomenon of death in a positive way, so that as much as St. Ignatius though in a very different fashion he finds "true life in death." When we ask how he does this, the answer seems to be that he sees in the total and irrevocable character of death the possibility of an *absoluteness* which belongs uniquely to death and contrasts with the *relativity* of every other possibility in human existence. To quote Kroner again, "he fills finitude with the meaning of infinity."[15] This point should be borne in mind for our later discussion.

But now let us notice a further point. Heidegger dwells on the connection between death and finitude, and we must notice that this particular connection is one which Christian theologians have tended to neglect. Christian theology has concentrated rather on the connection between death and sin, following the lead of the old mythology which represented death as the punishment for sin, and which might therefore seem to suggest that if there were no sin, there would be no death either, even for a finite existence. Heidegger too is aware of the relation between death and sin, or at least between death and what he calls "falling" or "fallenness," the existential-ontological structure that comes nearest to the idea of sin in his analytic. It is for fallen existence that death appears as the great evil that must be covered up. But if the transition is made from an inauthentic to an authentic existence, death is not removed nor is its essential character changed; what is changed is the attitude toward death, for this is no longer the reaction of flight and concealment, but the acceptance and taking up of death as the one possibility of transcending the senseless succession of "nows" so as to attain unity and totality. We must consider then whether Christian theology can learn something about the relation of death to finitude from such a philosophy as Heidegger's, and how this may bear upon the traditional theological concern with the relation between death and sin.

[15]*Loc. cit.*, p. 28.

This point may be raised by taking a look at a highly speculative but intriguing theological question. If man had never sinned, if he had never fallen, would there be no death in the world? Perhaps many Christian theologians of the past would have replied without hesitation that if there had been no sin, there would have been no death either. For instance, St. Anselm's theory of the atonement goes on the assumption that Christ could make satisfaction because there was no necessity to die, for one who had not sinned. But this assumption may be due to the fact, already noted, that Christian theology has been almost exclusively preoccupied with the Old Testament story that connects sin and death, and has given little thought to the relation of finitude and death. To Heidegger, it would seem foolish to ask whether if man had never sinned, he would be subject to death, for Heidegger sees death as an implication of finitude, not of sin. And Heidegger seems to be right about this. Even if there had been no sin, would there not still be an end—which we may call "death"—for any finite embodied existence in the world? Is it true that for one who had not sinned, there would be no necessity to die, or is it not more likely that for such a one also there would come an end or death (for we can hardly suppose that such a person would live on for ever in the world—indeed, even the world itself does not last for ever)? However—and this again can be learned from Heidegger—the attitude of such a person to his end might be quite different from the attitude of the ordinary "fallen" human being toward death; and in this sense, the end or death of the "sinless" person would be somehow different from death as we ordinarily know it, just as the death of Jesus has something "different" about it.

The question of sin, finitude and death has been brilliantly discussed from the theological point of view by Karl Rahner.[16] He acknowledges that the statement that death is the consequence of sin would seem to imply that before his sin the first man (to speak in terms of the myth) was not subject to death. But he claims: "It is not legitimate to infer from this proposition of faith that the first man in Paradise, had he not

[16] "On the Theology of Death" in *Modern Catholic Thinkers*, p. 152.

sinned, would have lived on endlessly in this life. Rather, it can be said with certainty that he would surely have experienced an end of his life, but in another manner." This "other manner" Rahner visualizes as "a pure active self-affirmation." The point then would seem to be that a transition has been made from a passive, fearful attitude in the face of the end to an active, accepting attitude. And Rahner goes on to point out that not everything in death is to be regarded as arising out of its connection with sin, and so as something "that should not have been so."

So there are two fundamental ways in which death can be understood. One view regards it as a hostile force which makes us its victims, tears us away from our world and disintegrates our existence. Seen in this aspect, death is an evil, and the more firmly we are attached to our world, the more unmitigated must the evil of death seem. On the second of the two fundamental ways of understanding death, it is not so much something that happens to us as something that has to be accomplished, and there is seen at least the possibility of a death that will be the highest act of fulfilment. It is presumably sin that gives to death the utterly destructive aspect which it has in the first of these two ways of looking at it, so that we can understand why death should have been represented as the punishment for sin. But for any finite embodied existence, there would need to be some end comparable to death, and from Socrates to Heidegger we see how in various ways and degrees men have sought to give to death a positive character that would belong to it in its own right, apart from any connection of death with sin.

Yet human life is such that no man's death could be understood only in positive terms as consummation and achievement. Every human death is at best a mixed phenomenon, sharing in both of the fundamental aspects delineated above. Even in the cases of Socrates, King Charles I and others whose deaths have won them renown in history, death was not just positive achievement, for it also had its dark side of waste, loss, separation from friends. To some extent, this is no doubt due to the universality of sin, so that no human death could be, in Rahner's expression, a "pure active self-affirmation." But is the dark side not due also to the very finitude of human existence? Finitude is such that every serious decision involves pain and loss; for to decide for one possibility (let us say, a lifelong vocation) inevitably implies that other possibilities that were open in the situation are relinquished. Moreover, finitude implies that there is no prevision of what the decision will accomplish, so that every important decision is taken in risk, and against a background of anguished doubt. Now, to decide for the absolute possibility of death (as in martyrdom) would imply that altogether apart from the question of sin, there would be present in a pre-eminent degree the darkness and poignancy that belong to finitude itself. For to die is not to relinquish this or that possibility in favour of a chosen one, but to relinquish *all* possibilities other than dying itself; and for this there would be required the highest act of faith, which would need to be matched by a corresponding abyss of doubt.

These matters become important when we return to the death of Jesus, as the paradigm of "true life in death." This death above all is affirmative, as the death that expresses perfect self-giving, which is at once the essence of obedience to God and of Christian love. This death is also not just something that happened to Jesus, but something that he took upon him to do at some point in his career, so that we remember it as his supreme deed, and in the teaching of the Church it has become the act of atonement or reconciliation. The Church has affirmed further that this was a death accomplished without sin. Yet even this death must have had its dark side, and this is recognized in the tradition. The agony in the garden, the cry of dereliction, the parting from his mother, the descent into hell—these are only a few traditional characteristics of the death of Jesus which show us that even in this most affirmative of deaths, the elements of loss and suffering are not absent but are even in some ways heightened. So even in this death there lurks the element of negativity, and indeed it would be senseless to talk of Jesus *enduring* the cross or *suffering* under

Pontius Pilate apart from such negativity. This was really death, not just a play. "He really, and not merely in appearance, was crucified and died," writes St. Ignatius[17] against some docetic heresy. Christ's genuine humanity is attested by his genuinely human death. How then are we to relate the dark and negative factors to the positive ones which equally belong to the death of Christ?

We take our point of departure from the question of Jesus' sinlessness. By this negative expression, we cannot mean an empirical judgment on the actual deeds of Jesus, for we know only a few of them. We mean rather a value-judgement on this person who encounters us in the Church's proclamation, and furthermore, this is a judgment that is affirmative rather than negative in what it asserts. For if sin is essentially separation from God, sinlessness is essentially union with God. Christ's "sinlessness" is a doubly negative expression which therefore expresses an affirmative conception. This affirmative conception is that of the incarnation, the union of God and man in Christ. Christ's sinlessness is also expressed in positive terms by Kierkegaard as his "limitless love"[18] whereby the separation of sin is overcome. Yet this limitless love (which is presumably divine love) has appeared in the flesh, that is to say, under the conditions of a limited finite existence. We affirm the unity of Christ with the Father, but we say also that the revelation of the Godhead is somehow veiled in the flesh, and that we see the Infinite through the glass of the finite. Again, we contrast Christ's first advent with his coming again "with glory," and whatever else this may mean, it implies that the first advent has a relative character that falls short of the greater glory still to be manifested. Finite existence implies being in a situation where only some possibilities are open, and even these are partial and relative, not total and absolute. Hence in a finite existence it would seem that only a relative perfection is possible, and this means that we have to ask how Christ could manifest a "limitless love" or how he could be in that

[17]Trall. 9.
[18]*Works of Love* (London: Collins, 1962), p. 170.

perfect unity with the Father which would allow us to talk of an incarnation. On the other hand, it would obviously make no sense to talk of an incarnation if we did not believe that Christ was really at one with us in our humanity, and so involved in all the relativities and ambiguities of finite existence. While we affirm his sinlessness and perfection, we must also recognize, as John Knox has expressed it, that "the larger social reality of which he was the dynamic centre was certainly not sinless or perfect; and it was in this social reality—the concrete body of relationships between Jesus and his own—that the incarnation occurred."[19]

It seems to me questionable, however, whether one should go on with Knox and others to hold that although Christ was himself sinless, it was "sinful flesh" that he assumed. My complaint is perhaps not so much with the idea as with the language (even if it happens to be Pauline!) which seems to me misleading as concealing the existential and personal nature of sin. The expression "sinful flesh" inevitably suggests that sin is a property inhering in some abstraction called "the flesh"; whereas sin is rather a possibility in which a concrete existent stands. Even if this possibility is universally actualized in the human race, it remains nevertheless an alienation from, rather than an essential characteristic of, authentic existence. But if what is meant by saying that Christ assumed sinful flesh is that he stood in the possibility of sin and was involved in the relativities of the human situation, this must be conceded, in spite of the traditional christological doctrine of his impeccability, that is to say, that because of the aseity of the divine nature, Christ had not even the possibility of sinning. This seems to make nonsense of his humanity, and is another symptom of the tendency toward docetism that has run through the history of christology. Certainly Christ could not be genuinely man if he lived in a dreaming innocence such as, to speak mythologically, we may suppose to have belonged to the first man in Paradise.

[19]*The Church and the Reality of Christ* (New York: Harper & Row, 1962), p. 135.

But is all this not adequately granted in the recognition of the radically finite character of Jesus' existence? The word "flesh" appears to be used in the New Testament in two senses—sometimes in a pejorative sense where it definitely implies a sinful existence, but sometimes in an ethically neutral sense where it asserts only finitude.[20] Here again we must remind ourselves that the ontological categories are not opposed to the ethical, but underlie them. Whereas sin is a perversion of man, finitude belongs to his constitution in its very basis. Ideally, at least, there could be genuine humanity without sin, but there could be no genuine humanity without finitude. The latter is not itself sin, but it is the condition for the possibility of sin. The dark side of Jesus' death arises out of his genuine participation in finite existence, so that while his death was supremely *creative*, it was also experienced as a *creaturely* loss of being-in-the-world; and while it was the sublime *act* of saving love, it was also the *passion* that had to be met (again, *pace* the traditional christology) in the finite "theological virtues" of faith and hope.

But whether we use the language of finitude or of sinful flesh, we have now to ask the question of how Christ, once we have located him so firmly in the relativities of the human situation, can become the redeemer of that situation and somehow break out of it. Even if he had lived on indefinitely, performing deeds of love, he could never have surmounted the limitations of a finite existence, or manifested anything more than a relative perfection and a relative love. However, we have already seen that the only possibility open to a finite existence for transcending the relativities of everyday existence, the only possibility that is characterized by something like totality and even absoluteness, is death. By his death, Jesus realizes his love as "limitless love," finitude gets filled with the meaning of infinity, and indeed, as Paul Tillich has so clearly recognized, the human Jesus with his relativity is sacrificed to become the Christ of faith.

[20]See my book, *An Existentialist Theology* (London: SCM Press, 1955), pp. 104-8, where I discuss the word "flesh" and claim that it has a neutral as well as a bad sense, appealing for support to Rudolf Bultmann's *Theology of the New Testament*.

Here we may permit ourselves one further speculation. At what moment did the incarnation take place, the union of God and man in Christ? At the conception, as St. Thomas taught? At the baptism, as some Protestant theologians have surmised? Must we not rather say, at the cross? Or better still, must we not rather get away from the idea of an instantaneous incarnation, and recognize that Christhood, like selfhood—and possibly Christhood is simply perfect selfhood—is not conferred ready-made as a "nature" at birth or whenever, but is achieved and hammered out in actual existence? This notion of growth is entirely in line with the teaching of the gospel.[21] Then the cross would not be so much the "moment" of incarnation as rather the consummation of the incarnation, the completion of the process in which God and man come together in the person of Jesus Christ. It is worth recalling that the nineteenth-century German theologian, I. A. Dorner, thought of the incarnation in this way, as a process which was perfected in death, though admittedly the background of his thinking was idealist rather than existential.

Such a theory does not separate the death from the life, but recognizes (quite in accordance, as had been said, with the New Testament) a growth in the person of Christ. In death the progressive manifestation of the divine love leaps, as it were, on to a new level, the level of "limitless love," so that the relative is raised to the absolute and the human Jesus is by death itself exalted to consummate unity with the Father in complete Christhood. Dorner expressed this very well as follows: "With Christ's death, not merely is his earthly work finished, but also the consummation of his person established. The lowest stage of his outward humiliation is itself the beginning of his exaltation."[22]

Our exploration of the expression "true life in death" has brought us therefore to the central mysteries of the incarnation, the coming together in unity of God and man. St. Ignatius used the expression to

[21]Luke 2: 52.

[22]*A System of Christian Doctrine* (Edinburgh: T. & T. Clark, 1896), IV, 125.

illuminate the meaning of Christ, but he understood it also as a pattern for all Christian existence, as indeed could be expected if Christhood is the perfecting of selfhood. Christian existence meant, for St. Ignatius, the imitation of Christ's passion. The word "imitation" should not be taken too seriously; it is not a kind of external copying to be done by our own unaided effort, as if Christ were merely the example set up before us. St. Ignatius conceives the process as taking place "in Christ," and he can talk of "dying into his passion."[23] So the "imitation" that he has in mind is not an outward modelling of life upon Christ, but a genuine participation in Christ.

This, in turn, takes place in the Christian community. In the sacramental life of the Church, life is found in death, and this not merely in the future but in the present. The Christian life is, in the Heideggerian expression, a being-toward-death, but specifically a being toward the death of Christ. It begins as such in baptism, which St. Paul describes as "burial with Christ" so that we may walk in "newness of life."[24] It continues in the sacramental existence of the community where every eucharist is a re-presenting of the death of Christ, and his Body is not only the sacramental host but also the congregation of the faithful. It finds expression in the Christian ethic which summons us from every worldly security to the adventure of outgoing love.

"True life in death" sounds like nonsense, but according to the Christian religion, it is nothing other than God's mysterious destiny for our being. John Baillie has reminded us that " 'Christianity' is not itself a New Testament word. The earliest equivalent of it is simply the 'way' or the 'road,' and the first Christians spoke of themselves as following this road. When our Lord asked his first converts to follow him, he meant that they should take the road with him in a quite literal sense. And I believe," Baillie goes on, "that when the Christians of the next generation spoke of the way, they meant that they were recapitulating the way he had travelled, his journey up to Jerusalem

[23]Magn. 5.
[24]Rom. 6: 4.

and to the crucifixion."[25] This is only what Christ himself is reported to have taught: "If any man would come after me, let him deny himself and take up his cross daily and follow me. For whoever would save his life will lose it; and whoever loses his life for my sake, he will save it."[26]

[25]*The Sense of the Presence of God* (London: Oxford University Press, 1962), p. 137.

[26]Luke 9: 23-24.

The Seven Gifts of the Holy Ghost

17

"Thou the anointing Spirit art, who dost thy sevenfold gifts impart." So run some well known words from an English version of the ancient hymn, *Veni Creator Spiritus.* In other hymns, both ancient and modern, and in devotional literature, the seven gifts of the Holy Ghost, or his sevenfold "energy" or sevenfold "mystery," are familiar themes. What are these seven gifts? Traditionally, the Church has listed them as wisdom, understanding, counsel, fortitude, knowledge, piety and the fear of the Lord. The present purpose is to attempt a theological inquiry into this venerable Christian tradition.

At first sight, this may not seem to offer very promising material for a theological study. Does not the idea of the seven gifts belong to the devotional and practical life of the Church, rather than to its theology? It must be confessed that the list of gifts, both in regard to its content and to the order in which the gifts are mentioned, strikes one as somewhat haphazard. The very occurrence of the number seven makes us suspicious right away, for it suggests an arbitrary selection drawn up to conform to all the other sevenfold lists that have come down to us from earlier ages of Christian piety—the seven sacraments, the seven penitential psalms, the seven corporal (and seven spiritual) works of mercy, the seven joys (and seven sorrows) of the Blessed Virgin Mary, to say nothing of the seven deadly sins.

Why then should we be asked to concentrate attention on these seven gifts, no more and no less? St. Paul mentions some quite different gifts of the Spirit:[1] wise speech, faith, healing, miraculous powers, ecstatic utterance, prophecy and—most excellent of all—love or charity. Elsewhere too he writes[2] of the "fruit" or "harvest" of the Spirit, and mentions love, joy, peace, patience and other qualities besides; and such fruit or harvest of the Spirit is hardly to be distinguished from the gifts of the Spirit, unless indeed we wish to be very meticulous and say perhaps that the harvest is related to the gifts as a course of action is to the attitude which it expresses. At any rate, St. Paul shows us that there are many gifts of the Spirit that are not mentioned, or at least not explicitly mentioned, in the traditional list of seven. If then we concentrate our attention on this list, it is not because we suppose that it sets out exhaustively the gifts of the Spirit, but because the Church has attached a special importance to this particular group of gifts, and presumably has thought that there is some reason for doing so.

One other feature of the traditional list of seven gifts may strike us as somewhat strange. Does it not show a curious lack of balance, in so far as it seems to put a considerable premium on what might be called "intellectual" gifts? Whereas St. Paul gives a prominent place to love in both of the passages to which I alluded, the word does not occur in the traditional list, where the stress appears to be on wisdom, together with understanding, counsel, knowledge. It is not even clear how these are distinguished from each other. Does not wisdom overlap with counsel? And how are both of these related to knowledge and understanding? Yet when we recall that in the New Testament[3] the Holy Spirit is also called the "Counsellor" or "Paraclete," and the "Spirit of truth," and it is declared to be a specific function of his that "he will teach you all

[1]I Cor. 12: 1 ff. [2]Gal. 5: 22.
[3]John 14: 16 and 26; 16: 13.

things" and that "he will guide you into all the truth," then perhaps we should not find it surprising that characteristics peculiarly associated with the appropriation of truth preponderate in the list of the gifts of the Holy Spirit. We shall see in any case that these characteristics are not to be understood in any narrowly intellectualist sense. They are moreover linked to the further gifts of fortitude, piety and the fear of the Lord, and it will become clear to us as we go along that one of the most remarkable features of this traditional list of the seven gifts is the way in which it brings into unity the different aspects of human life, cognitive, volitional and affective, thereby opening up for us a very profound insight into the complex structure of our own human existence. It may also be the case that the very stress which the traditional list lays upon gifts of the mind gives to it its special theological interest, since theology itself is an intellectual enterprise within faith, seeking to bring to explicit understanding the convictions that are rooted in faith.

If these preliminary remarks have done something to answer the questions or even the doubts which we might raise about the usefulness of a theological inquiry into the seven gifts, let me now sketch the form which the inquiry will take. It will fall into three parts. The first part is exegetical and historical; it will briefly review the tradition of the seven gifts as it has arisen from the biblical sources and as it has subsequently taken more definite shape in the thinking of the Church. The second part will inquire into the theological presuppositions of the tradition; here we shall ask what is meant by a "gift" of the Holy Ghost, and how we can conceive the operation of the Holy Spirit in the bestowing of such gifts, both in relation to the economy of the Godhead and in relation to the structure of our own responsible human existence. The third part of the inquiry is concerned with the actual content of the tradition–the seven gifts themselves, the contribution of each, and the way in which they are interrelated. When these tasks have been carried out, we should be in a position to evaluate the adequacy of the tradition as a description of Christian existence, conceived as a life in the Spirit.

I

As is well known, the origin of the tradition of the seven gifts is found in an utterance of the prophet Isaiah:[4] "The Spirit of the Lord shall rest upon him, the spirit of wisdom and understanding, the spirit of counsel and might, the spirit of knowledge and the fear of the Lord." There are differences of opinion among commentators about the provenance of this passage, but it seems probable enough that it goes right back to the eighth century before Christ, and envisages an ideal ruler of the line of David—a ruler who would embody in himself all the finest kingly qualities. These qualities are not explicitly called "gifts" by Isaiah, but they are certainly not conceived as natural human qualities, for they are referred to the "Spirit of the Lord" resting upon the ruler. They are all qualities that are highly esteemed in the Old Testament, and that are associated with God's operation on men. Presumably it was from such prophetic visions of ideal kingship that the full-blown messianic hope was eventually to arise in Israel.

Right away, however, we notice that Isaiah mentions not seven qualities but six, and six is obviously the number required by the rhythm of the Hebrew text, where the six are arranged in three pairs. The additional quality which makes up the number to the traditional seven gifts comes in the Septuagint. Here in the Greek version we find "piety" inserted between "knowledge" and the "fear of the Lord." It is hard to assign any reason for this addition, except by simply referring it to the freedom which the translators apparently felt to make certain curtailments or expansions in the text when they saw fit. It may be that in this particular case they felt that the number of qualities ought to be seven. As everyone knows, the number seven exercised a peculiar fascination among all the religions of the Near East. Probably this fascination goes back to the days of primitive astralism and the cult of the sun, moon and five planets known to the ancient world; but whatever the origin of the idea may have been, it would certainly have seemed ap-

[4]Isa. 11: 2.

propriate to a Jew living at the time when the Old Testament was being translated into Greek that the Spirit should bestow seven distinctive qualities rather than six. Wisdom had come to be regarded as the supreme gift of God, the one which Solomon had preferred to any other and which he was said to have received in a superabundant degree.[5] The panegyrics on wisdom, both in the Old Testament and in the Apocrypha, conceive this wisdom almost as a hypostatic divine emanation.[6] It is said that "she has set up her seven pillars,"[7] and whatever this expression may mean (it could be astralism again), it may have contributed to the expectation that a list of Spirit-given qualities headed by wisdom should be sevenfold. Somewhere along the line too there arises the idea that the Spirit of the Lord is also sevenfold. In the Revelation of St. John there are several references[8] to the "seven spirits," an idea derived from a Jewish background and associated, it may be, with the seven archangels of Jewish angelology or with the seven-branched candlestick as symbolizing the divine Spirit. But we have spent enough time over these occult ideas, and the precise disentangling of origins is not our business. It suffices to notice that the Septuagint expanded the six qualities to seven, and that when St. Jerome translated the Bible into Latin, the seven gifts passed in turn into the Vulgate and so into a secure place in the tradition of the Western Church. And even if the additional gift of piety found its way on to the list almost by accident, we may find that this extra item turns out to be a valuable and worthwhile enrichment of Isaiah's original saying; for it need hardly be said that here we are concerned not with anything like a strict exegesis of the biblical text, but with trying to interpret an idea from the text as something that has already been interpreted and worked over by generations first of Jewish and then of Christian thought.

Before leaving the Septuagint expansion of Isaiah's text, we should notice one further point. The additional gift of piety was not, as we

[5]I Kings 4: 29.
[6]Prov. 8: 1 ff.; Wisd. of Sol. 7: 7 ff.
[7]Prov. 9: 1.
[8]Rev. 1: 4 etc.

might have expected, simply tacked on at the end of the list. It has been inserted between the fifth and sixth items in the Hebrew version, and this procedure looks as if it was deliberate. Certainly at a later time importance was attached to the order in which the gifts are arranged, St. Thomas Aquinas, for instance, claiming that "the excellence of the gifts corresponds with the order in which they are enumerated."[9] But even in the Old Testament there are several passages which affirm a remarkable connection between the first and the last of the qualities which Isaiah enumerates. "The fear of the Lord," we are told, "is the beginning of wisdom,"[10] and this may well have suggested that Isaiah's list of qualities is not just a collection of unrelated properties set down in any order, but a unity, either a circle of related gifts in which the last returns to the first or a kind of stairway of gifts in which the lowest, the fear of the Lord, is the first step toward the highest, wisdom itself. Hence if piety got on to the list almost by accident, its position is probably not accidental, for this position still leaves wisdom and the fear of the Lord at opposite ends, even when the list gets expanded from six to seven.

The next important step in the development of the tradition brings us on to the New Testament and the primitive Church. All the evangelists associate the baptism of our Lord with the descent upon him of the Holy Spirit, and their thought clearly is that the Spirit rested upon him in the fullness of its divine energy. It is true that none of the evangelists explicitly refers to Isaiah's list of the gifts of the Spirit, though indeed another saying of this prophet about the Spirit of the Lord is associated with Jesus.[11] But who can doubt that at a time when the Church was searching everywhere for messianic predictions in the Old Testament, the particular passage concerning the gifts came to be applied very early to our Lord? From there, the next development is a very natural one. The Christian life is one that is conformed to the life of Christ, and so it too must be conceived as a life on which the Spirit rests and in

[9]*Summa Theologiae*, 1a2ae, 68, 7.
[10]Prov. 9: 10; cf. Ps. 111: 10.
[11]Luke 4: 18.

which the gifts of the Spirit are manifested. Thus evidences of the presence of the Holy Spirit speedily become the distinguishing marks of the Christian in the New Testament. As the Spirit had descended and rested on Christ at his baptism, so its descends upon the Church at Pentecost, and subsequently on those baptized into the Church. St. Paul is able to speak of the gifts of the Spirit bestowed upon Christians, while St. Peter, in what may well be an allusion to our text in Isaiah, assures those Christians who are being persecuted for their faith: "You are blessed, because the Spirit of glory and of God rests upon you."[12]

This brief survey shows us the scriptural foundation of the tradition of the seven gifts of the Holy Ghost, and the way in which the words of the Hebrew prophet eventually came to be interpreted. It would be a long story to attempt to trace the further development and elaboration of the tradition in patristic thought, and it would be irrelevant to our purpose. It may suffice to say that by the time of St. Augustine the tradition of the seven gifts had assumed the definite shape in which it has come down to us. In several passages of his writings,[13] St. Augustine discusses the "sevenfold operation of the Holy Ghost, of which Isaiah speaks," and clearly attaches considerable importance to the idea. Some of the things that he says are taken up by St. Thomas in his discussion of the gifts[14] and indeed many of St. Augustine's remarks are so illuminating that we shall have occasion to look at them later, when we seek to analyse the content of the seven gifts. But enough has been said for the present on the historical side, and we must now turn to the specifically theological inquiries.

[12]I Pet. 4: 14.
[13]*Our Lord's Sermon on the Mount*, I: 4; etc.
[14]*S. Th.*, 1a2ae, q 68.

II

Our next task is to ask about the theological presuppositions of the tradition of the seven gifts, and this is bound to open up for us a very wide field. On the one hand, we have to consider how we can visualize the operation of the Holy Spirit in relation to the triune God, while on the other hand we have to consider the structure of the human existence upon which the Holy Spirit operates. It seems to me that there are two major pitfalls to be avoided in these considerations.

One of these pitfalls is the danger of separating the Holy Spirit from God—and even if this sounds absurd, it is a real danger. The danger is probably increased by the person-language that we use about the Holy Trinity, and by our tendency to understand the word "person" in its modern sense as a self-contained autonomous entity. We may even find ourselves slipping into a kind of tritheism. Much traditional talk about the Holy Spirit has been infected with this error, so that he is represented as a kind of intermediary between God and man. But the Holy Spirit is not an intermediary. The Holy Spirit is nothing other than God himself in one of his ways of being; and without the Holy Spirit, God would not be the triune God of Christian faith. Hence we must be careful to think of the Holy Spirit and his operation as integral to the whole Godhead. Even though we speak of "gifts of the Holy Ghost" we must not forget that this means that these are gifts of God, and that it is by a kind of theological convention of speech, called traditionally "appropriation," that we assign these gifts peculiarly to the Holy Spirit, as the person of the Godhead most closely connected with their bestowal.

The other major pitfall is the danger of thinking of the gifts of the Holy Ghost in such a way that the integrity and responsibility of human existence is destroyed. Bultmann points out[15] that even in the New Testament—and the same would hold good *a fortiori* of the Old Testament—the Spirit sometimes appears as a quasi-magical force, tak-

[15]*Kerygma and Myth*, p. 6.

ing hold of a man from outside, as it were, and using him as a merely passive instrument. An illustration of this would be provided by the more ecstatic kinds of *charismata*, such as speaking with tongues, where, to put it bluntly, the man concerned has become a kind of marionette at the disposal of a ventriloquist, and whatever force operates upon him does so in a subpersonal manner. But when we are thinking of such gifts as wisdom, fortitude and the like, we must conceive their bestowal in nothing less than personal or existential terms, preserving on the one hand the initiative of the Spirit as the author of the gifts, and on the other hand the free response of the man who makes them his own and actively employs them.

If we begin by considering the operation of the Spirit within the triune Godhead, it may be worthwhile first of all to remind ourselves of the revolution (for it can hardly be deemed less) which is even now going on in theology concerning the fundamental idea of God. Traditional theism has thought of God as another being or entity—indeed, as the supreme being or entity, the *ens realissimum*—standing outside of the familiar world of beings or entities (including ourselves) as that world's Creator and Governor. This old metaphysical scheme is under heavy fire, as is evidenced among other things by the breakdown of the traditional natural theology. The place of the old scheme is being taken by the thought of God as Being itself—and however we may think of Being as such, it manifestly cannot be conceived as itself a being or entity, not even as the *ens realissimum*. We must rather think of Being as the condition that there should be any beings whatsoever, and if we think of Being as itself a being or an entity, we cannot avoid falling into antinomies. The contemporary theological prophets of this point of view are, of course, men like Paul Tillich and the Bishop of Woolwich. However, a still clearer analysis of the issues involved is to be found in the philosophical writings of Martin Heidegger.

I do not wish to deny that such ways of thinking about God may be disturbing, or to minimize their revolutionary character—they are perhaps just as revolutionary as was metaphysical theism itself when it displaced the still older mythological understanding of God as located in the sky above. But we should not be unduly alarmed by the current developments, partly new, partly the recovery of lost insights. We may well find that they open up exciting new possibilities in theology, and in particular that they can bring to expression the mystery and transcendence of God as the older categories could not. So far, however, only the merest beginning has been made (even by Tillich) in trying to rethink traditional Christian doctrines in conformity with the revolutionized conception of God. What follows may be regarded as a contribution toward such a rethinking of trinitarian doctrine, though before long I hope to work this out much more fully elsewhere.

Let me then without more ado proceed to sketch, in the barest outline, a trinitarian doctrine in terms of God as Being—a doctrine which will prove to be helpful in elucidating our particular theme of the seven gifts of the Holy Ghost. The Father we may call "primordial" Being. He is the source from which all proceeds, the condition that there should be anything whatsoever. But in the Christian religion we do not think of God or Being as a static, motionless "uncarved block." Being has a dynamic character and manifests itself in time through the multitude of particular beings that come into being and go out of being. In theological language, we talk of the Son as eternally "generated" by the Father, and the Son is also the Logos, the agent of the Father in the creation and recreation of the world. So we may call the Son "expressive" Being. He it is who manifests the otherwise hidden character of the Father's primordial Being, in the world of finite particular beings and supremely, as Christians believe, in the particular being of Jesus Christ. But the outpouring of primordial Being through expressive Being obviously involves what we may call a "risk"—the risk namely of a split in Being itself. The risk becomes acute with the creation of particular beings such as man, who have a limited freedom to order their own being and the being of nature and have thus been constituted guardians of Being. They may choose to be for themselves, rejecting or forgetting their dependent or steward-like status, and so ceasing to be manifestations of the Being which it was theirs to express; or, as we say in theological language, losing the image of God in which they were created. So as well as primordial Being and expressive Being, we must also posit unitive Being, and in this we recognize the operation of the Holy Spirit. This is not the return of particular beings to primordial Being, in a kind of Hegelian dialectic. The facts of sin and rebellion, if taken at all seriously, make it clear that there is no such automatic return taking place, and even if there were, and all was to be reabsorbed into the Absolute, creation would seem to have been pointless in the first place. We have to visualize a more complex kind of movement, one that maintains the particular beings in their particularity without either separation from or absorption into primordial Being. A clue to this more complex movement is provided by the Western theological tradition which teaches that the Holy Spirit "proceeds" from the Father and the Son. This doctrine of a double procession suggests a twofold movement in which primordial Being and expressive Being come together in a new unity—a richer unity since it now holds in itself diversity. And do not the prayers of the liturgy speak often of the Father and the Son "in the unity of the Holy Ghost"?

An illustration will help to make clearer what is being indicated here. Why was it that St. Peter recognized Jesus as the Christ, the Son of God, while the Jews thought of him only as a troublesome character who was upsetting the existing order and had to be got out of the way? Both saw the same life, heard the same words, and presumably started with much the same background of beliefs. The Jews perceived only a particular man, St. Peter perceived the same particular man *in depth*, as revealing the Father and manifesting Being. These different reactions remind us that the revelation of God in Christ is not read off automatically, and this would seem to be a sufficient refutation of the view that the Spirit and the Logos are one and the same, and that we need think of the divine Being under two aspects only, not three.

St. Peter recognized the Christ not by "flesh and blood,"[16] in the ex-

[16]Matt. 16: 17.

pression employed by one of the evangelists, that is to say, not by simple observation. There happens in the very being of St. Peter himself a moment of illumination which may be fairly described as the coming together in unitive Being of expressive Being and primordial Being (and of course, whether this happened during the ministry of Jesus or after the resurrection is of no importance here). What happened in this case is indeed what happens every time that we hear a word of man as the Word of God, and it is what theologians have sometimes called the "inward testimony of the Holy Spirit."

This has been a longish excursus into a somewhat speculative flight of theology, but it has brought us around at the end to man, in whose existence the illuminating activity of the Holy Spirit takes place. And it will be recalled that we had a second question to investigate—how can we conceive of the Holy Spirit's operation on man in such a way that it does not violate the integrity and responsibility of our human existence?

Man not only is, he exists, in the technical sense in which the word "exist" is used in existentialist philosophy. That is to say, along with his being, man has some understanding of that being, and likewise responsibility for it. He makes his essence by his choices and decisions. He either lays hold on his potentialities for being, or lets them slip. As St. Athanasius noted long ago, man is on his way from the nothing out of which he has been created toward the being to which he is called, but he can either go forward or slip backward. Trees, rocks, rivers, horses—these too have being, but they do not exist as man exists. Their essence is given with their being. Man alone is open to Being, so that he exists in the light of Being. His own being is already a question for him, and with that question comes also the question of the wider Being within which man lives and moves and has his being. He can understand himself in terms of the world of finite entities in which he finds himself as just such an entity, and this we may call a "secular" understanding. Or he can understand himself, to use one of Heidegger's expressions, as the "guardian" of Being, the only particular entity known to us to whom

Being has entrusted itself and whose responsible co-operation it demands. This we may call the "religious" understanding of life. Incidentally, it should perhaps be added that this way of understanding "secular" and "religious" should not be confused with some of the ways these words get used in current discussions of "religionless" Christianity and "secular" interpretations of the gospel.

But how is man awakened to his relation to divine Being, and called out of that secular self-sufficient understanding of himself as one finite particular entity among other such entities in the world? The Christian faith has always asserted that this comes about by a movement from the divine to the human, in experiences of revelation and grace where the initiative lies with God and which we associate especially with the operation of the Holy Spirit. One of the defects of much contemporary theology is its lack of a proper doctrine of the divine immanence. It may be that the immanence of God was stressed overmuch in the days of idealist philosophy, so that by way of reaction theology has been driven to overemphasize his transcendence. But such overemphasis always makes anything like revelation or grace seem arbitrary and imposed. I think we are saved from these excesses (typified in Barthianism and neo-Calvinism) when we think of God in terms of Being, and of the triune God in terms of primordial, expressive and unitive Being. The transcendence of God is certainly preserved since Being utterly and incomparably transcends all particular beings, and is of a different order so that one may even define "transcendence" as the relation of Being to beings—probably a better definition than the metaphysical one that visualizes God as "outside" or "beyond" the world, or the mythological one that thought of God as "up there." But the immanence of God is also preserved, for Being has presence in and expresses itself in every particular being, that is to say, in everything that *is*.

The unitive Being of the Holy Spirit, conceived as the coming together (as double procession) of primordial Being and expressive Being is possible in man because of his openness to Being, his ex-sisting in the light of Being, which distinguishes him from every other entity that we know. The most percipient observers of such experiences as grace and revelation have frequently remarked that in them God appears to be on both sides. Talking of love towards God, for example, W. G. de Burgh remarks: "God is not present simply as the object of man's response, as though *his* love towards *us* called forth *our* love towards *him;* our answering love is the very Spirit of God working within us. God is present, so to speak, on both sides of the reciprocal relation."[17]

But this happens without any submersion of man's personal and responsible existence, and even our way of talking about such matters makes this clear. For we may think of trees, rocks and the rest as having a relation to God—they participate in being as created things, and we might even think that in their intelligible structure they express something of the divine Logos. But we would never talk of the Holy Spirit's operating upon a tree in the mode of grace, let us say. This can happen only with man, whose essence is not given, but who stands before possibilities. The Holy Spirit does not impose anything on him, but awakens him and empowers him to possibilities which he can either seize or let slip.

We now have before us a way of understanding what is meant by a "gift" of the Holy Spirit. It is nothing less than a gift of God, though as we are awakened to it through the unitive mode of the divine Being, we associate it especially with the Spirit. It is given to us as a potentiality placed within our grasp, but on which we must ourselves lay hold. The basic gift is simply existence itself—the particular existence to which each one is elected with all its possibilities of fulfilment. The details of this fulfilment in the Christian life and the reason for considering this under the form of a sevenfold gift will occupy us in the final part of our study.

[17]*From Morality to Religion* (London: Macdonald & Evans, 1938), p. 259.

III

We now have to consider the actual content of the tradition of the seven gifts of the Holy Ghost—the qualities or attributes of wisdom, understanding, counsel, fortitude, knowledge, piety and the fear of the Lord. What total picture emerges, and how adequate is this list as a description or phenomenology of the Christian life?

I have already hinted that although there was an element of arbitrariness involved in the putting together of the list and in its working over, nevertheless it should not be treated as just a collection of seven unrelated items, set down at random. Certainly, Christian thought came to think of the list as representing a unity. As has been pointed out, the reiterated Old Testament assertion that the fear of the Lord is the beginning of wisdom links together the first and the last of the seven gifts, and has also been taken as bringing together those that lie between, so that these seven gifts are conceived as interrelated. Moreover, we took note that the gifts have to do with the wholeness of human existence, with the entire man as thinking, willing, feeling. So even the prominence given to such ideas as knowledge, understanding and wisdom does not indicate an intellectualist bias. As used in the Bible and in much of the history of Christian thought, these terms do not have a narrowly rationalistic sense, but have a practical and existential connotation. In the same way, when it is said that the Holy Spirit will lead the disciples into all truth, this does not imply that his primary function is to impart some theoretical knowledge, but rather to illuminate (make unconcealed) all the dimensions of our human existence.

The first question to be decided concerns the order in which the gifts may best be studied so as to bring out their interrelatedness. The traditional order, taken from Isaiah himself, begins with wisdom, and we may suppose that it ranks first among the gifts. It might indeed be claimed that the fullest wisdom contains within itself all the other gifts, so that if we began with this divinely given wisdom, then by a process of analysis or unpacking we would find ourselves being led through the gamut of all the other gifts. For purposes of exposition, however, it is probably simpler and better to begin at the other end with that fear of the Lord which is said to be the beginning of wisdom, and to build up from this towards the gift of wisdom.

It is worth recalling that in two passages where St. Augustine discusses the traditional seven gifts, he treats them in reverse order, beginning with the fear of the Lord and ending with wisdom. In his treatise *On Christian Doctrine*,[18] he speaks of "seven steps" to wisdom, and describes the progress or ascent of the soul through the various gifts until "such a son ascends to wisdom, which is the seventh and last step, and which he enjoys in peace and tranquillity." In his exposition of *Our Lord's Sermon on the Mount*,[19] he makes an interesting comparison between the seven gifts of the Holy Ghost and the Beatitudes. Both, he claims, depict the same pattern of life, and he draws ingenious if not always convincing parallels between the details of each scheme. The main point he makes, however, is that the two descriptions proceed in opposite directions. Isaiah's list of the seven gifts, according to St. Augustine, begins with the more excellent, whereas the Beatitudes begin with the inferior. The "poor in spirit" of the first Beatitude, called in the *New English Bible* "those who know that they are poor," correspond in St. Augustine's thought to the gift of the fear of the Lord in the sevenfold list; while at the other end, the peacemakers are those who have attained to wisdom, or, as St. Augustine puts it, "the contemplation of the truth, tranquillizing the whole man and assuming the likeness of God." In his own exposition, he again shows a preference for the ascending order.

Of course, St. Augustine's remarks have a neo-Platonist colouring. They may suggest too much the mystical ascent of the soul to the ethereal heights of pure contemplation, and in particular we may find it somewhat repugnant to hear St. Augustine laying such stress on the "tranquillizing" character of the highest exercise of the spiritual life.

[18]II: 7.
[19]I: 4.

St. Thomas too speaks of the contemplative gifts as preferable to the active gifts.[20] But even if we follow St. Augustine's order of treatment, we are not compelled to follow all the details of his interpretation, of the gifts of the Spirit. The temper of our age (and probably also the temper of the Old Testament from which the list of gifts is originally derived) demands a more practical interpretation, even of wisdom and the so-called intellectual gifts; or perhaps we should say that it demands that any sharp distinction between "intellectual" and "affective" or "conative" be modified, and the various gifts seen in the "existential" unity of the entire man.

We should not be misled either by St. Augustine's talk of "steps" or "stages." This does not mean that the earlier stages are left behind as we proceed to the later and higher ones. Rather, they are all present together in the unity of the Christian life. Nor does the adoption of the ascending order mean that man rises up by himself to the knowledge of God. Such a misunderstanding forgets the giftlike character of the whole movement, for every step on the way and the way as a whole is a gift and is dependent on the divine initiative.

Let us begin then with the fear of the Lord, the seventh of the traditional gifts but, as the beginning of wisdom, the first in ascending order. The expression "fear of the Lord" is nowadays somewhat old-fashioned, and it is in any case very misleading. Fear, as it is described by modern psychology and physiology, is an organic state produced as the response to some threatening situation that has arisen in the environment. The suprarenal capsules pour adrenaline into the bloodstream, the heartbeat quickens, various activities of the body, such as digestion, are suspended, and the whole organism is tensed to meet the emergency. If this is what is understood nowadays by "fear," then the word can be used only in a remotely figurative way when we talk of the "fear of the Lord."

The psychosomatic description of fear is not, however, an exhaustive one. As persons who have sometimes ourselves been afraid, we have

[20]*S. Th.*, 1a2ae, 68, 7.

access to the understanding of fear not only through the descriptions of overt fearful behaviour offered by psychologists or physiologists, but through our own experience of fearing. We know fear from the inside, so to speak, as an affective state of mind. In such a state of mind, we become aware of the precariousness of our own being, through the emergence of some state of affairs that is taken to threaten our being. Fear is perhaps the most typical member of a whole family of affective states, all of which in some way or other bring to awareness the precariousness of human existence. Most languages have a wide variety of words to express the different shades of feeling that are possible within this general area of experience. In English we talk of "fear," "terror," "panic," "dread," "fright," "alarm" and so on.

The basic state of mind, of which all those others may be considered as variations or modifications, is the one made familiar to us by contemporary existentialist philosophy as anxiety, often designated by its German name as *Angst*. Anxiety may be paradoxically described as the state of mind in which we become aware of nothing. It comes upon us in certain moods when our accustomed securities fall away and there is disclosed to us the human condition as basically characterized by finitude, guilt and death—that this existence of ours is permeated through and through with nullity. Anxiety brings us to the awareness that we all the time exist over an abyss of nothing.

This anxiety might be called the "religious *a priori*." It is the encounter with the nullity inherent in his own existence—the shock of possible non-being, as Tillich has expressed it—that makes man ready for the encounter with Being, or in religious terms, makes him ready for the approach of God. It is the experience of nothing that summons him out of his secular self-understanding as one entity among others in the world, recalling him from what Heidegger calls the "forgetting" of Being, and empowering him to recognize the Being that lets him be, and sets him before the possibilities of fuller being. St. Augustine was not mistaken when he saw a relation between the seventh gift of the Holy Ghost, the fear of the Lord, and the quality belonging to those who are declared blessed in the first Beatitude, those who know how poor they are. "Near to essential anxiety, as the terror of the abyss," writes Heidegger, "there dwells awe (*Scheu*)."[21] And "awe" is perhaps the best English word to describe what was once called the "fear of the Lord," where "fear" stands by metonymy for that group of experiences that bring to awareness the precariousness of our human existence, and so open our eyes to the wonder of the Being that gives itself to us.

One further point may be mentioned before we pass from this first gift of the Holy Spirit. The fear of the Lord is the beginning of wisdom, and the fear of the Lord has been interpreted in terms of the affective state that leads from fundamental anxiety to awe before the majesty of Being. One of the great contributions of contemporary existentialism has been its work on affective states, such as anxiety, and its recognition that such states are also disclosive states, that is to say, they are not merely emotions but carry with them an implicit understanding. The artificial barriers which in old-fashioned psychology were supposed to separate the cognitive, affective and conative sides of human nature (a superstition which still lingers in the artificial division of language into "informative" and "emotive") have been broken down so that we can see man as he really is in his total existence, which is always involved in cognition, affection and conation together. So the wisdom which has its roots in the fear of the Lord cannot be an "apathetic contemplation" in the neo-Platonist sense. This wisdom rises out of pathos and concern, and we shall see that it remains concerned.

We can afford to spend a shorter time over the next gift to which we come as we continue to read the list in reverse order—the gift of piety. It will be remembered that piety was the additional quality inserted into Isaiah's list of six, and I expressed the view that this addition might turn out to be an enrichment rather than a mere intrusion. Such an enrichment it does indeed constitute, for piety adds something that rounds out the gift of awe or the fear of the Lord.

[21] *Was ist Metaphysik?*, p. 47.

When we speak of "awe," and still more when we use the word "fear," the emphasis is on the overwhelming majesty of Being as the wholly other to all particular beings. Being does indeed have this character, reflected in such expressions as the "wrath of God." But Being does not only encounter us in strangeness, but also in kinship, for we ourselves *are*, we participate in Being. Here again a doctrine of sheer transcendence can be dangerous, if it loses sight of the divine immanence. Being does not appear as just the *mysterium tremendum.* As Rudolf Otto reminds us in his classic work on the subject, the numinous meets us as *mysterium tremendum et fascinans.*[22] Equiprimordial with the overwhelmingness of Being is the grace of Being, in constituting us guardians of Being; and equiprimordial with awe is reverence, the awakening of that love and loyalty which is signified by the gift of piety. We are all acquainted with the natural piety that a man may show toward his family or people or country—the kind of piety of which Aeneas is a famous exemplar. But the piety which is the gift of the Spirit is called forth not by any particular being but by Being itself, and therefore has in it the seeds of a love that is not particular but universal—the love so well described by Kierkegaard as that which always has God for its third term.[23]

The fear of the Lord and piety, as we have seen, are primarily affective states, but in them as in all affective states there are cognitive elements. The bringing of these cognitive elements to the level of conscious awareness is the content of the third gift, knowledge. The inclusion of knowledge among the gifts of the Spirit is what is likely to be most puzzling or even offensive to the non-Christian. Is not knowledge so far from being a gift that men have had to work very hard and sometimes endure very great dangers in order that they might painfully increase the sum of human knowledge over the centuries? Do Christians then claim to have a shortcut to knowledge—as perhaps they have indeed claimed in some of the unfortunate controversies between scientists and theologians?

[22]*The Idea of the Holy*, pp. 31ff. [23]In *Works of Love.*

It need hardly be said that the knowledge which is a gift of the Holy Ghost is primarily the knowledge of God; and it does not need much reflection to show that there are different kinds of knowledge, and that they are acquired in different ways. The knowledge of facts, the kind in which science deals, can be gained only by patient and laborious study, and we may well be thankful for this knowledge and the benefits it has brought in delivering the human mind from ignorance and superstition, and in improving the conditions of life. This factual kind of knowledge is attained by what Heidegger appropriately calls "calculative thinking." In such thinking we objectivize whatever is to be known, and in wresting the truth from it, we gain the mastery over it. As has often been pointed out, our knowledge of other people is of quite a different kind, and is differently gained. We do not and cannot wrest such knowledge from them. We get to know them as they are willing to open themselves up to us, and in so far as they do so, they may fairly be said to be conferring a gift. But this relation of person to person, which is one of mutuality and equality, still does not show us what is the structure of our knowledge of God, and is at the best an analogue. There is to be recognized a third kind of knowing, in which we neither stand over against an object nor yet over against another subject on the same level as ourselves, but are rather brought into subjection. This is the knowledge of Being or of God. In contrast to calculative thinking, Heidegger recognizes also an "essential" or "primordial" thinking. This essential thinking he understands as an occurrence of Being in us, so that it is the kind of thinking in which we are submissive. With his usual fondness for etymologies, Heidegger relates this "thinking" to "thanking," so dramatically calling attention to its giftlike character.

Incidentally, Heinrich Ott sees in Heidegger's theory of thinking the most important contribution that his philosophy has to make to theology, and draws a parallel between the primordial thinking of the philosopher and the reflective thought of the theologian, who operates within the framework of faith. It seems to me, however, that Ott's appreciation for Heidegger is too restricted, and consorts ill with the Barthian, christocentric elements in his theology. I would want to go much further than Ott, and claim that Heidegger's views offer a possible basis for an epistemology of revelation and indeed for an entire new-style philosophical or natural theology.

From the way in which the knowledge of God or Being has just been described, it could not be regarded as a mere intellectual contemplation. It is a knowledge that arises through involvement and participation, and that issues in commitment. This is entirely in line with the biblical conception of the knowledge of God. In his article on the subject in Kittel's *Wörterbuch*, Bultmann writes that in biblical usage, "to know God or his name means to recognize him, to confess him, to give him honour and do his will."[24]

Hence it is entirely appropriate that next among the seven gifts as we ascend the scale is fortitude, which more than any of the others that we have so far considered, suggests the life of action. Fortitude, or might, speaks of the new man who has been transformed through the fear of the Lord, piety and the knowledge of God. He understands himself as summoned out of nothing into the potentialities of being and selfhood, out of the life of anxiety into the life of faith.

St. Athanasius, as has been said earlier, envisaged man as standing between nothing and Being, and fortitude designates the way by which man advances into fuller being. One of the paradoxes of his life is that he makes this advance not by concerning himself with his own particular being or trying to maintain and increase it, but by going out of himself in committing himself to something greater than his own being. He has to lose his life to find it. He is strengthened in his being precisely as he commits or engages himself beyond the narrow range of his own being, and of course the ultimate commitment is the commitment to that which really is ultimate—to Being itself, or God. This is what is sometimes called the "paradox of grace." It is well expressed by St. Paul, who ascribes his very being to the grace of God in his life,

[24]*Gnosis* (London: A. & C. Black, 1952), p. 17.

yet he has not ceased to be himself: "By the grace of God I am what I am, and his grace toward me was not in vain. On the contrary, I worked harder than any of them, though it was not I, but the grace of God which is with me."[45] Perhaps in view of all that has already been said above on the operation of the Holy Spirit, something of the meaning of this paradox will have become clearer to us. But our consideration of fortitude has certainly brought out more clearly that the conferring of every gift brings with it a task. The gift is given as a potentiality which requires labour and obedience for its fulfilment if it is not to be a gift offered in vain.

These remarks bring us immediately to the next gift—counsel. Faith does not come as a permanent possession in which we can securely rest, but as something to be continually renewed in every situation; for each situation demands again fortitude, and what Tillich has called the "courage to be." Thus, as we have already noted, the various gifts are not stages of such a sort that each may be left behind as we proceed to the next. Man needs to be constantly receiving all the gifts.

The nature of counsel can be seen if we attend to one of the most noteworthy characteristics of the life of the earliest Church, as it is depicted in the Acts of the Apostles. We cannot read far in this account without noticing that the disciples, whether acting individually or corporately, never took any decisive step without having, as they believed, the guidance of the divine Spirit. Again and again we read how the Spirit is supposed to have counselled them in their actions. This does not mean that the Christian hears some interior voice which lays down precise instructions about what he is to do in a given situation, thus relieving him of his own responsibility; though admittedly the New Testament seems on occasion to speak as if the Spirit did act in almost an automatic way. But if we need not take the meaning that the counsel of the Holy Spirit has a quasi-magical character, at least, if we take in any serious sense the operation of the Holy Spirit at all, we must suppose that there is a real way in which God can be said to

[25] I Cor. 15: 10.

"speak" to men. This is what happens every time an incident or something said by a fellow human being or perhaps a verse of scripture (it may be one that we have often heard before) or a passage in a sermon takes on for us a depth of meaning, speaks to our very problem and throws light on what we have to do. I have in mind the kind of thing that happened when St. Augustine read St. Paul's words on the new life in Christ and so arrived at a new understanding of himself in relation to God; and all the innumerable other cases in which God "addresses" men through some agency or other within the world.

No doubt psychology can offer some explanation of the mechanism involved in such experiences, but it must also be claimed that on a deeper level of explanation we must recognize here the "inward testimony of the Holy Spirit." The scriptures of the Christian religion are still relevant, the ministrations of the Church in the sacraments and in preaching lead to new self-understanding, Christ himself is present reality, because the Word of God is not something belonging to the past but something that comes alive again and again as we expose our lives to the counsels of the Holy Spirit, above all in the life of the Church as the guardian of the sacraments, worship, prayer, instruction in the faith.

Passing naturally to the gift of understanding, we may now consider the specific place of theology within Christianity and within the community of the Spirit. Not everyone is called to be a theologian, but every mature Christian has a duty so far as he can to think out, to understand and appropriate the meaning of the faith within which he belongs. It is a tragedy that the dimension of understanding in the Christian life, though it stands high among the gifts of the Spirit, is sometimes despised, for there has been plenty of evidence in history to show that a faith which has not rooted itself in understanding can be a very weak and transient affair. And surely the need for a sound understanding of the Christian faith is very great in the world today, when it is challenged by so many and formidable rival ways of understanding life.

Theology is no doubt partly itself to blame for the suspicion with which it is sometimes regarded, even within the Christian Church. From time to time in its history it has lost touch with the life of the Church and so lost itself by falling into abstruse speculation and arid disputes, by becoming something that tries to exist for its own sake. But theology is not a coldly detached study of religion. It is *fides quaerens intellectum*, it is rooted in the fear of the Lord and all the other gifts of the Spirit, and its own specific gift of understanding is just as much a gift as the others, though like the others it imposes its own task.

Yet this does not imply on the other hand that theology has got to be narrowly biblicist, or that it should be shut up within the narrower life of the Church. The theologian will see the world too as the potential Church. Because he speaks from the standpoint of faith, he recognizes all genuine understanding as ultimately a gift of the Spirit, and so he is prepared to learn from the philosopher or from the adherents of other religions or from anyone else who can enlarge his understanding and fit him better for his own peculiar work of bringing to as clear and consistent expression as he can find the content of that faith in which he stands. In this connection it may be well to remind ourselves that the Holy Spirit "blows where it wills"[26] and does not necessarily confer its gifts through the sometimes sadly constricted churchly channels, and still less in a manner that would always be approved by our ecclesiastical machinery. Often it has been the case that genuinely Christian insights have got lost in the Church, and we have had to be reminded of them by persons outside. Such persons may not indeed think of themselves as acting under the Holy Spirit—like the men whom St. Paul found at Ephesus, they might even say, "we have never even heard that there is a Holy Spirit"[27]—but who would deny that they may be in fact recipients of the gifts of the Spirit?

[26]John 3: 8.
[27]Acts 19: 2.

All the gifts are summed up in wisdom, and by this time it is unnecessary to stress that such wisdom is no merely intellectual contemplation. It belongs to, or rather, it is conferred upon the whole man. It may seem to us disappointing that the list of gifts does not culminate in love, and we may hazard a guess that had St. Paul been its author, then love would have had the highest place. There is perhaps often a tendency within the Church to exalt other categories at the expense of love. John McIntyre has pointed out[28] that in most contemporary theology, the regulative or normative category is not love but revelation. But the absence of an explicit mention of love in our traditional list is mitigated when we remember that wisdom is for the whole man, and is not a purely intellectual category. It has to do with life, and as such it conduces to love. St. Thomas, who distinguishes virtues from gifts, and rates the virtues higher, nevertheless can say that "the gifts of the Holy Ghost are connected together in charity; so that whoever has charity has all the gifts of the Holy Ghost, none of which can be possessed without charity."[29]

When we remember the practical bearing of wisdom, then we will not suppose for a moment that the gift of wisdom unlocks all mysteries, or that the Church makes the arrogant claim that all things on heaven and on earth are opened to its gaze. Wisdom may indeed be sufficient for the needs of life, but an important part of wisdom is just to know where the limits of our human powers lie. This is indeed the beginning of wisdom, for it is the same as the fear of the Lord, man's recognition of his own finite and dependent status. It is surely no accident that possibly the most celebrated example of secular wisdom stresses precisely this point. Long before the time of Christ, Socrates was told by the Delphic oracle that he was the wisest man in Greece. Knowing only too well his own lack of wisdom, he was at first astonished by the saying. Then the meaning of it dawned on him. He was wiser than others just because he perceived his own limitations. He was like those

[28]*On the Love of God* (London: Collins, 1962), p. 26.
[29]*S. Th.*, 1a2ae, 68, 5.

mentioned in the first Beatitude who know that they are poor, and this, says St. Augustine, is the fear of the Lord and the beginning of wisdom. It is not surprising then that St. Justin could name Socrates among those whom he regarded as "Christians before Christ," for his wisdom too bears the mark of being a gift of the Spirit–as perhaps all genuine wisdom is.

The wisdom which the Spirit confers is to see our own being and all our actions in the light of Being itself, that is to say, of God. Wisdom has the same basic structure as Kierkegaard claimed to see in Christian love, with God as the third term. This wisdom may be contrasted with what St. Paul calls the "wisdom of this world." To the wisdom of the world, the Christian wisdom conferred by the Spirit looks like folly. The wisdom of the world is the wisdom that has to do with beings and nothing else, and which aims at the mastery and manipulation of beings. Christian wisdom is certainly not indifferent to beings, but it looks through them to what the "world" regards as the "nothing else," to transcendent Being, and sees the beings in the light of this. This is the distinction between the secular and the religious attitudes to life, and the choice that confronts us today.

What then are we finally to say about this venerable tradition of the seven gifts of the Holy Ghost? It is certainly not an exhaustive list, and indeed we could not list exhaustively all the treasures that flow from the mystery of divine Being. The list has been put together somewhat arbitrarily, and perhaps we miss in it some qualities that we would have liked to see emphasized–above all, the most excellent gift of love. Yet it does give us a remarkably comprehensive view of the structure of the Christian life under the Spirit, the life in which man is summoned out of his nullity into that fullness of being for which God has destined him. The Church did not err when it singled out this particular group of gifts for special attention. Nor do we err when we say of their author, the Holy Spirit, that he is "the Lord and Giver of life, who proceedeth from the Father and the Son, who with the Father and the Son together is worshipped and glorified."

Index

PRINTED AT
RUNGE PRESS LIMITED, OTTAWA
DESIGNED BY ROBERT R. REID